# The Ghosts of Consciousness

# OMEGA BOOKS

The OMEGA BOOKS series from Paragon House is dedicated to classic and contemporary works about human development and the nature of ultimate reality, encompassing the fields of mysticism and spirituality, psychic research and paranormal phenomena, the evolution of consciousness, and the human potential for self-directed growth in body, mind, and spirit.

John White, M.A.T., Series Editor of OMEGA BOOKS, is an internationally known author, editor, and educator in the fields of consciousness research and higher human development.

**MORE TITLES IN OMEGA BOOKS**

BEYOND THE HUMAN SPECIES: The Life and Work of Sri Aurobindo and the Mother, *Georges van Vrekhem*

KUNDALINI: EMPOWERING HUMAN EVOLUTION
Selected Writings of Gopi Krishna, *Edited by Gene Kieffer*

KUNDALINI EVOLUTION AND ENLIGHTENMENT
*Edited by John White*

LIFECYCLES: Reincarnation and the Web of Life
*Christopher M. Bache*

THE MEETING OF SCIENCE AND SPIRIT
Guidelines for a New Age, *John White*

THE RADIANCE OF BEING: Understanding the Grand Integral Vision; Living the Integral Life
*Allan Combs, Foreword by Ken Wilber*

THE SACRED MIRROR: Nondual Wisdom and Psychotherapy
*Edited by John Prendergast, Ph.D., Peter Fenner, Ph.D., and Sheila Krystal, Ph.D.*

# The Ghosts of Consciousness

## *Thought and the Spiritual Path*

by

*Herbert S. Demmin*

PARAGON HOUSE
St. Paul, Minnesota

Published in the United States by

Paragon House
2285 University Avenue West
St. Paul, Minnesota 55114

The Omega Books series from Paragon House is dedicated to classic and contemporary works about human development and the nature of ultimate reality.

Library of Congress Catalog-in-Publication Data

Demmin, Herbert S., 1959-
  The ghosts of consciousness : thought and the spiritual
path / by Herbert S. Demmin.
     p. cm. -- (Omega books)
Includes bibliographical references and index.
  ISBN 1-55778-825-1 (pbk. : alk. paper)
  1. Thought and thinking. 2. Self-perception. 3. Consciousness. I.
Title. II. Series: Omega books (New York, N.Y.)
  BF441.D395 2003
  153.4'2--dc22
                                    2003015114

10 9 8 7 6 5 4 3 2 1
For current information about all releases from Paragon House,
visit the web site at www.paragonhouse.com

# Contents

## *Foreword:* A Personal Journey

W HEN I WAS TWELVE years old I became aware of something strange happening to me. Quite suddenly, the way I was experiencing myself seemed very different. I knew it was a mental change. Amazingly, my sense of self was greater than ever before because I was more tuned into and aware of my thoughts. I remember being very confused and frustrated as I grappled with this greater awareness of my thoughts and self. Agonizing, I told my mom that I didn't know of any words to describe what was happening in my head regarding this change in my awareness. I doubted that such words even existed. Despite my skepticism, she was confident that such words did exist and that someday I might identify and put together these puzzle pieces of my mind.

For the past twenty years I have been trying to do just that. During college I read a book by J. Krishnamurti that described the illusory experience of duality created by thought. He said that reflective thinking creates a mirroring effect that engenders a separate sense of self seemingly set apart from all other forms of experience. He also described how the thought-induced experience of the separate self leads to many forms of human suffering. I sensed that what Krishnamurti was saying was true. But he didn't detail how reflective thinking created this mirroring effect, resulting in the experience of duality; of a self-sense separate from "its" internal and external experience. Consequently, I was determined to find someone who could further clarify this phenomenon of the thought-induced separate self.

Much to my amazement, nine years of study in psychology and sixteen years of professional practice have yielded little to help me better understand the questions prompted by my earlier reading of Krishnamurti. It seems that the field of psychology as a whole has largely ignored the study of thinking (as a process) and its co-occurring phenomenological manifestations. Instead, the *contents* of thought (primarily beliefs) have been closely scrutinized and utilized in order to develop theories of pathology and modes of psychological treatment.

As a contrast to Western psychology, Eastern religious traditions seemed to offer much more about the nature of thinking per se and its experiential manifestations. Further readings of several Buddhist masters fascinated me. They wrote beautifully and convincingly about the nature of mind and reality, the sources of suffering, Buddha nature, the illusory forms of experiencing, and so on. They saw the separate sense of self as largely created by reflective thinking, a major source of human suffering, and obscuring awareness of our true natures. Unfortunately, my understanding of how this reflective thought process evoked a separate self-sense remained unclear to me, and I continued to feel very troubled by it. As a result, I took Krishnamurti's advice to look inside myself for the answers to my questions rather than totally rely on anyone else's experiential understanding of the thought process and the illusions it creates.

Thus, over many years and countless instances I have intermittently tuned into my thoughts during my normal day-to-day waking experience, trying to catch myself just before, during, and after discrete thought-moments. In addition, I have often engaged in a state of internal absorption where I closed my eyes and allowed my mind to wander in thought and internal experience. I also intermittently reflected on these thoughts and moments of internal reverie as a way to take note of their experiential qualities. I often struggled during such moments of reflection to recapture the sequence of how one, two, or three thoughts unfolded. I tried to capture how sequential thoughts were related or how one seemed to lead to the next. I attended to the experiential differences between moments when I had been consumed in thought and those of reflecting on them. In particular, I focused on differences in my experience of self-awareness as a function of changes in the direction of and objects of my attention. Thus, much of what I write about here is an account of a personal, introspective journey of trying to understand the thought-induced nature of my experience of self. This introspective journey was accompanied by the task of trying to clearly describe this evolving understanding.

Presented in the pages ahead is a detailed description of the phenomenologically based structure and process aspects of thought and how a separate sense of self and other illusory manifestations are engendered. This description may be entirely unique in its detail and specificity. Consequently, the first two chapters are very technical in nature because a necessary foundation for understanding the thought process is being laid for perhaps the very first time. Therefore, I ask for your patience as you read chapters 1 and 2. They set the stage for understanding many insights about yourself in the chapters ahead, insights that I believe you will find very rewarding. I also ask that you not get too bogged down or frustrated if you don't understand something in the first two chapters. The important concepts are repeated many times in different ways throughout the book, so I trust that your understanding will be forthcoming.

In addition, I want to note that the contents ahead represent a description of the phenomenology of thinking and self-awareness. This description is partly theoretical because I posit a number of ways in which different manifestations of self-awareness are engendered by thinking. I cannot presume that my descriptions are absolutely correct or accurate, hence the word "theoretical." I leave this accuracy for you and other readers to determine as you compare my words against your own internal experience.

Last of all, I want to note that certain conclusions I make in this text are relevant to the thought-process only, and not to other higher forms of consciousness or unusual, altered states of consciousness that often preclude thought altogether.

# Introduction

O VER THE LAST ONE hundred years the field of psychology has developed an inferiority complex. To a large extent it lost its identity by trying to emulate the "hard" physical sciences, which employ the scientific method and rely upon empirical data to support their hypotheses (Wilber, 1995). Fifty years ago, psychology, in the form of behaviorism, espoused the extreme viewpoint that human behavior should be explained and accounted for by the scientific method and empirical data (Gardner, 1985; Chalmers, 1996; Paranjpe, 1998). Hypotheses related to motivation, for example, as a phenomenon intrinsic to understanding manifest human behavior, were rendered obsolete. Motivations, should they actually exist, cannot be seen or directly measured, and therefore are not valid candidates for "scientific" study.

In time the psychology pendulum began to swing away from exclusive empiricism in the form of behaviorism, to cognitive-behaviorism or cognitive psychology (Kihlstrom, 1987). Although mental structures and processes, including internal cognitions, cannot be seen from some external vantage point, they are recognized as playing an important role in human behavior. Nevertheless, cognitive psychology granted these structures and processes validity only to the extent that they were manifest in observable behavior (Wilber, 1996b).

Recent research suggests that cognitive psychology is now the most prominent school of psychology (Robins, Gosling, & Craik, 1999). In the 1980s, cognitive psychology sprouted cognitive science. As an interdisciplinary effort to unravel the mysteries of the human mind, cognitive science takes materialistic explanations of mind, psyche, and consciousness to an even more mechanistic level, comparing human mental functioning to central processing units, consciousness to working memory, and goal-directed human behavior to nodes representing processing goals (Kihlstrom, 1987). Cognitive psychology and cognitive science typically favor studying the surface structures and functioning of machines rather than the interior, subjective world of human beings. At best, they come closest to humanity by concerning themselves with mental states deemed relevant to the causation and explanation of behavior (Chalmers, 1996).

Some researchers believe that the human mind works just like a computer (Pylyshyn, 1981). Others rely on computer-based models to think about how the mind works (Robins, Gosling, & Craik, 1999). Such models are surface oriented and minimize or ignore the realities of what it's like to live and function with a subjective, human awareness. Trying to understand aspects of humanity as basic as thinking, consciousness, self-awareness, and memory, by comparing them with computer functions, is like discerning the taste of strawberries by comparing them to artificially flavored fruit roll-ups.

Where Western academic psychology has lagged behind, scholarly philosophy publications about consciousness and self-awareness have increased in recent years (Paranjpe, 1998). Generally such publications present philosophical arguments based on formal logic to refute or support theses about general mental states (Chalmers, 1996; Gennaro, 1996; Natsoulas, 1998; Searle, 1998). Unfortunately, such writings are not often accessible and understandable to the educated public. In addition, general and varied definitions of consciousness and self-awareness often seem irrelevant to the concerns of everyday life. Psychology and philosophy need to go beyond clarifying general mental states in favor of focusing on specific descriptions of mental acts to which readers can introspectively and experientially relate and apply to their lives.

An understanding of the interior realities of feeling, thinking, and experiencing one's self as a separate human consciousness seems to have died with William James over one hundred years ago (James, 1950; Paranjpe, 1998). At that time, philosophers and psychologists valued the study of subjective, human interiors and were unafraid of employing introspection as a method of observation and learning (Gardner, 1985; Paranjpe, 1998). Since then, however, psychology has missed her calling trying to emulate her big sisters, allowing them to harass her into feeling inferior because she has different interests, tastes, and preferences, ones that cannot always be elucidated and tested in ways her sisters' interests can.

As a contrast to the West, Eastern religious traditions have valued and respected the subjective interiors of sentient creatures for thousands of years (Wilber, 1995; Paranjpe, 1998). Their experiential exploration of mental phenomena has yielded remarkable discoveries beyond the imagination of Western science. Their language for conveying the insights and discoveries of human interior realities is generally anti-intellectual (Suzuki, 1970), in preference for experiential, practice-based teachings (Goenka, 1993; Paranjpe, 1998). Practices meant to confuse and frustrate one's intellectual mind are often drawn upon in the service of facilitating experiential learnings (e.g., koans) (Carrington, 1977).

Meditation is the single most important practice for understanding the workings of the mind in Eastern religious traditions. Eastern religious experts believe that fundamental insights about the nature of thinking and the illusions it creates are revealed through meditative practice. They believe that human emotions and motivations, belief systems, and a separate sense of self are largely driven by the habit of thinking, by the content of thought and its processes (Goldstein & Kornfield, 1987; Rinpoche, 1993; Paranjpe, 1998).

Perhaps the most personally important and fundamental internal human reality is the experience of a coherent sense of self. Most of us generally construe our sense of self as a basic human reality and absolute given of existence. The Eastern mind, however, sees it as an illusion generated by thought, and as creating unnecessary suffering (Da Free John, 1983; Mangalo, 1993;

Rinpoche, 1993; Thera, 1993). For example, because the seat of our sense of self is in our thoughts, we tend to be overinvested and attached to our beliefs and opinions, which creates unnecessary interpersonal conflict. Our objectified sense of self results in preoccupation with our failures, successes, and possessions. We are defensive about our flaws, mistakes, limits, and weaknesses. Such attachments, preoccupations, investments, defenses, and conflicts keep us on a perpetual roller coaster of emotional highs and lows. In the East, to preclude thinking altogether, or to observe how it proceeds and functions, helps lessen the overattachment to an objectified self-sense and the tendencies it produces (Suzuki, 1970; Goldstein & Kornfield, 1987; Rinpoche, 1993; Paranjpe, 1998).

In *Self and Identity in Modern Psychology and Indian Thought,* Anand Paranjpe (1998) has written a breathtaking comparative overview of Eastern and Western perspectives on self and identity. His analysis addresses the paradox of maintaining a sense of unity and sameness of identity in our lives despite the diversity and changes in our self-concepts. He suggests that the distinction between the experiences of self-as-subject and self-as-object represents a point of convergence between Eastern and Western perspectives on the nature of self. He summarizes a sampling of representative theories of personality, self, and identity that deny or minimize the existence of self-as-subject, or, in contrast, embrace it as an ever-present witness. One major difference between Eastern and Western theories of self, notes Paranjpe, is that Indian philosophies provide guidelines for how to dis-identify with various objects construed as self, so to awaken to the transcendental self in the witnessing mode. These guidelines emphasize a critical self-examination of all *objects* construed as self which are actually not-self.

Consistent with Eastern religious philosophies reviewed by Paranjpe, the theory developed in this book reflects the practice of critically examining the experience of self-awareness created by objects mistaken as the self. However, an understanding of the role of thought-objects in creating an illusory self-sense is shockingly absent among the theories considered by Paranjpe. Only one or two sentences of this voluminous text suggest that the sense of self is anchored in our current or most recent objectified thoughts (as witnessed), and tend to emphasize an overattachment to the beliefs reflected therein. In contrast, the theory of the microdynamics of thinking and self-awareness developed in the following pages indicates that observing "passing thoughts" is the most significant source of the illusory self, even apart from the beliefs reflected therein. This theory offers a detailed description of how observed thoughts create a sense of self, and why this self-sense is false. It also describes the structure and successive unfolding of thoughts. Lastly, like many Eastern religious philosophies of self examined by Paranjpe, *The Ghosts of Consciousness* promotes a process of transformation of consciousness by exposing the thought-based self-as-object as an illusion.

Despite the fact that many people have achieved insights about the relationship between thinking and self-awareness, I have not seen any detailed description of the structure of thought, the illusions created by it, or of how thought engenders them. William James (1950) began this process a century ago when he explained and described a general structure of thought, how reflective thought created a sense of self, and that reflective thought evoked certain illusory experiences. Since James, however, the structure of thought appears to have been ignored, and consequently, a theory of how thinking creates a sense of self and a number of related illusions has been impossible to outline.

In the following pages, a theory of the microdynamics of thinking and self-awareness is presented, where the "parts" and types of thought are distinguished based on their *phenomenal differences*. In addition, an analysis of their *process* aspects helps us understand their phenomenological manifestations. In other words, the theory describes how the "parts" of thought unfold and interact, and how different types of reflective thoughts create a sense of self and a variety of other experiential illusions.

The theory of the microdynamics of thinking and self-awareness is meant to firmly establish psychology in the realm of the subjective interiors of humanity once again. Reflected in this theory are intellectual insights about thinking that might motivate people to transcend their present manner of experiencing themselves and their world, consistent with the aspirations of Eastern religious and philosophical schools.

Lagging far behind Eastern religious and philosophical traditions such as Buddhism and Hinduism, which embrace teachings and practices relevant to consciousness, thinking, self-awareness, and so on, Western science has deemed the subjective interiors of humanity as largely irrelevant. Therefore, the theory of the microdynamics of thinking and self-awareness could serve as the initial core for a potentially new branch of transpersonal psychology: *cognitive phenomenology*. I envision *cognitive phenomenology* as the study of the subjective realities of thinking, its structure, types, process aspects, interactions, development, phenomenal and illusory manifestations, emotional, psychological, and behavioral influences, transpersonal and spiritual implications, and its relationship to self-identity, self-awareness, and self-esteem. Its most prominent tools would be introspection, meditation, and contemplation, its database, the interior, subjective world-space of the "I" and its data, the subjectively experienced and discerned mental images, thoughts, concepts, beliefs, their unfolding, interactions, phenomenal manifestations, significance, and influence. Its validating paradigm consists of the three strands of any knowledge quest: injunction or experimentation, interpretive data or apprehensions, and confirmation or consensual validation/rejection (Wilber, 1995).

Where cognitive psychology and science rely on concepts taken from computer structures and processes in order to understand and theorize about human mental functioning, cognitive phenomenology would emphasize more direct descriptions and representations of the subjective experience of mental events. Subjectively accurate descriptions of internal mental processes are as important as mapping unexplored geography. This descriptive goal is an end in and of itself rather than a means to a functional end, such as a better understanding of observable human behavior. This is not to say, however, that the phenomenally based descriptions, understandings, and insights of cognitive phenomenology wouldn't serve productive, helpful purposes applicable to our lives. To the contrary, theoretical insights reflected in this text have profound practical implications

Insights concerning the illusory nature of self, reflected in the theory of the microdynamics of thinking and self-awareness, are consistent with those of Eastern religious systems. However, the bases of these insights are more clearly articulated and specified in this theory, compared to its Eastern counterparts. Consequently, the theory of the microdynamics of thinking is an intellectually based adjunct and significant contribution to Eastern insights regarding the nature of self, thought, awareness, and so on. Despite this intellectual contribution, Eastern teachers and students of consciousness remain far ahead of Western society in *practices* based on such insights, resulting in transformations of consciousness not yet imagined by most Westerners.

A child's Slinky toy helps us discern the elusive, ephemeral structure of thought, and chapters 1 and 2 are its playgrounds. The paradoxical complexities of Slinky movement are shown to metaphorically parallel the structural and functional aspects of an evolving thought. Distinguishing thought in all of its Slinky-like features reveals invisible, living "ghosts" that have their own subjectivity, development, and influence. These "ghosts of consciousness" are surprising, unconscious aspects of thinking with whom we constantly interact.

Chapter 1 reveals that the preeminent ghost of consciousness is called an *excerpt*. An excerpt is a picturelike, mentally-based, meaning-laden, quasi-image, typically rising into one's awareness. It can be a memory association from one's past, a solution to a question or problem posed, a "piece" of meaning-laden "ground" from which a decision arises, a personally relevant, image-based reminder, or a "snapshot" of an object, person, event, or experience. Shocking is the fact that every thought is initiated by an excerpt, and we don't even know it!

Besides the excerpt, chapters 1 and 2 outline phenomenally and functionally distinct "parts" of thought, distinguished by using the Slinky metaphor: the *excerpt and excerptive-clip*, the *proactive* or *reactive excerpt-found reaction*, the *proactively or reactively identified excerpt*, the *reflective conceptual portion of the thought*, the *elaborative conceptual portion of the thought*, the *excerpt-searching reaction*, and *attentional surfacing* (also see glossary). An outline of the "parts" of thought, and of the process aspects of successive thoughts, offers amazing explanatory power for how the objectified sense of self is created. For instance, we can pinpoint the brief juncture among the unfolding "parts" of thought during which we feel temporarily self-aware and conscious of the object being thought about. In addition, we are unaware of the totality of any one thought, as if it were a minidream, perhaps becoming conscious of it only in retrospect.

Two general types of thought are defined and compared in chapter 1. *Elaborative thoughts* are like a waking dream. Most elaborative thoughts live a fleeting life without any recognition of their existence. *Reflective thoughts* are responsible for the experience of duality, where two actors relate on stage, when before there were none. In chapter 2, the new vocabulary of thinking is extended to five types of excerpts, the subtype of elaborative thinking called *implicit reflective identification* (IRI), a subtype of reflective thinking called *explicit reflective identification* (ERI), and two subtypes that can be elaborative or reflective: *reflective identification of excerpts* and *reflective identification of excerptive-clips of external objects*.

Chapter 3 identifies and describes the phenomenal differences between elaborative and reflective thought: during elaborative thinking, *thoughts seem to move forward, reflective moments seem fleeting or nonexistent, awareness totally embodies the object of attention,* and *there is no experience of time, place, or self;* during reflective thinking, *thinking seems to stop, reflective moments seem prolonged, self-awareness is experienced by attending to and objectifying a "passing thought," one can be conscious of the act of observing while being aware of the thought-object,* and can *experience self-awareness as a body-self and/or mental-self in space and time.*

Rarely prompting notice, thinking and self-awareness seem as natural as breathing. Like the eye blind to itself, chapter 3 outlines the processes through which you mistake the "passing thought" for your subjective presence, and at a level of greater complexity, of how your self-sense is continually reborn in the present, relative to a version of self that is sacrificed to the "past" and dies. Ghostlike in their felt, yet unseen presence, these two types of self-awareness are created by *noncomparative reflective thinking* and *comparative reflective thinking*, respectively.

Chapter 3 ends with a review of eight "parts" of thought and with a description of their respective phenomenologies. This is the culmination of a precise, theoretical formulation of the microdynamics of thinking. You will know more about thinking than ever before. A deeply personal and mysterious world will be revealed, and entirely new insights relevant to self-knowledge and understanding will begin to take root.

The structure of thinking, its unfolding, and phenomenology are like varied, amoeba-shaped cutouts, fitting the picture-puzzle of human development established by theorists and researchers. In chapter 4, ten types of thinking, with their particular phenomenologies of self, are here defined, clarified, exemplified, and placed within Ken Wilber's "full spectrum developmental model of consciousness" elaborative thinking, implicit reflective identification, explicit reflective identification, the reflective and elaborative forms of reflective identification of excerpts and reflective identification of excerptive-clips of external objects, noncomparative reflective thinking, comparative reflective thinking, and transparent reflective identification. Differences in the acuity and longevity of reflective awareness across these ten types of thinking are detailed and explained. A "holarchical" pattern of evolutionary development (across the human life span) reflected among these thought-forms is proposed and discussed. Lastly, each type of thought is associated with increasingly complex and expanded self-identities, creating a potential for genuine personal and spiritual advancement.

No matter how humble you *think* you are, reflective thinking elicits various shades of grandiosity, potentially embarrassing if you weren't so deceived. These qualitatively distinct yet overlapping experiences of self-inflation take four primary forms, and are defined in chapter 5.

Self-awareness is intermittent; sometimes it's "on" and sometimes it's "off." It's fascinating, however, that the conscious self only knows the experience of being "on" or present. Therefore, it believes it plays a creative and knowing part in all mental processes, experiences, and contents. In chapter 6, the conscious self receives the shock of its life, realizing that it only asks for and receives the gifts of its experience, rather than creating them as well. It learns that thoughts actually function as instructions to one's self, and are stimulus-prompts embodying the context within which associations from the unconscious mind rise into awareness (Jaynes, 1976).

The relationship between conscious and unconscious functioning is clarified in chapter 6. For instance, cognitive neuroscience reveals that clusters of neurons in the brain, functioning as autonomous modules of experiential knowledge, operate outside of awareness and are activated by internal or external conditions, thereby becoming part of one's awareness (Gazzaniga, 1985). In addition, research suggests that genetically and developmentally determined patterns of neuronal circuitry among the "small minds" of one's brain influence the nature of the contents of consciousness (Ornstein, 1986, 1991; Wade, 1996). Other unconscious realities influencing the nature and contents of consciousness, including one's personal and cultural history, as well as one's present emotional and physical condition (Wilber, 1995), are discussed in this chapter.

Experientially-based concepts derived from Ericksonian hyp-nosis are defined in chapter 6 in order to highlight the nature of and relationship between conscious and unconscious functioning (Erickson, Rossi, & Rossi, 1976; Erickson, Rossi, & Ryan, 1985). In addition, the scientific explanation of how a lightning bolt oc-curs (William, 1993), metaphorically parallels, in many surprising ways, the subjective realities of the conscious and unconscious as-pects of thinking.

Shaking the bedrock of one's sense of self and its relation-ship to all of reality, chapter 7 challenges the supposed separation between self and any experience the self "has." By drawing on the definitions of and distinctions among the "parts"and types of thought, the feeling of duality, of being a self-experiencer sepa-rate from and observing some objectified thought, is exposed as an illusion. For example, *during* an elaborative thought, you are never aware of the thought itself as it occurs. *During* a reflective thought, you become aware of a "passing thought" being observed and construe yourself as separate from it. However, reflective thoughts are actually a special kind of elaborative thought. There-fore, during reflective thoughts, the experience of being separate from thinking conceals an underlying elaborative phenomenol-ogy. Thus, the experience of duality is revealed as illusory because you are unaware of being immersed in one, unbroken experience as a splitting of experience seems to be occurring.

The mistaken belief of being *experientially* separate from environmental objects is also exposed in chapter 7. For instance, as a light-reflecting object, the tree you see in the back yard is manifested and enlivened through your sentient presence. Your experience of it is a function of being a living creature and of its unique physical properties interacting with stimuli that im-pinge on and in you. You can't ever separate yourself out of the equation in your relationship to the tree. You never know it as it is *to itself* because you're imbuing it with *who you are.* You and the stimuli from the tree combine to form a single experience, despite the reality of the apparent separateness between you, the self-experiencer, and it, the object of experiencing. Like a film projector casting images on a movie screen, the appearance of all reality is largely your creation. This is a central Buddhist insight for sentient creatures: in essence, that all of reality (as experienced) *is consciousness.*

Sensing the presence of ghosts in the attic, you finally face your fears, flashlight and flyswatter in hand. Exposing them—their tricks and antics—can bring longed-for relief from much of their habitually troublesome presence. In other words, the different types of *reflective thinking* give rise to various subjective experiences, many of which are exposed as illusions. Chapter 8 describes and challenges eleven illusions based on an understanding of the component "parts" of thought and of the different types of reflective thinking.

There are twins inside of you in mental form. They are twin kings ruling over an imagined kingdom of many. In the actual "kingdom" they are its only subjects. Being a king to yourself creates a number of chronic problems, which chapter 9 outlines. Based on an understanding of the component "parts" of thought, how they unfold and interact, and of the different types of thought, specific examples of how thinking engenders immediate happiness and suffering are presented. As a result, Eastern religious teachings are further specified and clarified. In addition, the teachings of several Buddhists provide a general understanding of the problematic nature of thinking and how it creates a great deal of human suffering. Having exposed the "mechanics" of the problematic nature and manifestations of thinking, meditation is briefly discussed as a common practice for learning to retrain and discipline attention so that it is not habitually drawn into thought. The positive outcomes of this practice are manifold, including the possibility of transcending one's present developmental level and moving up the ladder of consciousness articulated by Ken Wilber.

In the chapters ahead, a theory of the microdynamics of thinking is presented, beginning with distinctions regarding eight "parts" of thought. An introspective analysis drawing upon this structure and two, posited, general types of thought, results in distinctions concerning ten types of thinking, each with its own phenomenology and functional manifestations. These types of thinking are placed in a hierarchy based on their phenomenal differences, one that reflects an increasing acuity and expansion of self-awareness. Utilizing the eight "parts" of thought, the dynamic processes reflected in each type of thinking are outlined and explained, resulting in an understanding of how their respective phenomenologies are engendered. That most personally valued, fundamental, and significant of human realities—the experience of self-awareness—can now be understood in relation to its thought-induced mechanics across various types of thinking. That objectified sense of self-awareness created by these various thought-forms is revealed as an illusory phenomenon. The problematic manifestations stemming from this thought-induced sense of self can now be understood in light of its illusory nature, resulting in insights potentially motivating one to disidentify with the objective, thought-induced self-sense, thereby breaking the bonds of much suffering, consistent with Eastern religious premises and practices.

Meditation is a form of introspection on mental processes (Wilber, 1995). William James' (1950) insights and observations about thoughts were based on his introspective efforts. The insights and observations in this book are based on many years of introspection, culminating in descriptions of an evolving understanding of how thinking engenders many subjective experiences, especially of self-awareness. Along this journey I envisioned better understanding the mind, but I never anticipated meeting any ghosts along the way!

# Chapter One: Thinking

I MAGINE A REALLY CLEVER ghost who interacts with you all day, but prevents you from remembering any of it. You're relating to him all the time, and though you experience his presence in any number of ways, you're totally unaware that he even exists. But he really doesn't care because he's having great fun playing his sly, ghosty tricks!

Certain ghosts, like this one, leave you unaware of their daily presence in your life. You can't find them in your surroundings; they're actually "in" your head, "mind," or internal experience. You could call them the "ghosts of consciousness." Some people never discover them, while others get to know them quite well.

To acquaint ourselves with these "ghosts of consciousness"—with the hidden nature of thinking, self-awareness, the illusion of the objectified sense of self, intention, problem-solving, and the like—we must first outline the constituents of a discrete thought. These "parts" of thought form the foundation of a theory of the microdynamics of thinking and self-awareness. No such theory has been possible until now because a detailed account of the structure and phenomenology of thought has not been developed. With this structure firmly in place, we will be able to pinpoint the juncture at which we become self-aware in relation to the object being thought about. We will be able to clearly discern and define, by using our own mental experience as an introspective database, different types of thinking founded on specific combinations of the various constituents of thought. We will be able to understand how the interplay among the "parts" of various types of thought results in particular phenomenal manifestations, unique to each. We will be able to understand how different types of reflective thoughts engender different experiences of self-awareness. Understanding how the thought-induced sense of self is created will help us take our experience of self-awareness less seriously, thereby loosening our attachment to it and to the aspects of living that seem to support or threaten it. In other words, through a Westernized theory of the microdynamics of thinking and self-awareness, thousands of years of Eastern religious practices and philosophical teachings are clarified. The insights and understandings derived from this theory may motivate personal transformations and practical everyday changes in the way we experience ourselves and our world. But first, before attempting to conquer such feats, we must start with an analysis of a discrete thought.

### Thoughts

At first glance, thoughts seem as basic as the hair growing on your head. Upon close inspection, however, thoughts reveal a uniformity and sameness as well as a complexity and uniqueness. Let's define thinking in a general sense before exploring its hidden nature in greater depth.

A thought is a meaningful series of words about something often expressed mentally to oneself. When I notice my thinking, I'm aware of saying silent words to myself, "in my head." Because a thought is a string of words, it has a clear beginning and end, over a finite period of time. A single thought, therefore, appears to be a discrete, meaning-laden, conceptual reaction or response. It's an activity that moves in a progressive fashion from beginning to end in time. It is a momentary, presently occurring state of mind involving the exercise of concepts (Gennaro, 1996).

Franz Brentano (1973) says that processes like thinking and recollecting are always directed toward something in particular. Therefore, such processes, he says, are characterized by the concept of "intentionality." Similarly, in chapter 1 of *Self-Awareness: Its Nature and Development,* John R. Searle (1998) indicates that any mental state that is about something is intentional. Perceiving, believing, describing, hoping, fearing, wishing, and so on, are intentional states. In contrast, pains, itches, and tickles, as examples, are not. In other words, an itch is about itself, whereas a perception or belief is about something else. Searle says that intentional states function to relate us to our environment via representations that act on it.

Thus, a thought is an intentional state that is never isolated. A thought is always connected to an object of attention to which it is a response; it is always a reaction to something. It is an intentional process consisting of two essential aspects that are bound by relation: the conceptual reaction and the object of the reaction.

When thinking, one's attention, and hence, awareness, is initially and completely focused on the object to which the thought is a reaction. During this initial focus, that object is illuminated by and completely illuminates one's awareness. Any attempt to attend to something other than the object of that thought will interrupt the thought itself. Thinking requires your undistracted attention to be directed toward the object to which the thought is a reaction.

### Ghost Photographer

As stated above, a thought is a discrete, meaning-laden conceptual reaction about or in response to an object of attention. Before we outline the constituents of thought, let's explore what the thought is about and a response to.

"Excerption" is a term coined by Julian Jaynes (1976) in his book, *The Origins of Consciousness in the Breakdown of the Bicameral Mind.* Jaynes says of excerption:

> Excerption is distinct from memory. An excerpt of a thing is in consciousness the representative of the thing or event to which memories adhere, and by which we can retrieve memories. (p. 62)

Thus, to Jaynes, an excerpt is similar to a photograph of an aspect of a past event or experience from which memories spring.

Jaynes says that if you wish to remember what you were doing last summer, you first have an excerption of the time concerned, which may be a fleeting image of a couple of months on the calendar, until you rest in an excerption of a particular event, such as walking along a particular riverside. Then you build associations around that event and retrieve memories about last summer. Jaynes adds:

> Reminiscence is a succession of excerptions. Each so-called association in consciousness is an excerption, an aspect or image, if you will, something frozen in time, excerpted from the experience on the basis of personality and changing situational factors. (p. 62)

Generally then, excerpts are memory associations. If we think of them as mental pictures or snapshots of objects and aspects of experience, we realize that they are representations of "the past," just as a photograph captures a prior moment in time. I propose that excerpts are a basic constituent of thinking. More specifically, every thought is a reaction to an excerpt. Consequently, because excerpts are a form of memory, every thought is a response to a memory association which takes the form of an excerpt.

The proposal that thinking is directly related to memory is not a new one. The importance of memory in thinking has been recognized for hundreds of years. In his book *The Astonishing Hypothesis: The Scientific Search for the Soul,* Francis Crick (1994) reports that a hundred years ago it was recognized that consciousness or awareness involved a very short-term form of memory that is closely associated with attention. Crick seems to equate consciousness with thinking, stating that thinking helps one become aware of a particular aspect of experience. He also indicates that despite their differences, three present-day cognitive theorists who study consciousness generally agree that short-term memory and attention are involved in it (Johnson-Laird, 1983, 1988; Jackendoff, 1987; Bears, 1988).

In the East, the importance of memory in thinking and

consciousness has been recognized for thousands of years. East Indian philosophical and religious traditions have defined the "inner instrument" as the mind manifesting attentively, the intellect capable of making distinctions (via conceptions), and a structure of memories of past experience that prompt actions under appropriate circumstances (Paranjpe, 1998).

The researcher Jenny Wade (1996), drawing on a convergence among religion, philosophy, neurology, and psychology, concentrates on four basic essentials of consciousness, one of which is memory. Memory is an integral part of conscious experience, says Wade, because it binds each moment of awareness into a coherent pattern, providing a sense of personal continuity or an ongoing sense of self. Our subjective sense of self depends on having a historically bound stream of consciousness that we recognize as our own.

Given the relative consensus that memory is a significant aspect of thinking and consciousness, I propose that excerpts are the basic form that memory takes in all thoughts. In addition, excerpts are often triggered by any internal or external stimulus, situation, or context. As a result, they often rise into conscious awareness quite autonomously and by surprise. For instance, seeing my wife's checkbook on the kitchen table prompted an excerpt-image of my friend and me talking about going to a seminar together. In response to this excerpt, I thought, "I need to send a check to those seminar people."

In contrast, excerpts triggered by thoughts which are prompts to ourselves to remember something somehow seem less surprising or autonomous, as if we planned or caused them to occur. For example, Jaynes (1976) notes that giving oneself the thought-instruction to remember the events of last summer automatically produces appropriately related memory associations. In such instances, we take credit for our "excellent" memory ability because the self-instruction to remember initiates the autonomous process of remembering. We simply pretend that we are responsible for on in control of the entire process.

Most importantly, I propose that excerpts mark the beginning of each and every thought. In order to think about any one thing, it must first be excerpted, objectified, or given a mental representation. That object or aspect of experience is given a mental form the instant attention fixes upon it. And, in order to think about any one thing, we must first take up the object into our "mental space" via this transforming, "mentafying," excerpting process, where it is given mental form. The mental form excerpts take are typically picture-like or image-based. We don't see excerpts in the same way we see our surroundings but they seem to involve the sense of sight nonetheless; it's as if we "look" at them. Thus, one can say that excerpts are image-like embodiments which transform all stimuli into a mentally solidified ground from which a thought can arise. In addition, kinesthetic, auditory, olfactory, visual, gustatory, conceptual, or image-based stimuli can be excerpted. For example, I walk into my garage and suddenly notice a strange smell. My attention to the smell results in an awareness of it. It is absolute evidence that the smell was excerpted if a thought occurs in direct response to it. The excerpt of the smell serves as a mental, meaning-laden "ground" from which my thought about it arises.

Excerpts take different forms and are triggered by different stimuli. So far we've noted that excerpts mark the beginning of every thought and that they are often triggered by a variety of external stimuli, and by a thought-instruction to remember something. Excerpts can also represent internal stimuli. For instance, I might think, "Maybe I'll get a hamburger at Mc-Dougall's tonight." Then, as I reflect on this thought, thereby attending to and excerpting some of its meaningful content I think, "Nah, I'm more interested in Chinese." In this case, the excerpted identity of the thought about having a hamburger at McDougall's prompted an excerpt which the thought about having Chinese food took as its object.

I believe that excerpts also occur whenever attention fixes on a stimulus, whether external or internal, followed by a thought, emotion, behavior, or excerpt in direct response to any given one. For example, on a rainy day I took a drive down a busy street in town. When I returned home my girl-friend asked if it was tough driving in the weather. In response to this question, excerpts flashed into my awareness of seeing a son and father playing soccer in the down pour, of a big black crow by the side of the road eating a small dead animal, and of the muddy construction site on the corner of our street. I recalled these images because they had been singled out by my attention and awareness, and hence, excerpted during my short car trip.

Excerpts take different forms and are triggered by different stimuli. So far we've noted that excerpts mark the beginning of every thought, are often triggered by a variety of external and internal stimuli, and represent the full range of internal and external stimuli. Excerpts also arise as a natural part of or during an occurrent (i.e., present) thought. Such excerpts manifest as fleeting images to the mind's eye, of which we're barely aware, if at all. For example, as I think about going to a nearby lake I reflect on and attend to the fleeting image of the muddy road at the lake's entrance. Then I think, "I'll wait until it's sunny and dry." In this case, the excerpt of the muddy road was embodied in the thought about going to the lake.

Excerpts are also triggered by thoughts themselves. Some meaningful nuance in the stream of the "passing thought" prompts an excerpt somehow related to it. For example, the thought about buying a hamburger at "McDougall's" prompted an excerpt of the Chinese restaurant across the street from it.

As a rule of thumb, excerpts and thoughts typically follow each other in an alternating succession of excerpt-thought-excerpt-thought. This is not always the case, however. For example, in direct response to one's desire to remember the events of last weekend, a sequence of excerpts regarding that time might come into one's awareness before experiencing a thought in response to any one of them. For example, I might experience an excerpt-image of eating ice cream cones at a picnic table with my family; and then another excerpt-image of seeing a car accident only minutes after eating; followed by another one of sitting on the grass and feeling thankful that we're all healthy and happy. These excerpts might then be followed by the thought, "We had a lovely afternoon that day." In this case, each excerpt gave rise to the following one as a function of a situationally-based association. Despite the possibility that a number of excerpts can be triggered by a given thought, any one excerpt always precedes the thought which is a reaction to it.

Now that we have defined various types and functions of excerpts, a review of some of the research on mental imagery will bring some perspective to the "distance between" their experiential reality versus their "empirical" validaion. In his book *The Mind's New Science: A History of the Cognitive Revolution,* Howard Gardner (1985) discusses at length the empirical research on mental images. He notes that over one hundred years ago, Wilhelm Wundt and his followers made the study of the contents of mental life, including mental imagery, their goal. Followers of Wundt, says Gardner, explored their own internal imagery via introspection and carefully analyzed self-reports by subjects trained in this method. However, after twenty-five years or so, imagery was deemed unfit for scientific study because it was such a transitory and unreliable phenomenon. It appeared that not everyone had images and those who did often introspected on them in different ways. There was no way to define imagery in an experimental situation and no agreement on what an image actually is. The new "science" of psychology was hesitant to embrace such a nebulous mental construct. As a result, the ghostly mental image was an outcast for the next fifty years of psychological study.

Then, in 1971, Roger Shepard and Jacqueline Metzler exposed subjects to geometric figures and asked them to judge as rapidly as possible whether two figures seen from different angles matched eachother. According to Gardner (1985), their results indicated that the difficulty of the task, as measured by the time it took to give a response, depended on the number of degrees by which one of the two figures had been rotated. A figure that had been rotated eighty degrees took longer to identify as identical to the target than the one rotated forty degrees. It appeared that subjects were mentally rotating these figures, and that the greater the distance of the rotations, the longer it took to respond correctly. Subjects verified this based on their subjective experiences. The researchers concluded that human beings generated mental images of these figures and rotated them through some undefined mental space.

To some researchers such as Stephen Kosslyn (1980), Shepard's findings suggested that internal image-making abilities were a basic capacity of the cognitive system (Gardner, 1985). However, these researchers avoided the terminology that humans experience "pictures" in their heads, but they gave validity to the idea of an analogue mode of mental representation. Shepard's results challenged efforts to explain all of thought (e.g., problem solving and reasoning abilities) in terms of the serial, digital computer, which processes propositional information (i.e., in linguistic or symbolic form) stored in lists or networks. His results suggested that the brain may mimic ordinary processes, such as visual-perceptual ones, when physical stimuli are being attended to in the world (Gardner, 1985).

Later, Kosslyn and his colleagues (1978) completed research that supported the existence or independent validity and flexibility of mental imagery (Gardner, 1985). They then developed a comprehensive theory of mental imagery to account for their results. Avoiding the claim that human beings have pictures in their heads, they espoused the notion of a "quasi-pictorial" form of mental representation called "imagery." They deemed it a form of mental representation as important for understanding cognition as the propositional representation. Imagery was being seen as a basic property of human cognition, and as a primary way in which information can be symbolized or represented (Kosslyn, 1978, 1983).

Kosslyn (1978) believe that an image has a surface representation (the quasi-picture) which is accompanied by the subjective
reality of its experience (Gardner, 1985). He says that images are
temporary spatial displays in active memory that are generated
from more abstract representations in long-term memory. These
abstract representations consist of propositions and other kinds
of non-imagistic information, such as that embodied in concepts.
Thus, in the generation of imagery, adds Kosslyn, there is an
interplay between descriptive (languagelike) and depictive (picturelike) memories. Kosslyn also believes that a mind's-eye-like
device is necessary to interpret images or parts thereof.

Kosslyn's overall theoretical position has been supported by
research (Farah, 1984) which suggests that the image-generating
component of his model can be destroyed in isolation by dam-
age to the brain. Nevertheless, nearly every aspect of his research
has been severely attacked (Pylyshyn, 1979, 1981, 1984). Pylyshyn (1981, 1984), in particular believes that an individual has
much available knowledge embedded as propositions that are
drawn upon to construct what is subjectively experienced as an
image (Gardner, 1985). He says that cognition is computation.
He believes that the brain operates much as a computer does.
He believes that images are derived from basic propositional or
symbolic representations rather than being a distinctive form of
representation themselves.

Kosslyn, says Gardner (1985), concedes that there is a basic
propositional level of coding from which images may well be
generated, at least in part. Nevertheless, he believes that mental
images play a causal role in problem-solving and reasoning. Further research might reveal several imagery systems that capture
and transform other kinds of information, such as linguistic,
musical, or tactile.

Gardner (1985) concludes that philosophers, psychologists,
and cognitive researchers are often averse to the term "imagery"
because it implies that there are pictures in the mind that are being viewed. In addition, because "image" connotes "stasis" rather

than "process" they dislike the term (Shebar, 1979).

It is clear that the research on the existence of mental imagery is controversial. Such controversy is striking given that experimental subjects being asked to perform image-based tasks subjectively report the experience of mental images. If the existence of such images are being called into question under such circumstances, what becomes of the experience and concept of excerpts? Unlike the quasi-pictorial forms used during problem-solving and reasoning, excerpts, I believe, are an intrinsic aspect of the thought process itself. As such, excerpts would appear to be more fleeting than their experimental counterparts, resulting in little-to-no conscious awareness of their presence as a mental experience per se. Furthermore, they are likely more quasi-pictorial than their experimental and experiential cousins. Despite their phenomenal reality as a quasi-pictorial mental form, establishing their existence experimentally might prove difficult. Thus, at this time, the phenomenal basis of excerpts is all we have to go on. Invoking Gardner (1985), "…it seems self-delusion…to deny images to one's own phenomenal experience"(p. 323).

In sum, I believe that excerpts are quasi-image-based embodiments presented to our mind's eye in response to thought-based triggers as well as to a huge variety and number of stimuli. As such, they are the basic form that memory takes in the thought process. In addition, they mark the onset of each and every thought. Excerpts arise as a natural part of occurrent thoughts. Last, any internal or external stimulus can be excerpted as a result of being momentarily fixed in awareness through attention to it. Such an excerpt subsequently leads to another excerpt, thought, emotional, or behavioral reaction in direct response to it.

The following is a brief summary of what has been said thus far about how excerpts can be triggered, of what can trigger them, of what they represent, and of how they function.

- Excerpts can be triggered by external or internal stimuli.

- Excerpts can be triggered by a thought-instruction to

remember something.

- Excerpts can be triggered by a "passing thought."
- Excerpts arise as a natural part of or during a present thought.
- Excerpts can represent internal or external stimuli.
- Excerpts can embody or represent some meaning in a "passing thought."
- Excerpts mark the beginning of every thought.

Just imagine how many excerpts are being presented or created in your mind given the number of thoughts you have during any one day! Isn't it amazing that you are reacting to the content of each excerpt via a given thought without any awareness of their existence per se? Excerpts are truly a special class of ghosts among the "ghosts of consciousness." At the very least, they are an unrecognized partner in the unfolding of each and every thought.

Easily recognizable behavioral tendencies provide some indirect observable support for the existence of excerpts, but they tend to go unnoticed. In their book *Frogs into Princes,* Richard Bandler and John Grinder (1979) discuss eye-accessing cues. In order to determine whether you are a person who is more visually, auditorially, or kinesthetically oriented in the way you mentally experience information, Bandler and Grinder watch for the direction your eyes move when you are receiving or processing information. They have developed a chart that makes certain generalizations about the kind of information a person is likely accessing based on the angle and direction of eye movements he or she tends to make in response to questions. Whether or not these generalizations are valid is somewhat irrelevant because individuals introspecting on their mental experience in response to questions frequently report accessing information in a certain perceptual form, at the instant of eye-shifting.

Consider eye-accessing cues in relationship to excerption. While a person is looking up and to the left during a conversation, for example, he is excerpting. When you see him direct his attention away from you by fleetingly fixing his gaze as if out into space, this gaze-shifting reflects the fact that his attention is fixing itself on an excerpt rising from within.

Pay attention to your mental experience the next time someone is asking you questions. Perhaps you can discern the form that answers take as they rise into your subjective awareness. In addition, pay attention to eye-shifting when you ask someone questions. I think you'll notice that the timing of their verbalized answers will immediately follow an instant of eye-shifting, suggesting that he is fixing his "inner" gaze on excerpted information rising into awareness.

It is amazing that during such an instant of excerpting, external reality no longer exists in his awareness. His awareness is, in that instant, totally fixed on the content reflected in the excerpt at hand. Then, he reacts to that now-recognized meaning embodied in the excerpt via a thought that he verbalizes as while turning his attention back to you. He had temporarily lost you and external reality in his experience without any apparent awareness of having done so. The entire activity or process of excerpting, and hence, of "losing you," was unconscious. The ghost (excerpt) was there and he was directly interacting with it without even knowing it!

### *Elaborative and Reflective Thinking and Experiencing*

The intermittent awareness of self in relation to external reality is called the General Reality Orientation (Shor, 1959). It is essentially equated with our ordinary waking state of conscious awareness, of orientation and relation to the concrete reality around us. As a matter of biological preservation, this orientation includes attending to ourselves as a physical presence, to what we're doing, where we are, what time it is, and the people with us. It reflects the diffusion of attention and awareness over a broad range of contextual realities, in relation to our presence. When we're not totally absorbed in some activity we tend to be conscious of ourselves as a physical presence in relationship to the activity at hand and to aspects of our surroundings. It is the experience of being self-aware, in context.

The GRO can help us think about the distinction between what I call *elaborative* and *reflective* thinking. Generally, if I attend to, excerpt, and explicitly represent the meaningful identity of a "passing thought" (at the outset of the current thought), along with (the potential of) becoming aware of and representing the presence of the thought per se, I'm engaged in *reflective thinking*. For example, an *explicit* reaction to the excerpted content of a "passing thought" is *about* that content: "Oh, I was just thinking about…"

On the other hand, if at the outset of the current thought I attend to and excerpt some meaningful aspect of a "passing thought," resulting in some *implicit* reaction to that aspect, I'm engaged in *elaborative thinking*. For instance, an implicit reaction to the excerpted content of a "passing thought" (e.g., "I need to cash my paycheck") is a reaction *to* it: "Yeah, tomorrow I'll go to the bank." In addition, I'm engaged in elaborative thinking if I excerpt and implicitly react to any other excerpted object of attention directly prompted by the prior thought (other than the identity or "presence" of the "passing thought" per se). For example, immediately after the thought, "That's right, we're decorating the Christmas Tree tonight," an excerpt of the fireplace came to mind, and I thought, "I need to get some wood for the fire." In other words, it's the nature of the identified excerpt coupled with how the present thought is reacting to it that distinguishes elaborative from reflective thinking.

Reflective and elaborative thinking share parallels with what I refer to as *reflective* and *elaborative experiencing*. When we're so absorbed in the *behavior* at hand that we have no awareness of anything other than what it embodies, we're engaged in *elabo-*

*rative experiencing.* When totally absorbed in playing a musical instrument, or sport, for example, our awareness embodies this activity; we do not attend to the activity itself as an explicit object. During this absorption the mind-body action at hand automatically leads us into the next naturally unfolding action in an ongoing, elaborative fashion.

In contrast, we've all experienced moments of distraction from our immersion in the activity at hand in favor of focusing on the activity itself as an object of attention. For instance, if I'm shooting a basketball my awareness might be totally focused on the back of the rim of the basketball hoop and on nothing else. However, *if I attend to the fact* that I am presently looking at the back of the rim, I am engaged in *reflective experiencing.* It's during such reflective experiencing that a sense of self-awareness occurs, one of being a looker, along with an awareness of the object of attention at hand, the back of the rim itself.

During elaborative thinking and experiencing, the contents of the experience at hand are so illuminated by and so illuminate awareness, you become one with them, phenomenally. It's as if awareness is too immersed in those contents for anything else to exist. In contrast, reflective thinking and experiencing allow the illuminated, objectified contents of attention to become a mirror in which you see yourself as an observer, in your awareness of them. You experience an awareness of being a seeing, observing entity, along with an awareness of the objectified contents at hand. In verbal form: "I'm aware of myself shooting a basketball at the back of the rim."

The old game of "shooting marbles" supplies an analogy for elaborative and reflective thinking. Imagine that your awareness is in an old marble looking at and moving toward a new marble. When the old marble hits the new one, your awareness, like a form of kinetic energy, is transferred into it. Your awareness then looks forward and ahead as the new marble moves forward. This is much like elaborative thinking. In reflective thinking, by contrast, when the old marble hits the new one, your awareness is transferred into it, but it then looks back at the old one, seeing its movement and reflection in it.

Thus, during elaborative thinking and experiencing, I seem to "skip off of" my present experiencing in a progressive or forward movement. It's as if I use my present experiencing as a springboard for moving ahead. In reflective thinking and experiencing, however, it's as if I "greet" my "present" experiencing. As a result, I essentially end up "meeting" myself by becoming self-aware in relationship to some objectified, "present" self-experiencing.

The absorbing nature of elaborative thinking requires explication of the following fact: the presence of a particular thought always signifies that attention had just focused on an identified, excerpted object to which it reacted. In other words, during elaborative thoughts, awareness pulls away from the identified, excerpted object, totally losing sight of what the excerpted meaning was or that it even existed! That unique meaning-laden moment was filled with the life force of awareness, led a brief life, and is now dead, without the solace of ever being remembered. Only an extra moment of reflection could have prolonged its "life" or created greater consciousness of it. Similarly, an entire chain of elaborative thoughts can pass without the benefit of reflection. As a result, they will never be known to one's conscious mind. During elaborative thinking, one's awareness is simply too busy *being* the unfolding reaction at hand to notice anything else, including passing instances of itself. Thus, to itself, it doesn't even exist!

During elaborative thinking, one's awareness is consumed in, identified with, and absorbed by the current of meaning-laden changes and transitions that one loses sight of self, self-experiencing, and time and place. Thus, during elaborative thinking, one's awareness and the mental experiencing at hand combine to form a single, experiential reality. As a result, nothing other than the experiential reality at hand seems to exist.

It is quite interesting to be absorbed in elaborative thinking or experiencing for a substantial period of time. You can't be aware of absorption in either one while they're occurring. It's only when you discontinue either experience that you can have any reflective awareness of having been so absorbed. We all know what it's like to drive on a highway, for example, and suddenly realize that we've been so immersed in thought that we forgot we were driving. Later, we're shocked we didn't have an accident!

During that period of internal "reverie" we were essentially caught up in elaborative thinking. At any moment throughout that period, the object of our attention and our reactive experience to it, are one. Phenomenologically, our awareness in relation to that object is a single experiential entity. However, at the instant when reflective thinking occurs we realize that we've been absorbed in thought and we experience a sense of coming back to ourselves. We become self-aware in the form of attending to our objectified experiencing (as "passing thought") in relation to our surroundings in time and place.

During elaborative thinking and experiencing, our phenomenology exists in the form of a reaction that our awareness embodies. During reflective thinking and experiencing, however, our phenomenology becomes dual: we are both aware of observing (of being an observer), and of the object of observation. However, neither tends to know each other on a subjective, phenomenal basis. From the vantage point of the self-sense engendered by reflective thinking, there is no awareness of elaborative thinking, of thought existing as an unfolding process. It is generally only aware of thoughts as objects it seems to witness. Similarly, from the vantage point of elaborative thinking, there is no awareness of self. Such a self-sense is engendered by taking the closest thought at hand as an explicit object of attention. Since elaborative thinking never takes itself as an explicit object of attention, it doesn't even exist to itself. It simply exists as the embodiment of various contents of awareness. Generally, with these two types of thinking, when one is phenomenally "on" the other is phenomenally "off."

Below is a brief summary of the differences between reflective and elaborative forms of thinking and experiencing regarding their objects and the nature of their reactions to those objects.

- *Reflective thinking* takes immediately "passing" thoughts and their meaningful identities as excerpted objects of attention, followed by an explicit conceptual representation of them (e.g., becoming *aware of thinking about a movie*).

- *Elaborative thinking* can attend to some excerpted meaningful content of a "passing" thought (other than its explicit identity), or to any other excerpted content/object directly prompted by a "passing" thought, followed by an implicit conceptual reaction to that content/object (e.g., thinking *about* a movie).

- *Reflective experiencing* attends and explicitly reacts to any excerpted aspect of self-experience (e.g., becoming *aware of playing* a flute).

- *Elaborative experiencing* attends and implicitly reacts to any excerpted object other than the self-experiencing at hand (e.g., playing a flute).

In this chapter, we defined a thought as a meaningful series of words about something, usually expressed mentally to oneself. A thought is a temporally finite, meaning-laden, conceptual reaction to an object of attention. Amazingly, that object of attention is always transformed into an excerpt. Recall that Julian Jaynes (1976) coined the term and defined excerpts as memory associations. Then we elaborated upon Jaynes' definition: excerpts are quasi-image-based "snapshots" of objects or aspects of experience to which thoughts react. Experientially, excerpts seem to involve the sense of sight because we seem to look at them. Thus, excerpts are imagelike embodiments representing the transformation of stimuli into a mentally "solidified ground" from which a thought can arise and take as an object. Any internal or external stimulus can be excerpted as a result of being momentarily fixed in awareness through attention to it. Regarding internal stimuli, excerpts can represent some aspect of meaning embodied in a given thought, and they often arise within the stream of thought itself. On the one hand, a thought can prompt an excerpt somehow related to it and any excerpt can prompt a thought, another excerpt, and an emotional or behavioral reaction in direct response to it. Finally, it's mind-boggling that, despite the fact that we are experiencing excerpts all of the time, we are not conscious of their literal presence as experiential realities. The ghost was there and we interacted with it only to forget about it milliseconds after it's gone!

We also defined two kinds of thinking and experiencing: reflective and elaborative thinking and experiencing. Given these distinctions among different types of thinking and experiencing, we realized that much of thinking and experiencing is elaborative, and hence, unconscious; once instances of them are over, there is often no awareness of their experiential existence whatsoever. One's awareness is simply too busy being the unfolding (elaborative) reaction at hand to notice anything else, including passing instances of itself; to itself, it doesn't even exist. Last, through our new understanding of reflective thinking and experiencing we discovered that our phenomenology therein embodies a duality: we are aware of being an observer *and* aware of the object of observation. In other words, reflective thinking and experiencing engender the experience of the separate self-sense set apart from objects of experience.

# Chapter Two: It's Slinky Time!

I N THIS CHAPTER, THE structure of thought will be outlined based on the phenomenological changes experienced across any given thought or series of thoughts. Get ready: the description of this structure may "blow your mind" because you have never given thoughts a second glance. In other words, you may realize that thoughts are much more than you ever imagined. Moreover, given the descriptive insights about their structure you may be awestruck when you attend to thoughts and experientially validate much of their phenomenology.

By the end of this chapter, eight "parts" of thought will be described and defined, elaborative and reflective thoughts will be distinguished based on their respective "parts," and six different types of thoughts will be defined based on their phenomenological structure. In addition, four types of excerpts will be defined, along with another general type of excerpt that often represents a meaningful aspect of any given thought. Last, based on this entirely new description of the structure and microdynamics of thinking, we will be able to detail and understand the process by which different reflective thoughts engender different forms of self-awareness.

In chapter 1, we examined the nature of excerpts and their inherent function as the object of every thought. As a result, we can further examine their role in thinking and further distinguish the components of any given thought. Going back in time, a child's toy will help get us started.

Those who played with a Slinky as a child will remember its loosely coiled, flat-wire design that easily collapses into a tube shape. When pushed off a stair its forward momentum takes it down a flight of stairs, step by step, end to end.

With no clear beginning or end, the Slinky seems to push

and pulls itself down the staircase. Leaping off each minicliff, it seems alive and purposeful in its self-perpetuating determination to reach its goal. The original "cyborg" of steel moves with the sameness and precision that machines possess.

The paradoxical complexities of Slinky movement metaphorically parallel the structural and functional aspects of the evolution of a given thought. Distinguishing the elusive and ephemeral qualities of thought in all of its Slinky-like features reveals invisible, living "ghosts" that have their own subjectivity, evolution, and influence. These "ghosts of consciousness" are surprising unconscious aspects of thinking with whom we constantly interact.

Figure 1 shows a Slinky-thought unfolding from left to right with the passage of time. The Slinky in Figure 1 has three numbered parts and its action of going down stairs can be compared to the process aspects of thought.

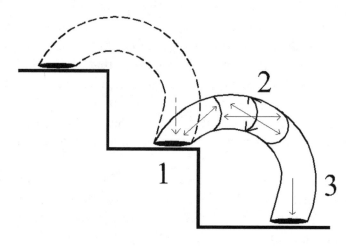

*Figure 1*

As we discuss the evolution of a given thought we will mix in elements of this moving Slinky metaphor. First of all, imagine that your awareness is inside the Slinky and that the Slinky is like a thought. Part 1 represents the onset of the thought, or in Slinky terms, one end of it is flowing down onto the stair, firmly planting itself there. As that end of the Slinky flows down onto the stair you experience a downward momentum of awareness toward and on top of it. That section of the Slinky that hits the stair represents the beginning of a new thought, where your awareness is focusing on and meeting an excerpt. The dotted-lined arrow pointing down toward the stair in Figure 1 represents this action of the immersion of awareness and downward momentum into the stair or excerpting moment.

The explanation of how an *elaborative thought* unfolds is as follows. At part 1 in Figure 1, a prior thought is ending as the downward momentum of the Slinky-thought's free end moves toward a new stair-*excerpt*. As it nears the stair, the excerpt, along with its meaningful identity, begins to coalesce, culminating in the appearance to awareness of a *fully identified* excerpt (after it hits the stair). Hitting the stair-excerpt marks the onset of a new thought and the end of the old one. Once one end of the Slinky-thought is firmly planted on the stair-excerpt, awareness reflects on and reacts to the excerpt's meaningfully identified content (as depicted by the solid lined arrow pointing to the except-stair at number 1). This reaction to and movement away from the identified excerpt is the *reflective conceptual portion* of a newly initiated elaborative thought. At the same time, the opposite, free end of this new Slinky-thought begins pulling away, moving forward, and then down the stairs.

In this description of an evolving elaborative thought, the action of identifying the excerpt *co-occurs* with its appearance to awareness during the cessation of the prior thought. In other words, identifying the meaningful nuances of the approaching excerpt-stair is initiated on the downward-momentum-side of the ending Slinky-thought as its free end nears the *appearing* excerpt-stair. This identifying *reaction* is called the *proactive excerpt-found reaction,* which results in a *proactively identified excerpt* as the excerpt fully appears to awareness after hitting the stair. During proactive excerpt-found reactions, one's phenomenal experience consists of *moving toward* an *increasingly* visible and identified excerpt.

The role of awareness when proactive excerpt-found reactions occur can be clarified with another metaphor. Imagine that your awareness is equally divided in and among one hundred puzzle pieces. Thrown into the air, the puzzle pieces magically fit together as they fall to the ground. Upon hitting the ground, awareness consists of a fully identified picture of an elephant, for example. As the pieces of the puzzle were coming together in the air, awareness was getting a preliminary sense of what the pieces were forming. This sense becomes increasingly solidified as the pieces move closer to the ground. By the time they hit the ground the full appearance of the elephant and its identity concurrently present themselves to awareness.

During proactive excerpt-found reactions, awareness is more than privy to past and present thought-content having a bearing on what the new excerpt will be because it exists in the form of that content. As one thought ends, awareness embodies the unfolding meaning at that moment. While a new excerpt comes into being, awareness embodies its preliminary form. Therefore, once the excerpt appears in its entirety, it's already (implicitly) identified because awareness was present during all of its evolution. As a result of this evolutionary process, the identified excerpt seems consistent with its predecessor thought. The excerpt seems to be a natural extension of the prior "current" of meaning, as natural as picking an apple after reaching for it. This meaningful consistency is also a function of meaning-laden "currents," influenced by and consistent with the just prior thought, which increasingly manifest in the form of the appearing excerpt.

When I reach to pick an apple off a tree, the picking is, in a sense, a natural reaction to and extension of the reaching. The picking is dependent on the reaching. This is true as well of elaborative thinking of the general type. By "general type" I mean to distinguish a basic form of elaborative thinking from more specific subtypes, which will be defined later. In a succession of general elaborative thoughts, my reaction following a particular thought does not involve any reflection on and excerption of that thought. My thought to clean the garage, for example, is a reaction to my predecessor-thought that the garage is dirty. Certainly, thinking about cleaning the garage is suggestive of having taken into account the prior thought of its dirtiness. My awareness subjectively embodied acknowledging the dirty garage, and hence, already "knows" that experience as lived. Therefore, the next thought is not necessarily so dependent on its predecessor that *it* had to be excerpted. Instead, the thought that the garage was dirty *prompted* an excerpt of the cleaning products I purchased last week, which I then reacted to by thinking, "I'll clean it today." Thus, a general elaborative thought is preceded by an *excerpt-searching reaction* that marks the end of its predecessor-thought. As that thought comes to a close, awareness goes searching for an excerpt prompted by that thought. Then a new thought is initiated by and is a reaction to a proactive excerpt-found reaction and the appearing, proactively identified excerpt.

Now that we have outlined the structure and unfolding of elaborative thoughts, let's discuss reflective thoughts. Similar to the onset of an elaborative thought, the beginning of a *reflective thought* occurs as the free end of the Slinky-thought moves down onto a new stair during the proactive excerpt-found reaction, resulting in a proactively identified excerpt appearing to awareness. This marks the beginning of the new thought as the prior thought ends. With one end of this newly initiated Slinky-thought firmly planted on the excerpt-stair, a momentum and movement away from that excerpt-stair occurs as awareness reflects on, reacts to, and *begins identifying the excerpt again.* Thus, during *reflective thoughts*, a second identifying *reaction* occurs in response to the proactively identified excerpt. This is called a *reactive excerpt-found reaction.* This second identifying reaction is subsequently brought to an end at the instant awareness is released from it and reflects on the reaction itself, resulting in an *explicitly* recognized and momentarily fixed excerpt. This excerpt is called a *reflectively identified excerpt*. Then, awareness *reacts* to this explicitly recognized excerpt via the *reflective conceptual portion* of the present reflective thought, or thought proper.

Thus, in contrast to an elaborative thought, a reflective thought places a second excerpt-found reaction on the pulling-away-side of an excerpt that has already appeared to awareness and been proactively identified at its outset. In other words, at the outset of a reflective thought, a reactive excerpt-found reaction occurs in response to a proactively identified excerpt that has appeared to awareness. During a reactive excerpt-found reaction, one's phenomenal experience consists of explicitly identifying an excerpt-image that has already appeared to awareness while looking toward and *moving away from* it. The appearing, proactively identified excerpt, coupled with a reactive excerpt-found reaction, marks the onset of all reflective thoughts. The reactive excerpt-found reaction is a second, more prolonged look at the proactively identified excerpt, resulting in an unfolding, explicit embodiment of its content, to which the *reflective conceptual portion* of thought can then react.

To recap: at the outset of a reflective thought, the first "look" at the excerpt occurs just before and during its evolution via the proactive excerpt-found reaction, resulting in an *implicitly and proactively* identified excerpt. The reactive excerpt-found reaction is a second, more prolonged look at the excerpt. Once awareness is released from and *fixes* on this reactive excerpt-found reaction, a second excerpting instant occurs, resulting in a reflectively identified excerpt, further solidifying its identity into explicit form. In other words, the *reflective conceptual portion* of the thought, or thought proper, initially reflects on the reactive excerpt-found reaction, essentially fixing it into an explicit, excerpted form or "snapshot." The remainder of the reflective conceptual portion of the thought is the conceptual reaction to this explicitly identified excerpt.

A reflective thought is preceded by a thought like, "I need

to mail those letters before I go to work." The release of awareness from this thought prompts attention to reflect back on it,
resulting in its proactively excerpted identity. Then a reactive excerpt-found reaction occurs in response to this implicitly identified and excerpted content. Next, attention fixes on the reactive
excerpt-found reaction at the outset of the reflective conceptual
portion of the reflective thought at hand, resulting in an excerpt
of the "passing thought's" explicit identity. The unfolding of
the reflective conceptual portion of the reflective thought, or
thought proper, consists of, "I was just thinking that I need to
send off the mail before I go to work."

As a side note: these phenomenally-based and functionally
distinct "parts" of thought only make sense when we consider
being absorbed in a series of thoughts. Their intuitive veracity
would not make sense if they were examined in the context of an
isolated thought, an experiential impossibility.

Regarding any one thought, the reflective conceptual portion of the thought occurs near its beginning and the *elaborative
conceptual portion* occurs during its middle to end (at #2 in Figure 1). The reflective conceptual portion of the thought occurs
as awareness reflects on and reacts to the meaningfully *recognized* excerpt, whether proactively or reactively identified. This
reflective moment always marks the beginning of the reflective
conceptual portion of the thought in response to a meaningfully
recognized excerpt.

During all thoughts, the more the reflective conceptual portion of the thought unfolds, the less the meaningful content of
the excerpt is being attended to in awareness. Instead, awareness
becomes increasingly immersed in the unfolding conceptual reaction at hand with no prolonged reaction to any one object of
attention, including the content of the excerpt. It's during this
period of immersion from the middle to the end of the thought
(#2 in Figure 1) that the *elaborative conceptual portion* of the
thought occurs. During this portion of the thought, awareness is
completely immersed in the unfolding, meaningful experiencing

at hand and not on any particular object of attention. When the elaborative conceptual portion ends, awareness surfaces from its immersion in-and-as the unfolding meaning at hand. Awareness then moves into the dark room of subconsciousness searching for an as-yet-to-be-found excerpt. This searching process is what I call the *excerpt-searching reaction,* where awareness is released from absorption in the experiential reality of the thought and is moving toward a new, *potential* excerpt (#3 in Figure 1). This searching ends as the proactively and implicitly identified excerpt begins to appear to awareness, marking the onset of the proactive excerpt-found reaction.

More generally, with successive thoughts, each thought is connected by a given, identified excerpt. In other words, the elaborative conceptual portion of the thought at the end of thought #1, and the reflective conceptual portion of the thought at the beginning of thought #2, occur together around the *identified* excerpt. Thought #1 ends as awareness exits a present thought and heads toward the as-yet-to-be-initiated excerpt for a new thought (e.g., the excerpt-searching reaction), and thought #2 begins as awareness reflects on the new, proactively identified excerpt. The identified excerpt is the most substantive experience marking the end of one thought and the beginning of the next. For example, I could be thinking, "The seats we had at the play tonight were really great." The meaningful nuances at the end of this thought prompt an excerpt of having sat near my old friend Sue. The excerpt marks the end of the thought about the great seats. In response to the identified excerpt, I think, "It was great to see her there" (an elaborative thought). The excerpt marks the end of one thought and beginning of the next thought.

In many ways thinking is similar to sitting inside the end of a large playground tube looking out toward a sand-castle. Imagine that you are suddenly sucked inside the tube watching the castle get smaller. As you are pulled through the tube, its twists and turns spin and disorient you so much that you forget the castle ever existed. Just as quickly, you are thrown out the other end of the tube, facing a merry-go-round.

How is the subjective nature of this "tube" experience similar to that of thinking? In thought, your attention is initially oriented to a certain, identified, excerpted object to which you begin to react, conceptually. This reflective conceptual portion of the thought is similar to being sucked back into the tube, still looking out at and reacting to that recognized sand-castle. But as the thought unfolds, its twists and turns are a reflection of changes in the unfolding, experiential meaning at hand. As your awareness of that original object ceases, you enter the elaborative conceptual portion of the thought, being swept through the thought-tube of meaning-laden changes (which your awareness embodies), until you come spinning out of it, and then "look for" a new object of attention.

Figure 2 summarizes the parts of a *reflective thought* across time with the "past" represented on the left of the figure as the thought unfolds from left to right with the passage of time.

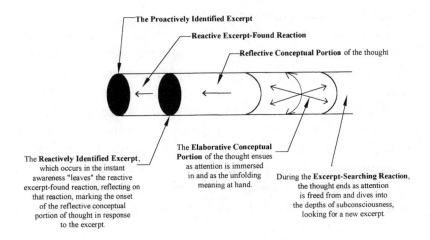

*Figure 2: Reflective Thought*

This Figure is supposed to represent a thought in the shape of a tube, within which awareness is contained and constrained. Assume that the dark oval on the far left of the diagram is an excerpt that was proactively identified. The dark oval to its right is the second excerpting moment or reflectively identified excerpt, which appears at the instant awareness fixes upon the reactive excerpt-found reaction at the outset of the reflective conceptual portion of the (reflective) thought. The excerpt-searching reaction at the far right of the diagram is just one way a reflective thought could end.

Thoughts are "speedy," and the parts of thought can be characterized by a series of movements and glances. Like driving a car, you are typically going so fast that you catch only glimpses of things: the squirrel darting into the trees to your left, a crow on the telephone wire, a fallen boulder on the side of the road, a father and son kicking a soccer ball. Later, if you were to reflect on your car trip, you might recall these images, which are as fleeting now as were the events themselves. At driving speed, a glance here and a glance there, a frozen image here and a frozen image there are all that is possible. There's no time to study anything, to watch anything evolve or unfold.

Similarly, a proactively identified excerpt is just a glance. Awareness glances at a stimulus, momentarily freezing it in time. Then I react to that image via the reactive excerpt-found reaction, for example. Then, a simple fleeting glance momentarily freezes that reaction (into an excerpt), initiating the reflective conceptual portion of the thought as a response to it. As the thought unfolds and is coming to a close, a glance may freeze the thought itself. Movements and glances, reactions and excerpts. The thought process speeds along while glances capture aspects of it, fleeting meaning-laden images from which reactions arise.

### The Complete Structure of Thought

Taking the basic constituents of thought and the two general types of thinking into account, we can introspect on our mental experience to further distinguish the structure and various types of thought. Once we complete this task, we will be in an excellent position to define different types of thought, further describe the phenomenology of thinking and understand how a sense of self is created by thought, outline the evolution of thought along a developmental hierarchy, better define the illusions of thought and the process by which they're created, and understand how the thought process engenders happiness and suffering, to name a few.

The basic components of thought discussed thus far include the proactively and reactively identified excerpts, the two types of excerpt-found reactions, reflective conceptual portion, elaborative conceptual portion, and excerpt-searching reaction. At this time I would like to complete our outline of the structure of thought. But first, let's briefly review excerpts, and define the different types of excerpts in thinking.

Recall that excerpts are quasi-images frequently triggered by certain thoughts, stimuli, and settings. They often rise into conscious awareness quite by surprise. They can be prompted by internal or external stimuli or by deliberate attempts to remember. In addition, any internal, external, or experiential stimulus can be excerpted by momentarily fixing attention to it.

The different types of excerpts can be further specified. An *excerptive reminder* is a spontaneously arising memory association prompted by some internal or external aspect of experience. Excerptive reminders relate to my personal sphere, but they are not directly autobiographical. For example, the coffee cup my client left behind prompted a flash-image excerpt of her and of the fact that she had surgery today. The coffee cup reminded me of her surgery. The excerpt of her surgery is the excerptive reminder.

Excerpts that are autobiographical memory associations from my past are called *excerptive memories*. An excerptive memory is a spontaneous memory association whose content is implicitly or explicitly recognized as personal or autobiographical in nature. I might be listening to some friends exchanging stories of traumatic injuries, for example, and experience spontaneous, flash-image excerpts of similar experiences from my personal history. Excerptive memories are synonymous with episodic memories which are particular autobiographical events from the past (Tulving, 1983).

*Excerptive solutions* are memory associations that are not explicitly personal or autobiographical in nature and have little to do with information from one's personal sphere. In other words, excerptive reminders are less personal than excerptive memories, and excerptive solutions are the least personal of the three. Excerptive solutions typically represent factual information as associations or answers, for instance, to academic questions or conversations about news events. They represent what we know about things outside of our most personal circumstances. Memory for what we know about things is also called semantic memory (Tulving, 1983). Excerptive solutions are the forms that semantic memories take.

In addition to these three types of excerpts, an *excerptive decision* embodies a prior moment's decision or has decision-influencing potential. The thought in response to the excerptive decision is the decision proper. For example, on the way home from work I notice the local video store, and an excerpt of the videotape under my car seat that I recently decided to return pops into my awareness. In response to this excerpt I think, "Oh yeah, I'll return it in the morning now." In this case, the excerpt embodied a *prior* moment's decision. Then, an excerpt of my girlfriend being angry if I'm late from work pops into my awareness and I think, "Nah, I'll return it right now." This is an example of an excerpt with decision-*influencing* potential. I believe that thoughts in response to excerptive decisions reflect the *experience* of intentionality, which we'll touch upon in chapter 5.

Many excerpts are spontaneous associations rising into awareness in response to various stimuli. However, the stimuli giving rise to such excerpts are often excerpts themselves. Any time awareness fixes on and mentally embodies a stimulus, where a mental or behavioral reaction occurs in direct response to it, that stimulus has been excerpted. For example, when my attention turns to an itch, transforming it into a fixed entity in my awareness, that itch has been excerpted. As a result, that itch exists as part of my mental experience. This excerpted itch then prompts the act of scratching it. It could just as easily prompt the thought, "What the heck bit me?" This excerpt could also prompt yet another excerpt embodying my recollection of the mosquito that bit me this morning.

A thought is also a stimulus that can be excerpted. Following the elaborative conceptual portion of a thought, attention can surface from and reflect on some meaningful aspect of it. At the instant this reflection occurs, some meaning embodied in that thought is excerpted. This excerpting instant immediately marks the end of the "passing thought" and the beginning of a new one. In other words, as awareness surfaces from its immersion "inside" a thought, the reflective action of attention fixes it in a mental form which embodies some aspect of its overall meaning. For example, I could excerpt the identity of the thought, "Maybe I'll go to the gym this morning." In response to this identified excerpt I might think, "What time is it anyway?" Alternatively, this excerpt could just as easily prompt another excerpt of my gym clothes in the basement.

Thus, any internal or external stimulus which has been momentarily fixed and mentally represented in awareness is an *excerptive-clip*. For whatever "reason," a given stimulus was singled out for representation by attention. That excerpted stimulus can then be reacted to via a thought or some other mental or behavioral act. For example, excerptive-clips often prompt excerptive reminders, memories, solutions, and decisions. When I heard my secretary state the date, an image of my friend Cindy came to mind because this is her Birthday. Hearing the date served as an excerptive-clip for the excerptive reminder of Cindy's Birthday. As another example, when my friend's words about her traumatic experience prompted an excerptive memory about a trauma of mine, some portion of her described experience served as an excerptive-clip.

When awareness surfaces from the thought at hand and reflects on it, followed by a reaction to some meaning embodied in that thought, an excerptive-clip of an aspect of its meaning or identity has occurred. I call the movement of attention leading to the creation of excerptive-clips of "passing thoughts," *attentional surfacing*. Something meaningful about the elaborative conceptual portion of the thought at hand, for example, brings awareness out of its immersion in the thought. This surfacing of awareness puts it in a position to reflect on, "clip off," mentally fix, and meaningfully "ground" either an aspect of or the identity of the thought. The action preceding this excerpting instant is that of attentional surfacing. This identified excerpt serves as a springboard leading to the reflective conceptual portion of the next thought where one is reacting to the meaningfully identified content embodied in it.

### The Different Types of Thinking

Thus far, we have distinguished and defined general elaborative and reflective thoughts. We have outlined a complete structure of thought noting the phenomenally-based structural differences between general elaborative and reflective thoughts. We have also discussed different types of excerpts which often mark the outset of a variety of thoughts. At this point, we are ready to outline additional types of thought, each of which consists of some combination of the possible constituents of thinking.

*Implicit reflective identification* (IRI) is a subtype of general elaborative thinking. At the outset of IRI, some meaningful aspect of the just prior thought is reflected upon and excerptively clipped. Subsequently, this excerptive-clip is reacted to via a new thought in the form of IRI. This excerptive-clip-thought dyad makes up

IRI. Like general elaborative thoughts, the reality of having taken into account some meaning embodied in the prior thought is subjectively implied in the present thought. For example, I might think, "I love her new car," followed by the thought, "Actually, the color of her upholstery is drab" (the instance of IRI). W*hile* I was thinking about how much I loved her new car, a fleeting image of her upholstery was part of my mental experience. The instant this thought "passed," I *reflected "back" on it* and excerptively clipped that image of her upholstery. Thus, IRI takes into account an aspect of its predecessor thought more directly than does general elaborative thinking. During IRI, an aspect *of* its predecessor thought is excerpted, whereas during general elaborative thinking, the predecessor thought *prompts* an excerpt to which a new thought reacts. Thus, there is more of a direct connection between a thought leading to IRI than between a thought leading to a general elaborative one. Implicit reflective identification, therefore, is preceded by attentional surfacing from its predecessor-thought, and is initiated by a proactive excerpt-found reaction and the simultaneously appearing proactively identified excerptive-clip of some meaningful aspect of the "passing thought."

If the second thought above had been, "I was just thinking about how much I love her new car," I would have been engaging in a subtype of reflective thinking called *explicit reflective identification* (ERI). As with IRI, an excerptive-clip of the former thought serves as a springboard for a new thought. But in one intermediate form of ERI, the excerptive-clip and the reaction to it *explicitly* represent the *identity* of the former thought, along with an implicit awareness about that prior thought as a presence. The identity of the "passisng thought," represented in the excerptive-clip at hand, can be explicitly represented in the new thought one is having in response to it. For example, I might think, "Maybe I'll go to the gym this morning." An excerptive-clip of this thought might then prompt the thought, "I was just thinking that I'd go to the gym this morning." This form of explicit reflective identification is preceded by attentional surfacing from its predecessor-thought, is initiated by a proactively identified excerptive-clip of that thought, a reactive excerpt-found reaction, a reactively identified excerpt, and a subsequent explicit representation of the identity of its predecessor.

There are three potential levels of awareness in response to the excerpted identity embodied in the excerptive-clip of the "passing thought" during three respective versions of ERI. During the least explicit form of ERI, there is an implicit conceptual reaction to the excerptive-clip of the "passing thought's" identity. In other words, I can implicitly identify the "passing thought" as embodied in the excerptive-clip at hand, and react to it in such as way as to suggest an implicit awareness of its identity. For instance, I can excerptively-clip the identity of the "passing thought" of wanting to go out for pizza and react to it by thinking, "I'll go to the Pizza Barn." In its moderately explicit form, there can be an excerptively-clippped, explicit representation of that thought's identity as reflected by the conceptual reaction to it, along with an *implicit* awareness of the thought as a presence per se ("I was just thinking about going out to the Pizza Barn). Lastly, in ERI's most explicit form there can be an excerptively-clipped representation of that "passing thought's" identity *and presence* as reflected by the conceptual reaction to it, but this is the least frequently experienced version of the three. During this most explicit form of ERI, I experience a heightened sense of self-awareness.

The differences between IRI and the moderately explicit form of ERI, for example, can be conveyed metaphorically. For instance, having checked my appearance as I walked past a mirror (i.e., a "passing thought"), IRI would equate to being aware of and representing some aspect of this (e.g., "Gee, I looked horrible!"). This has a more elaborative phenomenology in that I'm entirely immersed in my reaction and am aware of nothing else. In contrast, ERI would include being explicitly aware of having looked in the mirror, of my appearance reflected there, along with an implicit awareness of the mirror per se (e.g., "I just saw my reflection and thought I looked horrible"). Having *looked* into the mirror to check my appearance is explicitly represented by my reaction. My reaction reflects an awareness of a very objectified reality there, with me juxtaposed as an actor in a separate relationship to it. It has a more reflective phenomenology because I'm aware of myself in relationship to the awareness of another object of attention.

"*Reflective identification of excerpts*" (RI of excerpts) is another type of thinking which has an elaborative form and a reflective form. In its *elaborative form*, "RI of excerpts" is the implicit representation of the identity of a proactively generated excerpt. By *implicit* I mean that one is *reacting to* the content of the excerpt without explicitly representing that content. It is typically initiated when one is deep in thought posing a question to oneself. The question leads to an excerpt-searching reaction, resulting in the appearance of an excerpt that is proactively identified and implicitly represented as a response to it. For example, on my way home from work I ask myself if I bought cheese at the store yesterday. Then an excerpt-image of standing at the deli buying Swiss pops into my awareness. In response to this excerpt I think, "Maybe I should have gotten cheddar." This thought implicitly embodies the answer to my question, and implicitly takes into account the content of the appearing excerpt of buying Swiss. Similarly, when the proactively identified excerpt leads to another excerpt, or to an emotional or behavioral reaction, the elaborative form of "RI of excerpts" is also occurring because such responses embody implicit representations of the content of that excerpt.

We've all had the experience of being deep in thought only to get stuck on a question or problem. For instance, you might have posed a question to yourself, and no answer was forthcoming: "Where did we eat last Thursday night?" The lack of an answer in response to this question grabs your attention, "pulling" you out of your absorption in thought. Repeating it leaves you expectantly waiting for the answer(s) to come to you. Such a question often entails a reflective phenomenology that carries over into the arrival of the answer(s); your attention actively seeks and expectantly waits for the answer, which seems to come out of the periphery of awareness. With its appearance, your experience during the *reflective form* of "RI of excerpts" seems more reflective or conscious in contrast to the arrival of excerpts at the outset of general elaborative thoughts, the elaborative form of "RI of excerpts," and IRI. In this type of thinking the proactively identified excerpt-answer in response to a question is an immediate product of an excerpt-searching reaction that marks the end of the predecessor-thought-question. The proactively identified excerpt-answer then becomes the object of a reactive excerpt-found reaction, and this reaction then becomes the reflectively identified excerpt-object of a new thought which explicitly represents that excerpt's identity. Recall that the reactive excerpt-found reaction is an unfolding, explicit representation of and response to the content of the appearing excerpt.

Excerptive memories, reminders, solutions, and decisions are the frequent objects of the elaborative and reflective forms of "RI of excerpts." However, unlike most of the reflective forms of thought that react to excerpted content *inherent to* the "passing thought," both forms of "RI of excerpts" react to excerpts *prompted by* "passing thoughts" which seem to come from outside the stream of thought.

Remember that excerptive-clips are "snapshots" of internal or external stimuli. The instant attention fixates on a stimulus (a sight, sound, smell, taste, feeling, or thought) it becomes an excerptive-clip if a thought, excerpt, emotion, or behavior takes it as its object. This distinction, however, between internal and external stimuli needs further clarification. By internal stimulus I mean a "mental" object such as a thought or image. In contrast, an external stimulus that I'm experiencing always has a clear sensory component. That externally based stimulus has a sensory reality that is represented in or embodied by my awareness. When external stimuli become excerptive-clips they are objects of a type of thought called *reflective identification of excerptive-*

*clips of external objects.* Prior to the excerptive-clip, awareness surfaced (attentional surfacing) from its absorption in a thought or action and fixated on an external stimulus.

Like "RI of excerpts," "RI of excerptive-clips of external objects" has an elaborative and a reflective form. In its *elaborative* form, an excerptive-clip of an external object is implicitly represented in one's response to it. In my reaction to that excerptive-clip, I'm unconsciously aware of its content; it is an unattended-to-knowing. In other words, it is not an object of attention in my reaction to its proactively identified content. More often than not, the elaborative form of "RI of excerptive clips of external objects" is preceded by attentional surfacing from a prior thought or action, resulting in a proactively identified excerptive-clip of an external object and subsequent implicit representation of its identity in reaction to it. For instance, the excerptive-clip of my wallet on the car seat prompted the thought, "I need to go to the bank after lunch." The thought in response to that excerptive-clip implicitly embodied that clip's meaningful significance.

The *reflective* form of "RI of excerptive-clips of external objects" is preceded by attentional surfacing from a thought or action and its onset is marked by a proactively identified appearing excerpt, a reactive excerpt-found reaction, and subsequent explicit representation of the reflectively identified excerpt at the outset of and during the reflective conceptual portion of the thought at hand: "I just saw my wallet and remembered that I need to go to the bank after lunch." Figure 3 summarizes the differences among the different types of thought, including several we have yet to define. Each thought unfolds from left to right with the passage of time.

### *A Comparison of the Different Types of Thoughts and Their Components*

General elaborative thoughts are probably the most basic and frequently experienced type of thinking. In their essence,

## General Elaborative Thinking

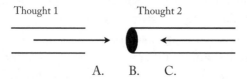

A. Excerpt-Searching Reaction and Proactive Excerptive Found Reaction
B. Proactively Identified Excerptive Memory, Solution, Reminder, or Decision
C. General Elaborative Thought

## Implicit Reflective Identification

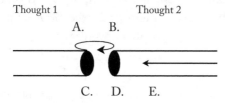

A. Attentional Surfacing
B. Proactive Excerpt-Found Reaction
C. Excerptive-Clip
D. Proactively Identified Excerptive-Clip
E. Implicit Reflective Identification

## ERI, NCRT, CRT, and TRI

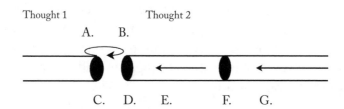

A. Attentional Surfacing
B. Proactive Excerpt-Found Reaction
C. Excerptive-Clip
D. Proactively Identified Excerptive-Clip
E. Reactive Excerpt-Found Reaction
F. Reactively Identified Excerptive-Clip
G. ERI, NCRT, CRT, and TRI (all defined later)

## Reflective Identification of Excerpts (Reflective Form)

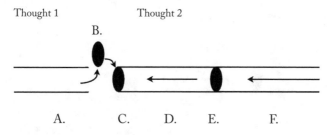

A. Excerpt-Searching Reaction
B. Excerptive Memory, Reminder, Decision, or Solution
C. Proactively Identified Excerpt
D. Reactive Excerpt-Found Reaction
E. Reactively Indentified Excerpt
F. Reflective Identification of Excerpts (Reflective Form)

## Reflective Identification of Excerpts (Elaborative Form)

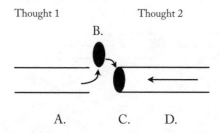

A. Excerpt-Searching Reaction
B. Excerptive Memory, Reminder, Decision, or Solution
C. Proactively Identified Excerpt
D. Reflective Identification of Excerpts (Elaborative Form)

### Reflective Identification of Excerptive-Clips of External Objects (Elaborative Form)

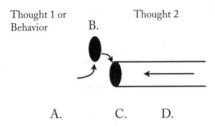

A. Attentional Surfacing
B. Excerptive-Clip
C. Proactively Identified Excerptive-Clip
D. Reflective Identification of Excerptive-Clip of External Objects (Elaborative Form)

### Reflective Identification of Excerptive-Clips of External Objects (Reflective Form)

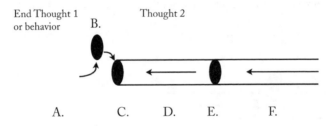

A. Attentional Surfacing
B. Excerptive-Clip
C. Proactively Identified Excerptive-Clip
D. Reactive Excerpt-Found Reaction
E. Reactively Indentified Excerptive Clip
F. Reflective Identification of Excerptive-Clip of External Objects (Reflective Form)

*Figure 3*

they embody the phenomenology of proactive excerpt-found reactions. The excerpts marking the onset of general elaborative thoughts have a thematically consistent relationship to their respective "passing thoughts," where each new excerpt is, in part, the fleeting culmination of unfolding, meaning-laden aftereffects of their respective predecessor-thoughts. The identity of such proactively generated excerpts increasingly coalesce as they appear to awareness. Their identity is known to awareness as lived, and represent unattended-to-knowings: the knowings themselves are not taken as objects of attention. In an earlier example of general elaborative thinking, my thought about the dirty garage prompted an excerptive reminder of the cleaning products I purchased last week. The next thought in response to this excerpt was to clean the garage. This excerptive reminder seemed to fly toward my mind's eye "proactively" as an increasingly clear and identifiable image. It seemed to be part of the internally absorbing, uninterrupted "stream" of thought. It served as a springboard for the next thought, which was an elaborative reaction to (not about) the excerpt.

Unlike general elaborative thinking, the subtype of elaborative thinking called IRI is preceded by attentional surfacing from its predecessor-thought and is initiated by an excerptive-clip of a meaningful aspect of that predecessor. Remember that the predecessor-thought to a general elaborative thought ends with an excerpt-searching reaction, following an excerpt which will seem to appear *"up ahead," within the stream of thought.* In contrast, the predecessor-thought to IRI ends when *attention surfaces* from and excerptively-clips some meaningful aspect *of the "passing" thought.* (However, both types of thought share proactive excerpt-found reactions, hence, their basic elaborative nature.) While I thought, "I loved her new car," a fleeting image of the upholstery was part of my experience. This thought ended as my attention surfaced from it. But the upholstery image was relevant enough to pull my attention back toward it; I reflected on and "proactively" moved toward the increasingly apparent and identified excerptive-clip of the upholstery aspect of that thought, leading to an instance of IRI. Having experienced it during the first thought, I then identified it "proactively" while it solidified as an excerptive-clip in my mind's eye.

In sum, a general elaborative thought is not preceded by

attentional surfacing from or an excerptive-clip of its predecessor-thought, as is IRI. Instead, the predecessor-thought for general elaborative thinking is terminated by an excerpt-searching (e-s) reaction which prompts an excerpt to which the general elaborative thought reacts. Furthermore, the phenomenology of the e-s reaction is one of leading to an excerpt as if "up ahead" within the stream of thought. This phenomenology stands in contrast to that which follows attentional surfacing, where excerptive-clips occur in relation to aspects of the "*passing*" stream of thought.

General elaborative thoughts share the same phenomenal components with the elaborative form of "RI of excerpts." In turn, these two thought-forms share the same components with the elaborative form of "RI of excerptive-clips of external objects," save one: the predecessor-thought (or action) to "RI of excerptive-clips of external objects" ends via attentional surfacing rather than an excerpt-searching reaction.

Just prior to general elaborative thoughts, the excerpt-searching reaction seems to lead to an excerpt "up ahead," as if within the stream of thought. Just prior to the elaborative and reflective forms of "RI of excerpts," however, the excerpt-searching reaction seems to take awareness out of the stream of thought, leading to an excerpt which seems to appear into the periphery of awareness.

All the types of reflective thoughts share the same phenomenal components, although the predecessor-thought to the reflective form of "RI of excerpts" ends via an excerpt-searching reaction rather than attentional surfacing, and results in any type of excerpt other than an excerptive-clip.

In general, all forms of reflective thinking (other than the reflective form of "RI of excerpts") are preceded by attentional surfacing from their respective predecessor-thoughts and are initiated by proactively identified excerptive-clips. The excerptive-clips are then followed by reactive excerpt-found reactions. The instant the reactive excerpt-found reactions are fixed in awareness by the reflective conceptual portions of the thoughts at hand, reflectively identified excerptive-clips exist to awareness, from which these portions of the thoughts react. Thus, reflective thoughts result in a prolonged period of reflectivity on proactively identified excerpts, transforming them into reactively identified excerptive-clips.

During reflective thoughts, awareness is "placed" in a more attentive "posture" in response to the proactively identified excerptive-clip at hand, rather than being flung headlong through a series of "tube"thoughts as a function of proactive excerpt-found reactions alone (as in elaborative thoughts). Thus, the "purpose" of reflective thoughts is to prolong one's awareness of the content of the proactively and implicitly identified excerptive-clip at hand so that it can be explicitly represented in the body of the thought.

In sum, general elaborative thoughts are preceded by excerpt-searching reactions that mark the end of their respective predecessor-thoughts and are initiated by proactive excerpt-found reactions and the variety of excerpts other than excerptive-clips. In contrast, reflective thoughts (other than "RI of excerpts") are preceded by attentional surfacing from their respective predecessor-thoughts and are initiated by excerptive-clips and reactive excerpt-found reactions. There is no overlap between general elaborative thoughts and reflective thoughts regarding these component parts.

Table 1 below summarizes the phenomenally based structural differences among these types of thought. Because I included the elaborative form of "RI of excerpts" under the heading "Elaborative Thoughts," I did not title the heading "General Elaborative Thought," as would have been the case otherwise. Included under the heading "Reflective Thoughts" is the reflective form of "reflective identification of excerptive-clips of external objects," explicit reflective identification, noncomparative and comparative reflective thinking, and transparent reflective identification, or TRI (the last three types will be discussed shortly).

| **Elaborative Thoughts**<br>(Exluding IRI and RI of excerptive-clips of external objects, elaborative form) | **Reflective Thoughts**<br>(Excluding RI of Excerpts—Reflective Form) |
|---|---|
| 1. Excerpt-searching reactions<br>2. Proactive excerpt-found reactions<br>3. The variety of (proactively identified) excerpts excluding excerptive-clips<br>4. Implicit representation of the identity of the excerpt during the reflective conceptual portion of thought | 1. Attentional surfacing<br>2. Proactive excerpt-found reactions<br>3. Proactively identified excerptive-clips<br>4. Reactive excerpt-found reactions<br>5. Reactively identified excerptive-clips<br>6. Explicit representation of the identity of the excerpt during the reflective conceptual portion of the thought |
| **Implicit Reflective Identification** | **RI of Excerpts (Reflective Form)** |
| 1. Attentional surfacing<br>2. Proactive excerpt-found reactions<br>3. Proactively identified excerptive-clips<br>4. Implicit representation of the identity of the excerpt during the reflective conceptual portion of thought | 1. Excerpt-searching reactions<br>2. Proactive excerpt-found reactions<br>3. The variety of (proactively identified) excerpts excluding excerptive-clips<br>4. Reactive excerpt-found reactions<br>5. Reactively identified excerpts<br>6. Explicit representation of the identity of the excerpt during the reflective conceptual portion of the thought |
| **RI of Excerptive Clips of External Objects (Elaborative Form)** ||
| 1. Attentional surfacing<br>2. Proactive excerpt-found reactions<br>3. Proactively identified excerptive-clips<br>4. Implicit representation of the identity of the excerpt during the reflective conceptual portion of thought ||

*Table 1*

### The Conscious and Unconscious Components of Thought

Now that we have broken down different types of thought into their constituents, we can examine the phenomenology of what we are and are not conscious of while experiencing each part. Concerning *elaborative thoughts*, once the excerpting instant has occurred and the content of the excerpt has been proactively identified, we experience the reflective conceptual portion of the thought in reaction to that excerpt's implicitly identified content. During the initial part of this reaction, we're usually so focused on the meaningfully recognized content reflected by the excerpt, and so absorbed in our response to it, we're only conscious of that content and of nothing else.

In relation to *reflective thinking*, however, the period of initial reflection on and growing awareness of the reflectively identified excerpt (of the "passing thought") at the outset of the reflective conceptual portion of the present thought can result in the experience of a subtle and fleeting awareness of observing. Awareness of observing only occurs as part of my experience during the outset of the reflective conceptual portion of a reflective thought. This reflective, reactive experience, both to the reactively identified excerpt and to the fact that I'm observing it now as a separating awareness, results in a sense of self or duality of experience. I'm simultaneously aware of the act of observing and of the observed object. I am aware of self in the form of an observing, separating entity in strict relation to the objectified content of the excerpt at hand. Along with the creation of the explicitly identified content of the excerpt-object, I am created as the separating awareness in relation to it.

An instant later, as the reflective conceptual portion of the reflective thought passes, my awareness of the meaningfully recognized content of the excerpt disappears, as does any potential experience of duality. As a result, awareness moves into and embodies the elaborative conceptual portion of the thought at hand. During this portion of thought I become one with the reactive experiencing at hand, with no prolonged awareness of any part of it as an object of attention.

Trailing behind the release of awareness from the elaborative conceptual portion of a reflective or elaborative thought are its meaning-laden nuances which often influence the content of the yet-to-be-found excerpt toward which awareness moves. If the release of awareness occurs in the "form" of an excerpt-searching reaction, awareness is so consumed in its action that I don't consciously experience this part of the thought either. Again, I become, in effect, the action of the release of awareness which is springboarding off of some meaningful aspect of the thought at hand.

Marking the end of the excerpt-searching reaction, I'm not conscious of proactively identifying the excerpt. I simply become this proactively forming excerpt as a form of consciousness. I'm also not conscious of the initial act of reflectively identifying or recognizing the proactively identified excerpt via the reactive excerpt-found reaction during reflective thoughts. I simply become this reaction as a form of consciousness.

Let's look at an example of an *elaborative thinking* sequence to highlight what we are and are not conscious of during thought. Upon my return home from work I notice that the house lights are off; a proactively identified excerpt. I then experience an excerptive reminder of my wife and daughter at a school function and think, "I forgot they were going to be gone tonight." Then I experience an excerptive reminder of my wife normally leaving dinner for me and I think, "Shoot, I'm going to have to fix something to eat." Then I experience an excerptive reminder of the half-sandwich I didn't eat last night, and I think, "I'll eat that sandwich in the fridge." Throughout this thinking sequence, the only "object" of which I was even fleetingly or barely conscious was the proactively identified, meaningful content embodied in the excerpt at hand *at the outset of the reflective conceptual portion of each thought*: the house lights being off; my wife and daughter being at school; my wife normally leaving me dinner; and the half-sandwich in the fridge. I'm implicitly aware of the meaningful content embodied in these excerpts as I initially react to each with a different thought. Every other part of the thinking sequence is totally unconscious; my awareness is caught up in *being* the excerpt-searching reactions, proactive excerpt-found reactions, proactively identified excerpts, reactive excerpt-found reactions (during reflective thoughts), reactively identified excerpts (during reflective thoughts), the middle-to-the-end of the reflective conceptual portions, and elaborative conceptual portions of the thoughts. Figure 4 illustrates a series of "connected" thought-moments.

Each circle stands for the excerpting instant, where awareness reflectively meets the excerpt, resulting in its appearance. The solid horizontal lines to which each solid-lined arrow is pointing stand for the *instant* when each excerpt's meaningful identity is objectified. This is synonymous with attention's reflection on, and hence, implicit identification of the proactively identified excerpt at the outset of the reflective conceptual portion of elaborative thoughts, and explicit identification of the reactively identified excerpt at the outset of the reflective conceptual portion of reflective thoughts. The solid-line arrows represent the action of awareness looking toward or reflecting on the proactively or reactively identified content of the excerpts

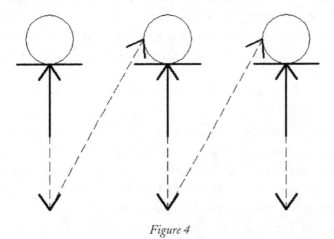

*Figure 4*

while it moves away from and conceptually reacts to them. This is the reflective conceptual portion of the thoughts, where awareness is *reacting* to the meaningfully identified or recognized excerpts. During the outset of this portion of the thought, we can potentially experience an awareness of observing while being conscious of the content of the excerpt at hand (e.g., at the outset of reflective thoughts). This phenomenon occurs as a function of the apparent separateness between a self-experiencer (the observing awareness) and a form of self-experiencing (the excerpted thought object). In this case, the object being observed is the "passing thought's" explicit identity, as reflected in the excerpt at hand. This sense of being a reflecting, observing awareness occurs along with the experience of being briefly conscious of the content reflected by the excerpt.

Thus, the solid lines in the diagram (other than the circles) represent being fleetingly conscious (whether implicit or explicit, depending on the type of thought) of the content reflected by the excerpt, and potentially, of the apparent fact that I am a separating, observing awareness beginning to conceptually react to that content. It's only during the *outset* of this reflective conceptual portion of *reflective thought*, when awareness is suddenly freed from, reflecting on, and conceptually reacting to the identified excerpt, that a sense of being conscious (of an object) as a separating, observing awareness can occur.

The dotted-line arrows in Figure 4 point in the opposite direction from the solid-line arrows and represent attention's movement away from its focus on the content reflected by the excerpted objects. Here, during the elaborative conceptual portion of the thoughts, awareness is immersed in-and-as the unfolding, conceptual meaning at hand. In other words, *my awareness feels no separate identity from that meaning*; it has no conscious awareness *of* that meaning because no sense of being a separate observer in relation to any observed meaning exists at this time. Awareness is the living embodiment of the unfolding meaning at hand, with no prolonged attention to and awareness of any one object of attention.

The long dotted arrows pointing at the circles at the front of each thought-moment stand for that period of time when awareness has been freed from the elaborative conceptual portion of each thought (excerpt-searching reaction or attentional surfacing). Once freed, it moves into the "darkroom" of unconsciousness, looking for an as-yet-to-be-found excerpt (e.g., the proactive excerpt-found reaction). This period of being freed from the immersion in the thought at hand, along with the period during which awareness is moving into the "darkroom" of the picture-taking process is also unconscious since there is no duality of experiencing. Coming full circle, the proactive excerpt-found reaction and excerpting moments of picture-taking, represented by the circles, are also unconscious in this sense. Last, the solid horizontal lines just under each circle stand for that *instant* when awareness reflects on, and hence, identifies the proactively appearing excerpt via the reflective conceptual portion of elaborative thoughts, or on the reactive excerpt-found reaction at the outset of the reflective conceptual portion of reflective thoughts, thereby objectifying the reactively identified excerpt's content. This instant marks the beginning of being conscious of the content of the excerpts (whether implicit or explicit) at the outset of the reflective conceptual portion of each type of thought.

Thus, the dotted lines of each thought-moment (including the circles) represent the periods of being totally immersed in-and-as the experiencing at hand with no awareness or sense of being conscious of something. The periods represented by the solid lines represent such an awareness. In short, the conscious period of thinking is all there is, to itself. Therefore, to itself, it always seems to be present. To itself, it's as if it is continually "on" or aware throughout the entirety of a given thought and across all thoughts. To this conscious, thinking self, the initial period of observation and consciousness of something is the entire experience of thinking. And this thinking-self experiences itself as always "on" or present during thinking because it can't be aware of the periods when it isn't "on" or present. But as you can see by the diagram, this experience, during a series of connected thoughts, isn't continuously "on." Instead, awareness of being conscious of something across a given thought or series of thoughts is more like a pulsing, on-off experiencing.

As you can see, each and every thought is a dual entity. At one end of the thought there is an identified excerpt or a represented experience to which a conceptual reaction arises. Therefore, there are two inherent "players" during the initial portion of a thought: a fixed, objectified, represented experience, in response to which the other "player," an unfolding, subjective, reactive experiencing arises.

Given the inherent duality of thought, the phenomenology of duality exists only at the outset of the reflective conceptual portion of reflective thinking, where there seems to be a separate experiencing between an awareness of the fleeting, explicitly identified content of the excerpted "passing thought" and that of our observing self: of this and that, of subjective experience in contrast to objective experience, of object and subject. These two entities co-occur, attached to one another by the extension of thought. They are seemingly separate "parts" contained in or subsumed by a more encompassing whole: that of the extending conceptual frame of the thought at hand. In a paradoxical fashion, they seem to be attached to each other as they are separating from one another along the extending length of the conceptual frame of the thought that subsumes them.

If we visually slice out the reflective conceptual portion of an elaborative and reflective thought, as depicted by the tube-cones in Figure 5, we can further establish their differences.

The meaningfully recognized, excerpted ends of the reflective conceptual portion of each thought are on the left side of each cone and phenomenologically, seem fixed or stagnant. Each thought unfolds in time from left to right. The unfolding right side of each thought "holds" awareness, which is looking at and reacting to its respective, excerpted object.

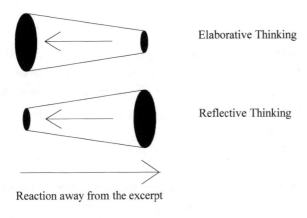

Reflective Conceptual Portion of the thought

Elaborative Thinking

Reflective Thinking

Reaction away from the excerpt

*Figure 5*

At the outset of reflective thinking, I am, as awareness, react-ing to the explicitly identified content of the excerpt of a "pass-ing thought" and can experience myself very acutely: either as a separate thought-self construed as existing in the form of the ex-cerpted "passing thought," or as an observing, separating entity in relation to the excerpted "passing thought." (We'll discuss this distinction in self-awareness later.) In other words, at the outset of reflective thinking, I can experience an awareness of myself as a thinking-self very strongly. In Figure 5, this experience of acute self-awareness is depicted by the larger darkened end or right side of the reflective conceptual portion of the reflective thought, which "holds" awareness.

In contrast, as one's attention reacts to the proactively iden-tified content of the excerpted object during the elaborative thought, there is only an awareness of the meaning embodied in that object, with no experiencing of self. The acuity of awareness of the meaningful object dominating one's attention at the out-set of an elaborative thought is depicted by the large darkened circle or excerpt on the left of Figure 5. The lack of experiential self-awareness at the outset of an elaborative thought, by contrast, is depicted by the smaller darkened circle on the right side of the figure.

Isn't it amazing that, despite experiencing thousands of thoughts a day, we're unaware that each and every one consists of a variety of "parts"?: the excerpt-searching reaction or attentional surfacing (marking the end of a predecessor-thought [or action]), excerpt or excerptive-clip, proactive or (potentially) reactive excerpt-found reaction, proactively or (potentially) reactively identified excerpt, reflective conceptual portion, and elaborative conceptual portion. Though we may have never given the actual experience of thinking much attention, we're now in a position to observe our thoughts and experientially identify these phenomenal, structural "parts" as or just after they occur. Pay attention and a whole new world will appear.

In sum, chapters 1 and 2 presented a theory of the microdynamics of thinking outlining a structure of thought which then helped us clearly define and experientially identify two general types of thinking and experiencing: elaborative and reflective. We have also identified a number of their subtypes (and respective component "parts"): implicit reflective identification, explicit reflective identification, reflective identification of excerpts (elaborative or reflective form), and reflective identification of excerptive-clips of external objects (elaborative or reflective form).

Please don't get lost in the technical details of the types of thought and their phenomenally based structure. Instead, consider the implications of being able to experientially recognize the different types of thought. For example, based on this new understanding of the "structure" and "process" aspects of thinking, you can better recognize what you are and are not conscious of during thought. My guess is that you once believed you were aware of every thought and every bit of the thought process, as if you were the conscious author of every word thought, written or spoken. Furthermore, because we delineated the "parts" of thought, you now know the juncture among them during which the sense of self is engendered. Had you imagined that something as basic as your experience of self-awareness as a thinking-self was largely a function of your thoughts and of how the parts of thought unfold in relation to each other while they interact with an observing awareness? Still further, had you imagined the possibility that certain kinds of thoughts create different experiences of self-awareness?

Just wait: the thought process by which your sense of self is created will be further specified in chapter 3 and the resulting insights may change your life. Two different types of reflective thoughts will be distinguished (as well as a third in a later chapter) based on their respective "parts" and unique phenomenologies of self-awareness. Upon this foundation of understanding how the "mechanics" of thought create a sense of self, you will achieve direct, experiential insights into its illusory nature. In other words, by observing and comparing your thinking experience against this new foundation of knowledge, you can subjectively discern the nature, structure, and functioning of your thoughts. The insights achieved may motivate and help you loosen your attachment to the experience of self generated by the awareness of "passing thoughts" as objects. Better yet, perhaps your experience of and belief in being such a self may explode under the firepower of your new understandings. As a result, you may engage in fewer problematic behaviors and consequent upsetting emotions that support and protect that self, as outlined in chapter 9. Moreover, the way you experience yourself and your world may be forever changed and expanded to include aspects of reality that you never imagined.

In this chapter, a basic theory of the microdynamics of thinking has been outlined. As a result, the structural and process aspects of thought are clearer. But the body of thought, what it is like to live and breathe as thought, awaits description. This is the task in chapter 3, where we move inside the phenomenal world of thinking, into its felt experiencing and life force.

# Chapter Three: The Phenomenology of Thinking

I N CHAPTERS 1 AND 2 a structure of thinking was developed based on experiential changes occurring during the evolution of a discrete thought and across thoughts. This structure, consisting of five or six "parts" of any one thought (out of a potential eight), is the foundation for a theory of the microdynamics of thinking. This theory provided a window into the world of thinking, allowing us to define seven types of thought. Moreover, it provided tremendous explanatory power regarding the objectively based, thought-induced experience of self-awareness.

In this chapter, the phenomenology of thinking and the "parts" of thought are further clarified. Describing the phenomenology of reflective and elaborative thinking, and the "parts" of thought, helps distinguish, highlight, and objectify the conscious and unconscious aspects of cognition, thereby lifting awareness out of its blind embeddedness in such processes. As a result, one may, for the first time, intermittently escape the problematic manifestations of thought-induced phenomenologies and their aftermath. Furthermore, while describing the phenomenology of reflective thinking, we will define two additional types of reflective thought, their respective mechanics, and accompanying forms of self-awareness. Lastly, William James' introspective insights about the phenomenology of thinking lend validity to the theory of the microdynamics of thinking presented in chapters 1 and 2.

Before addressing the phenomenology of reflective and elaborative thinking and their component "parts," we will consider Eugene Gendlin's understanding of thinking and experience, and further distinguish conscious (reflective) and unconscious (elaborative) mental processes.

### *Eugene Gendlin and Experiencing*

Discussing thinking in technical language distracts from the reality that thoughts embody vivid, fully lived experiencing. Thinking and experiencing go hand-in-hand, and few authors have written as clearly and comprehensively about these co-occurring realities as Eugene Gendlin. In *Experiencing and the Creation of Meaning: A Philosophical and Psychological Approach to the Subjective*, Gendlin (1962) defines and describes the central role of "experiencing" in our lives. Gendlin says that experiencing is so simple and such a basic given of existence that we rarely acknowledge it. He describes it as the always-available, concretely present flow of feeling. It is always "there" for us, he says.

When you feel your body from the inside, with the thousands of different feeling tones and felt meanings, you're in touch with that inner sense, that always-available referent for your inward attention, says Gendlin (1962). At any given time you can always put a few aspects of felt experience into words. But no matter how you define it in any given moment, no matter which symbols you use to specify aspects of it, no matter how you divide it, felt experience is always "there."

This experiencing or "felt-sense" is there for you in everything you do. It is the body and substance of every action. For example, Gendlin (1962) indicates that when you consider the meaning of any verbal statement, you have an experiential sense of its meaning. Its meaning is "in" your experiencing, located in that ever-present feeling mass that is a direct referent of inward attention. For instance, you "feel" any sentence's meaning, and in order to say now what it means, you must refer to that aspect of your experiencing that constitutes the meaning of the sentence to you. In other words, its meaning is part of your inward body sense; it is bodily felt. It is an aspect of your total body feeling that your attention specifies.

According to Gendlin (1962):

> Experiencing is a constant, ever present, underlying phenomenon of inwardly sentient living, and therefore there is an experiential side of anything, no matter how specifically detailed and finely specified… (p. 15)

As such, experiencing is involved in every situation and instance of behavior and thought:

> Experience, then, is a momentary cross-cut (that is, it is existential in space and time) …of all content that is or could under some circumstances be in an individual's phenomenal field. (p. 242)

Experiencing is a present and implicitly meaningful "felt datum" to which you can directly refer. Gendlin (1962) says that you can conceptualize it in many different ways, but it is not itself explicitly conceptual. Instead it is implicitly meaningful, and can therefore give rise to many concepts that can be checked against its implicit meaning. Whether these concepts are accurate or not, the felt datum itself will still be directly present. As Gendlin summarizes it, experiencing is:

> the felt datum of an individual's inward direct reference in his phenomenal awareness. It is a changing, organic, spatiotemporal process, a continuous stream of feelings and some explicit contents. It is the feeling process that continuously occurs in an individual's phenomenal field. (pp. 243–44)

According to Gendlin (1962), meaning is formed in the interaction between experiencing and symbolizing. Feeling without symbolizing is blind, and symbolizing without feeling is empty. We cannot know what a concept means without the "feel" of its meaning. This experienced dimension of feeling, of felt meaning, plays a vital function in the having and forming of all thinking, cognition, and knowledge.

Gendlin (1962) provides a brief list of some of the roles played by felt meaning in knowledge and cognition. He reminds us that John Dewey (1925) believes the "feel" of meaning "guides our inferential movements." For Merleau-Ponty (1945), felt meaning guides speech. Because felt meaning is experienced first, we know what we are about to say before we say it. In other words, suggests Merleau-Ponty, all words and symbols proceed from it. Discriminations regarding anything, says Gendlin, can be explicitly stated, whereas the gestalt of something can be had only as a felt meaning. Relationships among different aspects of a given question arise as a result of putting their felt meanings together. We feel or sense relationships first, and then symbolizations of these arise from within us.

Clearly then, thinking also requires experiencing. Thinking is the functional relationship between symbols and experiencing. Despite the fact that only a few considerations can be held in mind in explicit verbal form, thinking involves the simultaneous occurrence of many considerations, Gendlin (1962) believes, which are experienced in a felt way:

> "Let me see, now, there is this, and this, and that," we may say to ourselves, meaning a whole complexity by the word "this" and by the word "that." We know what we mean by "this" and "that" because we directly feel the meaning. (p. 6)

Felt experiencing, he says, makes up the greatest portion of our experience during thinking.

During the thought process, only a part of a presently held meaning is explicitly symbolized. A meaning always includes some implicit aspects that are not symbolized. Gendlin (1962) calls these aspects "fringe," as in a "fringe" of felt meaning. This fringe occurs in every instance of thought. Thus, when we explicate a meaning and focus on it, it is felt or experienced while being explicated. The thought of a particular something includes the "feel" of its meaning, and not only the fringe of what is being thought, but the salient aspects of meaning on which we are focusing or symbolizing.

### General Reality Orientation

As stated in chapter 1, the intermittent awareness of contextual, external realities is referred to by Shor (1959) as our General Reality Orientation (GRO). This GRO is essentially equated to our ordinary state of conscious awareness, of orientation and relation to the concrete reality around us. We've been trained and conditioned to "check out" our surroundings as a matter of biological preservation. This orientation includes attending to ourselves as a physical presence, to what we're doing, where we are, what time it is, and the people with us. Therefore, this ordinary state of consciousness reflects a diffusion of attention and awareness over a broad range of potential objects. When we're not totally absorbed in some activity, we tend to be conscious of ourselves as a physical presence in relationship to the activity at hand and to aspects of our surroundings. In fact, most of us consider this frame of mind as being our most typical and normal because *it is* the experience of being aware, as a self, in context. We're not so self-aware, activity-aware, and context-aware during other forms of experiencing. Thus, during our general reality orientation, we are essentially bringing a diffuse kind of conscious awareness to objects of attention that orient us in relation to our surroundings.

What I have called reflective experiencing is this experience of GRO. In other words, instead of being focused on and immersed in a specific activity or reactivity, as in elaborative experiencing, one is fixing attention on one's self, engaging in this activity, in this particular place and time. A given man might orient himself to himself by focusing on his awareness as a physical-bodily presence, playing tennis. He might orient himself to place by quickly noting his physical surroundings. He might orient himself to time based on his recognition of the meaningful significance of certain external realities (e.g., how much daylight is present) and sociocultural realities (e.g., people going to church).

At certain stages of development, we also experience the GRO in relation to particular internal-mental phenomena. The experience of GRO as a physical-bodily presence in relation to external-physical realities has its "internal" complement when one experiences a GRO as a mental-thinking presence in relation to internal-mental realities. The former GRO experience is an *externally based GRO* (E-GRO), and the latter is an *internally based GRO* (I-GRO). Generally, E-GRO is synonymous with reflective experiencing and I-GRO is synonymous with reflective thinking. Both result in a phenomenological experience of self-awareness as either a physical-bodily presence (E-GRO) or mental-thinking presence (I-GRO) when one is aware of attending to certain, present activities of the self. Further distinctions between these forms of experiencing are elaborated below.

Neither elaborative thinking nor experiencing reflect our focus on aspects of self-experience which result in orienting to self in time and place. Instead, they reflect our focus on an object that does not result in any form of self-orientation, and hence, self-awareness. Consequently, we can refer to elaborative experiencing as an external, physically based, object orientation. Similarly, we can refer to elaborative thinking as an internally based, object orientation.

The following is a brief summary of the general definitions of and relationships between the different types of GRO and reflective and elaborative forms of experiencing.

*Externally based general reality orientation* (E-GRO) includes the activity of reflective experiencing where, as a physical-bodily presence, my behavioral experiencing becomes a relatively prolonged object of attention, resulting in self-awareness, in this particular time and place.

*Internally based general reality orientation* (I-GRO) includes the activity of reflective thinking where, as a mental-thinking presence, I take my thoughts as relatively prolonged objects of attention, resulting in awareness as a thinking-self in this particular time and place.

*Externally based object orientation* includes the activity of elaborative experiencing where my awareness moves into some form of physical activity, taking specific, external, physical forms as objects of its absorption.

*Internally based object orientation* includes the activity of elaborative thinking where my awareness moves into some form of internal, mentally based thought activity, taking internal, mental forms as objects of its absorption.

Despite the fact that every thought has reflective and elaborative elements, I've made distinctions between reflective and elaborative thinking, which we've further differentiated in light of the experience of the GRO. Table 2 lists several subjective differences between these two types of thinking. Following the table is a description of the phenomenal aspects distinguishing each of these two types of thought. When discussing the phenomenology of reflective thinking, we will outline two new types of reflective thought, each of which engenders a different experience of self-awareness.

## The Phenomenology of Elaborative Thinking

At least four phenomenological aspects of experience occur during elaborative thinking.

### 1. Thoughts seem to move forward.

A particular unfolding thought, with its particular, unfolding, meaningful nuances, plays a significant role in the new object presented to awareness once the thought ends. While awareness is still immersed within the thought, but is no longer focused on the recognized content of the excerpted object to which the thought is a reaction, it embodies the meaning in which it's absorbed at that moment. During this elaborative conceptual portion of the thought, as one's awareness is so absorbed, it will suddenly "skip off" of some of the unfolding meaning at hand. That

### Elaborative Thinking Phenomenology

1. Thoughts seem to move forward.
2. Reflective moments seem extremely fleeting or nonexistent.
3. Awareness totally embodies the experience at hand.
4. No experience of time, place, or self-awareness.

### Reflective Thinking Phenomenology

1. Thinking seems to stop.
2. Reflective moments seem prolonged.
3. Experience of self-awareness by attending to and objectifying the "passing thought" (noncomparative reflective thinking).
4. Awareness of the act of observing while being aware of the objectified thought-object being observed (comparative reflective thinking).
5. Self-awareness as a body-self (E-GRO) and/or mind-self (I-GRO) in space and time

*Table 2*

meaning serves as an associatively-based springboard for *moving toward* and "finding" a new excerpt. Then a new thought-reaction in response to this new, identified excerpt occurs, within which awareness is always just as consumed. In other words, during an elaboratively connected series of thoughts, there seems to be a momentum in which awareness is always forward-moving, caught up in a new thought, and then another thought, and then another, without ever looking back!

During a series of elaboratively connected thoughts, awareness seems to be flying in the face of proactively identified excerpts. Because there's no prolonged awareness of such excerpts, they seem to barely exist at all. Awareness rushes forward not even knowing that the course it's now taking was influenced by the last excerpt it just noticed. In addition, because just "passing thoughts" are not being excerpted, they are experienced "as lived," as fleeting vehicles for awareness, which rushes forward from one thought to another.

In elaborative thinking, "connected" thoughts seem to skip ahead in much the same way a flat rock thrown over a lake gets more "air time" by skipping off of a stone in the water. The rock's first discrete period of "air time" is brought to an end by the stone it hits. This stone strongly influences the rock's direction as it moves into another discrete period of "air time." Similarly, one elaborative thought comes to an end by hitting the same identified, excerpt-object from which the next elaborative thought begins.

### 2. Reflective moments seem fleeting or non-existent.

Thinking occurs with amazing speed and fleetingness. Witness an elaborative thought: by the time awareness goes from immersion in an unfolding thought, resurfaces from within it, springboards off of some meaningful aspect of that thought to find a new proactively identified excerpt, thereby initiating the outset of a new thought, and reflectively reacts to the implicitly identified excerpt via the reflective conceptual portion of this new thought, perhaps only milliseconds have elapsed. Moreover, I will have no memory whatsoever of any portion of the process just "prior" to where I now find myself. It's all too fast, and paying attention to any part of the process stops it, like a dream vanishing before my eyes when I become aware of it.

The process of elaborative thinking is entirely unconscious, by definition, because it changes into reflective thinking if it takes any aspect of *itself* as an object. Therefore, reflective moments during elaborative thoughts seem fleeting or nonexistent. In elaborative thinking, one's awareness is simply too busy *being* the unfolding reaction at hand to notice anything else, including itself. Thus, to itself, it doesn't even exist.

The nature of elaborative thinking requires explication of the following fact: the presence of a particular thought always signifies that attention had just focused on an identified, excerpted object to which it reacted. In other words, during elaborative thoughts awareness pulls away from the identified, excerpted object so fast that it totally loses sight of what the excerpted meaning was, or that it even existed! That unique meaning-laden moment was filled with the lifeforce of awareness, led a brief life, and is now dead, without the solace of ever being remembered. Only an extra moment of reflection could have prolonged its "life" or created greater consciousness of it. Similarly, an entire chain of elaborative thoughts can pass without the benefit of reflection. As a result, they will never be known to one's conscious mind, and hence, are like dreams that are never remembered.

### 3. Awareness totally embodies the experience at hand.

During elaborative thinking (and the elaborative portion of all thoughts), one's awareness is so swept up in, identified with, and embodied by the current of meaning-laden changes and transitions, one loses sight of self, self-experiencing, and time and place. Thus, during elaborative thinking, one's awareness and the mental experiencing at hand combine to form a single, experiential reality. As a result, nothing other than the experiential reality at hand seems to exist.

At the outset of an elaborative thought, there is only an awareness of the meaningful content of the identified excerpt to which I'm reacting. That is all of which I am aware, at that instant. Once my awareness gets absorbed in the unfolding meaning at hand, in response to that excerpt, I am the living embodiment of that meaning. Thus, across every part of an elaborative thinking process, I exist in the form of the reaction at hand, as a singular experiencing. The object of my attention, and my reaction to it, are one experiential entity across every instant of elaborative thinking.

Thus, during any one elaborative thought, I am meaning-coming-into-being. It's as if my awareness is the head of a current of meaning-laden changes. In other words, each unfolding part of the elaborative thought reflects or embodies a mental-experiential reality. During each instant of thought, the conceptual-mental-representational-situational-experiential reality is right "in my face." During elaborative thinking, I'm totally absorbed in-and-as the flow and head of this current of mentally based, meaning-laden thinking changes.

While I'm immersed in the elaborative flow, I feel as if I'm at the head of a stream of unfolding meaning, as if I'm intimately connected with what I experience as natural, intrinsically connected fluctuations, changes, and transitions of meaning-laden current. It feels as if my awareness embodies these meaningful fluctuations. I am the living stream, alive with meaning, at one with these fleeting, reflective, and elaborative reactions, occurring around identified, excerpted objects of attention.

During elaborative thinking I am the embodiment of changing, meaning-laden experiencing. I am the changing, the reacting to, the shifting out of and into. I am the manifestor-creator who brings particular, meaningful form to experiencing. I am the combination and embodiment of being and creating. It's as if I'm the burning tip of the fuse of unfolding, meaning-laden experiencing, giving meaning-based form to each instant of contact with the fuse.

Successive elaborative thoughts may not seem logically consistent, in retrospect. Looking back, it's almost impossible to discern exactly how one thought led to another. Even so, the "reason" why one thought gives rise to another feels totally natural and makes perfect sense to the "traveler" of the thoughts. In other words, the fact that one thought reminds me of something in response to which I then experience a new thought, feels just right to the awareness absorbed in being each part of that process.

I believe that the consuming, absorbing phenomenology of elaborative thinking is reflected in the experience of daydreaming. Consider your experience of daydreaming; my guess is that you can't easily describe it. You don't really know what it consists of because you can't bring a reflective knowing to the experience without interrupting it. You tend to be so consumed in the experiential reality of the daydream that there's no room for an observing awareness to get to know it in any other way than by *being* it. Consequently, there is little to no experience of duality and hence of self-awareness during a daydream. Instead, one's experience is inextricably bound to and one with the unfolding internal/mental reality at hand.

Thus, during elaborative thinking, my awareness is being swept through a conceptual tube of unfolding, meaning-laden changes and is an embodiment of that meaning in each instant. It is then shot toward a new object of attention and subsequent conceptual tube without any conscious awareness of how it got there. It's as if one meaning-laden nuance associated with a particular portion of the elaborative thought at hand provides the force and angle for the direction I go, and hence, to the next object of attention I find. In elaborative thinking, then, there is no conscious awareness of the transitional aspects of elaborative meaning that "shoot" me to a new object or aspect of experience. Awareness is so thoroughly embodied by the meaning-laden fluctuations of the thought, by the time it shoots to a new aspect of experience, it has no idea of how it got there. Like day or night dreaming, I can be so consumed in my experiencing during the dream that when I awaken, I instantly lose sight of it. Similarly, while I'm the living, experiential embodiment of unfolding meaning in an elaborative thinking sequence, I have no conscious awareness of this fact. *I'm awareness itself*, as much as the unfolding, meaning-laden changes at hand. If and when I try to reflectively catch that prior elaborative thinking experience, it easily slips from my grasp.

### 4. No Experience of Time, Place, or Self-Awareness

When I am in my "normal" state of consciousness (GRO), I am attending to aspects of my experience in relation to my surroundings. My awareness is somewhat diffusely and fleetingly attending to various aspects of self-experiencing in this time and place. In fact, when I orient myself to any one of three facets of experiencing—time, place, or self-experiencing—the other two are somewhat present in my awareness as well. For example, it is difficult to be explicitly aware of the physical space I am in without also being aware of myself in relation to it. And how could I be explicitly aware of stimuli indicative of time without also being aware of some aspects of the co-occurring physical space, and hence, of me in relation to this space? Thus, I believe that during my normal consciousness (or GRO), I am, at the very least, diffusely aware of all three of these overlapping facets of experiencing.

By definition, during elaborative thinking, we are not taking the overlapping realities of time, place, or self-experiencing as explicit objects of attention. For example, the experience of time does not exist during elaborative thinking. Most of us have driven a car and become so lost in thought, we're later surprised (as we move back into our GRO) a whole thirty minutes had passed. Similarly, we're aware of the phenomenology of losing a sense of space when we voice surprise that we didn't get into an accident or didn't miss our exit. At times like these, we literally lose a sense of self until suddenly becoming aware of the fact that here we are, driving our cars, at this particular time and place.

### The Phenomenology of Reflective Thinking

At least five phenomenological aspects of experience occur during reflective thinking.

#### 1. Thinking seems to stop.

Earlier I touched on an example of shooting a basketball as a potential form of elaborative experiencing that then changed to reflective experiencing. When shooting a basketball, my awareness can be so focused on the back of the rim as I shoot the ball nothing else exists for me in that moment. I am so immersed in the play at hand, my awareness embodies this activity, and nothing else.

When someone is very absorbed in an athletic activity and playing extremely well it is often said that he or she is "unconscious" or "in the zone." This "zone" epitomizes elaborative experiencing. In contrast, if he or she suddenly attends to the act of playing itself, reflective experiencing is occurring. Any athlete or musical performer can tell you that by becoming conscious of the activity at hand, and of themselves in relation to it, their performance deteriorates rapidly.

When conceptually reacting to an explicitly recognized excerpt regarding the identity of a particular "passing thought," I am engaged in reflective thinking. (Further distinctions about different types of reflective thinking will be discussed later.) When I suddenly move out of elaborative thinking and into reflective thinking, my experience tends to be that of stopping what seemed to be a flowing, thematically consistent, elaborative process. Instead of having an experience where thoughts just skip ahead in a seemingly progressive and forward-moving direction, as in elaborative thinking, thought seems to stop altogether at the outset of reflective thinking.

At the outset of reflective thinking, I seem to move away from *being* thinking to becoming aware of or *capturing* thinking. This awareness is engendered by turning thought into an object of attention and excerpting it. As a result, it's as if I'd literally captured it alive in the hand of my awareness. Instead of allowing my thoughts to run wild in their natural elaborative domain, I seem to bring them to a standstill in the cage of my reflective awareness.

### 2. Reflective moments seem more prolonged.

Many of us have had the experience of anxiously waiting for the time to pass in anticipation of something we desire or would rather avoid. We also know that this "clock-watching" is usually an unpleasant experience because it seems as if time slows down when we pay attention to its passage.

I believe that the phenomenology during "clock-watching"

is consistent with the experience of the GRO: we're aware of ourselves even as we're aware of watching the clock and waiting for the time to pass (e.g., as in reflective experiencing). Our awareness of any activity makes it seem to last longer. The cliché "Time flies when you're having fun" refers, in contrast, to the common experience of losing ourselves and the contextual elements of time and place by being immersed in the activity at hand. Many of us have been surprised when we realize how much time has elapsed after having been absorbed in some engaging experience, as in elaborative experiencing.

During the reflective conceptual portion of a reflective thought, I can be aware of myself as a separating, observing entity and of an objectified thought. I'm aware of this observing, reflective moment, and this alone makes it seem longer. Time suddenly exists as I become aware of myself reflecting on, observing, attending to, or separating from the thought-object at hand. Depending on the type of reflective thinking in which I am engaged, my awareness of the experience of observing (the thought-object) can be implicit or increasingly explicit. The more explicit this awareness, the more conscious one is of the passage of time, and hence the longer the reflective moment seems to last.

In sum, during reflective thinking, one is attending to an explicitly identified and excerpted, "passing thought" object as an apparent movement away from that thought. Depending on the type of reflective thinking in which I'm engaged, I can be implicitly or, to varying degrees, explicitly aware of this reflecting, observing, separating movement. Thus, across the various types of reflective thought, I'm increasingly aware of the passage of time. The more I attend to this reflecting, separating, observing movement, the greater my awareness of it and the more prolonged this reflective moment seems to be.

## 3. Experience of Self-Awareness by Attending to and Objectifying the "Passing Thought" (Noncomparative Reflective Thinking)

Most children between the ages of seven and eleven identify

themselves according to the roles assigned to them by others. Older children on the other hand can learn to identify themselves according to what they believe. Their beliefs reflect, in part, who they are as unique personalities. Their thoughts and beliefs about themselves and the world are construed as the truest reflection of self (Wilber, 1995).

An adolescent has an increasing ability to become aware of a given "passing thought," yielding a new experience of self-awareness in the form of an objectified thinking-self (Wilber, 1995). A younger child is a thinking-self, too but is simply too absorbed in *being* a thinking-self to be consciously aware of it. In contrast, an adolescent's or adult's self-identity is engendered in large part by taking her thoughts as objects per se and hence as instances of present subjectivity. For example, she could be sitting at her desk and find herself reacting strongly to a character she's reading about: "That Robert is a real drag!" In this instance, she's not only aware of the content of that thought but of its existence as an objectified thought per se. In this instance, she's not only aware of the content of that thought but of its literal existence as an objectified thought per se. In addition, as she looks at and identifies it as, "My thought about Robert," it's all that she's aware of at that moment. It completely fills her awareness. Furthermore, she's experiencing herself as personally embodying that observed thought-object: "That's me!" Her present subjectivity is being equated with that thought-object. She is personifying it as the most immediately present instance of self. All that exists in that moment of observation is that objectified instance of her which completely fills her awareness.

This experience of self-awareness engendered by reflecting on thought is similar to that of Narcissus. Narcissus came upon a quiet pool while walking with the nymph, Echo (D'Aulaire & D'Aulaire, 1982). Bending down to drink he suddenly stopped and stared, for in the reflecting surface of the water he witnessed the most handsome face he'd ever seen. He was spellbound by the stranger in the water, not knowing it was his own image.

There he sat, so in-love, and infatuated with himself that he forgot to eat or drink, until at last he wasted away and died.

Unlike Narcissus, who mistook his image for a stranger's, you become transfixed by the thought-object witnessed because you mistake it for yourself. Seeing your reflection in "passing thought," you become transfixed because you construe them as instances of the actual you.

Most of us, adolescents and adults alike, take the objects of our thoughts as instances of our immediate subjectivity. I call this type of reflective thinking *noncomparative reflective thinking* (NCRT). It's "noncomparative" because, by capturing the thinking-self in the form of the thought-object at hand, one loses sight of the subjective awareness doing the capturing. That thought-object is construed as one's subjective self. There's no comparative awareness between the subjectivity doing the capturing and the thought-object being captured. Interestingly, most of us become fascinated with and addicted to the reflective actions that engender these instances of self-awareness.

Here we have yet another kind of ghost. This ghost, with its "host" at the stages of adolescence and adulthood, can pose as *you* in the form of the thought-object. It's an impostor version of yourself, having great fun fooling you about your true identity!

### 4. Awareness of the Act of Observing While Being Conscious of the Objectified Thought-Object Being Observed (Comparative Reflective Thinking)

For most adolescents and adults the act of reflecting on and becoming explicitly aware of the presence of a "passing thought" results in construing it as the most immediate and truest instance of subjectivity. During this experience of NCRT, that thought-object dominates their observing awareness so much nothing else seems to exist at that moment.

With time and attention, however, I may begin to discover that the observed thought-object is not the truest manifestation of my subjectivity. Instead, I may begin to realize that there is an observing self, or witnessing awareness, that is the truest subjectivity, rather than the thought-object at hand. I may realize that this witness is always more immediate and present than its thought-object. This realization may come via the repetitive discovery that the witness (in the supposed form of the "passing thought") cannot actually be captured or objectified. I discover this by realizing that whenever I try to capture the witness by objectifying it, I can always then replace it with what I come to believe is an even more recent and hence truer version of my subjectivity in the form of another thought-object. In other words, the witness can capture itself as a thought-object in this instance, only to replace it with another instance of itself (as a thought-object) in the next moment.

Therefore, I realize that there is always an immediately present witness who cannot be captured, seen, or objectified. As a result, I begin to associate my sense of self with this observing awareness which unfolds in relation to the objectified thought-self (at the outset of the reflective conceptual portion of thought). That is, this reflecting awareness *begins* to manifest itself in the form of a thought unfolding in relation to an excerpted and objectified thought-self. Consequently, this type of reflective thinking is called *comparative reflective thinking* (CRT). It's "comparative" because, at the *outset* of the reflective conceptual portion of the reflective thought at hand, the individual compares the "passing thought" to the reflecting awareness and subsequent thinking-self unfolding in relation to it. This process will be elaborated on later, but for now let's compare it to the experience of looking into that pool of water and seeing your reflection. This time, however, you're aware that your reflection isn't the actual you because there's a truer you doing the looking.

The experience of self-awareness engendered by CRT is more or less present in all forms of reflective thinking because the witnessing awareness is the truest reality embodying all such forms. In the lesser forms of reflective thinking, this witnessing awareness is blind to itself as it construes its thought-objects as the truest instances of itself, or as experiences that it "has." (We will elaborate on this in chapter 5).

Comparative reflective thinking, in particular, and its co-occurring phenomenologies can be compared to descriptions of "out-of-body" experiences. A friend of mine once described his experience of being in a car accident as of it happened in slow motion, as he became while being aware of (and remembering) only a few aspects of the trauma. For example, he was aware of the other driver's face at one instant and of the sound of crushing metal at another. He was aware of excruciating pain as he was pulled from the car and of feeling the grass against his body.

Lying on the grass, his vantage point and subjective experience suddenly changed. He was no longer lying down, feeling the grass, his pain, and seeing others moving above him. Instead, he discovered that he was *looking down* at himself lying on the grass. His new subjective state was one of great mental clarity. He was in a calm, pain-free, and surprised state of mind as he witnessed himself below. He had moved from one subjective vantage point to a totally different one and was aware of this unusual experience as it happened. He felt himself as separate from that person below while recognizing and *identifying* with that self's experiencing by remembering what that self appeared to be going through now. Thus, from his more subjectively alive vantage point above, he experienced a sense of separateness from that self below. Yet he also found himself disidentifying with that self below: from "above," his subjective reality was more holistic, vivid, alive, and immediate; he had this new vantage point plus the one he was witnessing.

Simultaneously, my friend was aware of his subjective past as it contrasted with his subjective present. He experienced himself in terms of his subjective past (as object), while experiencing something more in terms of his subjective present (as subject). His present subjectivity included the entirety of his remembered subjectivity, but was other than and something more than it, as well. Consequently, the present subjectivity seemed experientially truer, more meaningful and all-encompassing than that subjectivity which seemed to be past, a contrast to, and lesser than it.

Digest this: during all instances of reflective thinking this "out-of-body" experiencing is occurring in the form of "out-of-thought" experiencing during that instant when awareness is freed from and reflecting on thought. As a result, during every such reflective instant a seemingly newer and more meaningfully significant you is born!

At the outset of the reflective conceptual portion of CRT, for example, the reflective-self's "out-of-thought" experience is one of feeling greater, more alive, pertinent, informed, and permanent than the thought-object construed as no longer present and alive with subjectivity. Looking back on that conceptual skin and former version of subjectivity, I, who just shed it say to myself, "Ah, here I am, newer, better, and more alive!"

These "out-of-thought" experiential realities are unconsciously or implicitly experienced during ERI, the reflective forms of "RI of excerpts," "RI of excerptive-clips of external objects," and NCRT. In other words, such experiential realities are unattended-to-knowings: they are part of one's experience but are not objects of attention, and hence are not explicitly conscious. Such realities are more consciously or explicitly experienced during CRT and TRI (to be defined in chapter 3), existing as attended-to-knowings.

By becoming increasingly familiar with the reflective thought process, I may begin to recognize that there's a more immediate subjectivity or witnessing self construing a thought-object as self. In other words, as I attend to the "passing thought" as a presence, I construe it as my most recent conceptual home, conceptual skin, or "temporary housing" for my subjectivity. This contrasts with my earlier tendency to construe that thought-object as myself. Now that thought-object is just one manifest form of my subjectivity. Therefore, as I reflect on that thought-object,

I give it credibility as a "prior" version of me.

From the vantage point of awareness at the outset of the reflective conceptual portion of CRT, I take that thought "over-there" as a prior instance of my subjectivity, wearing the "clothes" of a specific conceptual reaction. Thus, I experience that thought-self as an object which is "behind" this thought-self as subject attending to that object. As unfolding subject, I am engaged in conceiving the differences between myself and the objectified version of myself being witnessed. In addition, because of my greater awareness of an always more immediate, witnessing-self, I'm in a position to attend to and become fleetingly aware of the witnessing awareness as it unfolds in relation to the thought-object at hand.

At the outset of CRT, a witnessing self-as-subject grounded in immediacy begins to recognize and conceive the difference between itself and the stagnant, objectified, less present self-as-object. Thus, the present "I-that-sees" is noticing the difference between itself and the "I-that-is-seen." This experience creates a sense of self-awareness and self-experiencing split in two: of a self-experiencer "over-here" that becomes self-aware by comparing itself to another apparent form of self-experiencing "over-there." Several potential pairs of sensed differences arise as a result of this comparative process: a "me-over-there" versus a "me-over-here" a "me-of-then" versus a "me-of-now" a "past-me" versus a "present-me;" and a "less-than-me" versus a "more-than-me." I have essentially created two me's in one moment as a function of the excerpt-thought dyad, one end of which is a stagnant, excerpted, objectified thought-self out of which an unfolding, conceptual, and subjective thinking-self emerges. Two me's occur in this moment, an objective-me and a subjective-me, both identified with and by their respective conceptual forms.

As my present, unfolding, conceptually different instance-of-me recognizes and compares itself against the objectified, "passing," conceptually different instance-of-me, a sense of time is created; a more personally bound and significant sense of time than any other. It's created as the present instance-of-me recognizes itself as different from the past, objectified instance-of-me. The recognition is one of, "This isn't that." "This isn't that" *is literally experienced as an extension of self* over mental space and time. It's *as if my experience of self is being stretched* in mental space and time. I simultaneously experience myself as here, in the process of stretching away from a different form of self over "there." It's as if a me is dying into an objective past and is being born to itself in an always more immediate present. And this newborn-me seems to be literally stretching away from the now-dead-me.

The comparative process between these two me's embodies a sense of difference and literally creates the experience of a self-awareness that feels newer, better, and more alive than its objective counterpart. This sense of difference is primarily based on the perceived contrast between *conceptual* "positions." The objectified thought is an instance-of-me with a specific conceptual identity. If one subjectively lived thought was, "Tomorrow is Sheila's birthday," as an object it becomes, "There's that thought about Sheila's birthday." The subjective awareness taking that thought as an object compares itself to and recognizes "This isn't that." It recognizes that its present position of knowing (about the thought regarding Sheila) is different from that past, objectified position of knowing (about Sheila). Again, the recognition of difference between these two sets of knowings is based on recognized conceptual differences.

Two me's are experienced as a function of the conceptual differences noted between the unfolding conceptual "I," comparing itself to the stagnant, conceptually identified, and objectified "I." One "I" compared to the other "I," recognized as two differing, manifest forms of the same, supposed subjectivity. I, as subject, identify with the objectified experience at hand as a "passing" version of me while also sensing another more present self extending from it. At bottom, this comparative reflective thinking process creates and engenders an entirely new experience of self-awareness.

In summary, during adolescence and adulthood an individual's sense of self normally exists in the form of the (objectified) thinking-self. And the actual thinking-self can't know itself in any other way than to be itself, unless it takes itself as an object. Despite the fact that two forms of the same subjectivity can't exist in the same instant, I can seemingly make it happen anyway! This thinking-self becomes aware of itself in the same way it becomes aware of anything else: by excerpting an experience for the mind's eye to see. By excerpting my "prior thought" I create a thought-object for my mind's eye. I then construe it as the most immediate and truest manifestation of who I am. My construal of this thought-object as my actual self fills and illuminates my awareness so completely nothing else exists for me at that moment. This is called noncomparative reflective thinking. Later, however, I can learn that the thought-object being reflected on isn't the truest instance of my subjectivity. Instead, through CRT I experience a sense of self-awareness as a witnessing and subsequent reflecting thought-self, taking that objectified thought as a prior version of me, and this engenders an entirely new experience of self-awareness.

### 5. Self-Awareness as a Body-Self (E-GRO and/or Mind-Self (Partial I-GRO or I-GRO) in Space and Time

An earlier discussion about the GRO indicated the possibility of orienting to self in space and time based on bodily and external stimuli (E-GRO). One can also do so based on internal, mentally based stimuli (I-GRO). This I-GRO is synonymous with reflective thinking while the E-GRO is synonymous with reflective experiencing. The I-GRO, explained below, is engendered by reflective thinking during adolescence and adulthood and exists in a slightly different form in adulthood if one progresses developmentally.

Most adolescents and adults experience a partial, mentally

based GRO by attending to and construing the thought-object per se as the self (partial I-GRO or NCRT). This process is mentally-based and hence is not observable from any external vantage point. As an object, that thought has been internally and mentally represented and can only be seen by the mind's eye of the person at hand. However, this is a *partial* I-GRO because, developmentally, that person continues to orient himself to time based on the significance of certain external, physical, and socio-cultural realities (E-GRO). Furthermore, he still orients himself to place by taking stock of his immediate physical surroundings (E-GRO).

Like most adolescents and adults, when I reflect on a "passing thought" per se I construe it as the truest and most immediately present version of self. As I progress developmentally, however, a comparative reflecting process can occur in relation to that thought-object which is construed as a "past" instance of subjectivity (CRT). I create a past or "what was" of my subjectivity, as well as perceiving it as "over-there."

It must be understood that experiences of change, movement, difference, and time are *created* when the unfolding thought (at the outset of the reflective conceptual portion of CRT), which "holds" one's subjectively felt awareness, *compares* itself to a "prior" subjectivity in the form of the thought-object at hand. This comparing process is based on the conceptual differences and recognitions between these states, both of which adhere to the experientially and conceptually extending framework of the unfolding thought at hand. At the outset of the reflective conceptual portion of the comparative reflective thought, I become aware of an apparent *movement* from a less-than state of conceptual knowledge to a more-than state of conceptual knowledge. This comparative process engenders an experience of change and difference. This experience of a more-than state of knowledge is created by recognizing what that thought (as recent subject) knew about whatever object it was reacting to, while also knowing more about that thought (as object) now as I see it from here in its *entirety*. I simultaneously experience that objectified thought as less-than while unfolding as more-than in relation to it. I'm also becoming aware of a death of one instance of my subjectivity as I'm born into a new instance of subjectivity. As a result, a past instance-of-me seems to exist alongside a present instance of me.

During CRT, my conscious awareness is on the thought-object as a contrasting experience to the reflecting awareness observing it. Consequently, I am not only having the experience of being a separating observer (bound in imediacy) being aware of a "present," separate, objectified thought construed as "past," I am explicitly representing this experience as such. My awareness experientially embodies this duality (because it's happening) is attending to and being aware *of* it, while conceptually representing it. In other words, while I am experiencing, *as* awareness, this duality of self-experiencing, I am attending to experiential aspects *of* this fact and am conceiving of it.

Given the above, when a person is capable of CRT, he may experience an I-GRO (versus partial I-GRO) by attending to his experience as an unfolding, meaning-laden, present-thought-subject existing here and now in relation to an internal, meaning-laden, past-thought-object. He may place himself in time by reaffirming his greater subjective presence as a thinking-self in the immediacy of now. He does this by attending to and construing the objectified thought as a "passing" instance of self. He may place himself in "mind-space" by attending to the experience of being a separating, subjective awareness "over here," witnessing a separate thought-self as object "over-there."

### The Phenomenology of the Parts of Thought

Before addressing the phenomenology of the "parts" of thought, a brief overview of their unfolding is in order. The excerpt-searching reaction or attentional surfacing marks the end of a discrete thought. The next thought begins with the appearance of the excerpt or excerptive-clip. That excerpt's appearance co-occurs with seeing it. In thoughts with reactive excerpt-found reactions (reflective thoughts), I then begin identifying or recognizing that proactively appearing and identified excerpt. My reaction to it is one of identifying, recognizing, or knowing it. My reaction is a kind of reflection of it, and hence, my awareness embodies a form of knowing the content of that excerpt. Because my awareness embodies both the content of the excerpt as an object as well as a subsequent reaction to it, that objecitified content seems to be *a part of* my experiencing *stretching* away from me. That content seems to exist, and I, as an identifying reaction, begin to separate from and extend away from it.

Next, the instant I reflect on the reactive excerpt-found reaction (reflective thought), the content of the excerpt becomes explicitly or "formally" identified: "That's what you are!" This, in abstract, is my response to what I now "see" and explicitly know in "front" of me. The outset of this verbalizing, out loud or silently, is the reflective conceptual portion of the thought. At this point, I'm essentially knowing that excerpt's explicit identity as I react to and extend away from its *now*-objectified and explicitly identified content. Thus, at the outset of the reflective conceptual portion of reflective thought, a second stretching of experience seems to be occurring: my reactive experience is one of knowing, and seems experientially attached to yet pulling away from an objectified form of knowledge.

Then, as my awareness comes to the end of the reflective conceptual portion of the thought, it is consumed in a transition period embodying an experience of not knowing because there is no longer a separate object to which it is attending. During this elaborative portion of the thought, I'm immersed in a transition period between objects of attention. I'm awash in the experience that *follows* my conscious response to the objectified content to which this thought is a reaction, and which is prior to the searching or surfacing period in which I will soon be consumed. Here, as in much of dreaming, I'm the embodiment of rich, vivid, and real mental experiencing, but the dreamer is nonexistent.

In summary, during every single thought there is a prior moment of searching, or surfacing from a predecessor-thought, an instant of seeing an object where the seeing and its appearance are synonymous realities, a reaction of explicitly identify*ing* or know*ing* that object (in reflective thought), a moment of reflecting on, reacting to, and knowing a now *objectified*, explicitly identified knowledge (in reflective thought), and moments of a dreamlike experience without the sense of a dreamer.

### The Phenomenology of Excerpt-Searching Reactions

A thought can end when awareness exits and then begins searching for the next object to be thought about. This is the excerpt-searching reaction. Considering this reaction by personifying "awareness," it's as though I, Awareness, abruptly leave the room, searching for the house keys. Moreover, upon leaving the room, it's as if I'm amnestic to myself, being alive, having left the room, and being somewhere else. I, and all of living temporarily disappear.

As Awareness was searching for the keys, I and all of the world disappeared phenomenally. Likewise, between thoughts, the apparent nonexistence of all experiencing during the excerpt-searching reaction seems to give way to an existent experiencing in the form of the appearing excerpt at the end of the proactive excerpt-found reaction when awareness reflects on it at the outset of the reflective conceptual portion of an elaborative or on the reactive excerpt-found reaction at the outset of a reflective thought.

### The Phenomenology of Attentional Surfacing

Imagine swimming like a dolphin with your dorsal fin knifing through the surface of the water. As you speed ahead, ocean creatures enter your field of vision. You're totally awash in the experience of the constantly changing ocean view in front of you.

Then, leaping out of the water, you see below the world where you dwell. Escaping and witnessing it ever so fleetingly is an amazing and wonderful experience.

During a lifetime of dreaming I'm living a totally separate existence from my waking life. Like a dolphin leaping out of the water, I achieve fleeting glimpses into the nature of this dreamworld. In generally, I live with little to no awareness of it.

Through glimpses into dreaming you realize being immersed in an experiencing that is as alive, rich, vivid, and real as your waking life. You sometimes become dimly aware of the fact of your dreaming and experience in the dream. You seem to surface out of the dream ever so slightly while still experiencing it. You see it while living it, only to become totally immersed in its flow moments later. If you surface out of the dream too much it disperses or fades away and your waking experience comes to the fore.

In the same way I experience reflective glimpses of living a dream when rising out of it ever so slightly, I catch sight of the dreamlike, elaborative, transitional flow as I delicately surface from thought. This glimpse seems to fly into the "face" of my awareness as a flash-image. Where a moment earlier all of awareness dissolved into the rich experiencing of thought, I suddenly sail above it as a focal point, a witness of a hidden world containing a secret life. Unaware that this fleeting insight marks the end of a thought, I dive into a new one and disappear once more. Onward I go, as if immersed in the currents of the ocean. I might as well be a dolphin swimming in a rhythm of successive and alternating movements both under and over the water.

### The Phenomenology of Excerpts

Excerptive-clips prompt and are the objects of IRI, and all the types of reflective thinking. Regarding thinking, for example, my awareness is absorbed in a thought, surfaces from and reflects on it, resulting in an excerptive-clip of its some meaning embodied in it. This excerpt marks the end of that thought and the beginning of a new one as my awareness reflects on and reacts to that clip.

The phenomenology of excerptive-clips is quite distinct. The phenomenology of excerptive-clips prompting IRI, for example, can be compared to riding a bicycle. I am casually riding my bike down a quiet street enjoying the pleasant sights in front of me. I'm simply taking in the sights in a relaxed fashion. Nothing in particular captures my attention as I stray from one object to another. I'm barely and only fleetingly conscious of one stimulus to the next.

Up ahead in the bush by the street I see a cat. For a moment I glance away from it. Then it suddenly it darts in front of me almost running into the wheel of my bike. I quickly squeeze my brakes and make a sharp turn to avoid hitting it. I watch it hurdle the curb as it runs into the neighbor's backyard. In seconds I've resumed my ride but on a different side of the street. In addition, I've completely forgotten my encounter with the kitty.

Just prior to an instance of implicit reflective identification, for example, I'm casually engaged in the natural flow of elaborative thought, as if everything is going as it should. And it seems as if I'm going somewhere; I have direction. Yet, there's nothing significant enough to notice really, nothing toward which I should feel any concern. Suddenly, the casual flow of thought is interrupted by an image rushing into my mental vision. It's abrupt and startling. It captures my attention, just like the cat I first noticed and which subsequently surprised me in an even more noticeable fashion. As a result, I excerptively clip the image and the flow at hand is disturbed; yet the startling excerpt-image seems to be part of the flow. The excerptive-clip represents an abrupt change and eruption *in* the flow but seems part of the flow nonetheless. It also seems to represent a change in the direction of the flow as my attention relaxes, watches, and reacts to that somehow familiar image. In a moment, however, I've completely forgotten my encounter with it.

The phenomenology of excerpts during a series of elaborative thoughts, some of which occur at the outset of IRI (which consists of excerptive-clips of prior thoughts), the elaborative forms of "RI of excerpts," and "RI of excerptive-clips of external objects" is much like this bicycle ride as well. During a series of elaborative thoughts these erupting excerpts are part of what seems like one continuous, uninterrupted flow of stimuli which my awareness embodies. I'm immersed in one, seemingly continuous absorbing experience consisting of occasional, startling, noticeable, and abrupt shifts. The "traveler" of the thoughts doesn't realize that each excerpt marks the death of one discrete thought and the birth of another. Despite the fact that these discrete shifts of attention are occurring, leading to discrete thoughts, the sensation is of being absorbed in one, uninterrupted, continuous, flowing experience.

General elaborative thoughts prompted by excerptive reminders, memories, solutions, and decisions are phenomenally similar to thoughts prompted by excerptive-clips. Here's how: as with IRI, and all the types of reflective thinking prompted by excerptive-clips, general elaborative thoughts are prompted by excerpts that also seem to appear as *part of the flow in the stream of thought.* They too seem to fly into the "face" of awareness, like a tropical fish swimming into a snorkeler's goggles.

In contrast to any type of thought initiated by excerptive-clips, instances of the reflective form of "RI of excerpts" are prompted by excerpt-searching reactions and subsequent excerptive memories, reminders, solutions, and decisions. Where an excerptive-clip is *of* the "passing thought," excerptive reminders, memories, solutions, and decisions seem to come from "somewhere" *outside the stream of thought.* They are not taken from or intrinsic to the prior thought. Consequently, their phenomenology is slightly different.

For example, I'm going on another bicycle ride, but this time I have an agenda. I'm going to take a ride through the town where I grew up. I haven't been there for a long while so I'm interested in what has changed. As a result, my bike ride is less casual, experientially speaking, than the one noted above. Now I'm on the lookout for changes.

As I come to the third block of Main Street everything is as I remember. So far my ride has been relaxing and uneventful. After pedaling a little farther, I deliberately shift my gaze to the right to see what the old general store looks like. I'm surprised to discover that it's gone. I'm not too surprised, however. I'm on a journey of expectant exploration. I knew there would be some changes in town and I was on the lookout for them. Thereafter I stay my course, steady even in my speed, curious as to what else I'll discover.

During the reflective form of "RI of excerpts," prompted by excerptive reminders, memories, solutions, and decisions, I'm often on a journey of expectant exploration as well. Excerptive reminders, memories, solutions, and decisions are often triggered by the thought at hand. When I ask myself—"Where did we go on vacation last year?"—I shift and focus my attention, waiting for certain images of possible locations to flash into my mind. When they come, I'm not surprised by the images. I expect them to come. They're so experientially familiar, I take their literal presence for granted.

When I smell the wet ground after the first winter thaw and a memory-image of a spring visit to my grandmother's house enters my awareness, I notice and react to it again, without surprise. Similarly, when I ask myself—"Which year was it when Bruce Jenner won the gold medal?"—specific images of events during that year come to mind, and I notice and react to them. When these excerpts come to mind, I implicitly recognize that they're consistent with the thought that prompted them. I expect some version of them to be triggered by the thoughts. Oftentimes I wait for them to come. In fact, I often "step out" of the thought at hand and actually look for their arrival. I may even track the relevance of the content of the appearing excerpts to the task at hand as well as the progress toward my goal.

As a function of this task-orientation and expectancy, the appearance of excerptive reminders, memories, solutions, and decisions seem to come from outside the periphery of my mind's eye or outside the stream of thought. In contrast, excerptive-clips and excerpts prompting elaborative thoughts seem to fly in the "face" of awareness.

### The Phenomenology of Proactive and
### Reactive Excerpt-Found Reactions

Proactive excerpt-found reactions occur during the outset of every type of thought. Recall that after an excerpt-searching reaction or attentional surfacing, either of which mark the end of the predecessor-thought, awareness moves toward an as-yet-to-be-discovered excerpt. The excerpt becomes increasingly clear and proactively identified as awareness moves toward it. The instant its appearance and identity is fully established, a new thought is initiated in response to it via the reflective conceptual portion of an elaborative thought or the reactive excerpt-found reaction of a reflective thought.

Phenomenally, proactive excerpt-found reactions can be compared to skydiving. Imagine jumping out of an airplane over an African wildlife preserve, focusing on a particular spot in the grasslands below. As the ground nears, that spot becomes increasingly clear. The instant its full detail is revealed, so is its identity as a lion, for example. Its full clarity and identity progressively and concurrently appear to awareness.

In contrast to proactive excerpt-found reactions, which occur at the outset of all thoughts, reactive excerpt-found reactions occur only during forms of reflective thinking. Following a predecessor-thought, a proactively identified excerpt suddenly appears to awareness, as if right in its "face." The instant awareness reflects on and pulls away from this implicitly identified excerpt, a reactive excerpt-found reaction begins to explicitly identify it. Then this reaction is reflected upon, thereby fixing, grounding, or solidifying its explicit identity.

Phenomenally, reactive excerpt-found reactions are like walking through the park and being knocked down by an object that suddenly hits your forehead. Gathering yourself on the ground, that object is right under your nose. Its appearance is there for you immediately, but it's too close to completely identify. Upon seeing it, you rise and can suddenly recognize it as a baseball.

### *The Phenomenal Teleology of Thinking*

The term "teleology" refers to natural processes shaped or explained by a purpose, where the end point of a system (of processes) tends to "pull" the system toward its actualization (Werner, 1980). In my opinion, such processes include thinking, which seems as natural and autonomous as a flowing river. Unlike a river, our thoughts have a logical order and coherence because of their conceptual nature. Furthermore, because many events in our surroundings seem to unfold in a sequentially logical, predictable, and causal fashion, our thoughts representing those events reflect that logical coherence. For example, when it rains it's natural to assume that things outside will get wet. If I thought of how dry the ground became after excerpting the fact that it's raining, it would be safe to assume that I was crazy. Thus thoughts generally reflect a logical order and unfold accordingly.

In a thematically consistent line of thoughts, prior thoughts have a logically consistent bearing on present and future thoughts. Moreover, when an excerpt-searching reaction, for example, comes to an end and a proactively identified excerpt begins to appear to awareness, an excerpt-"ground" is "geographically" forming, and from this "ground" a thought will sprout. The instant awareness reflects on that excerpt-ground, I experience an extremely fleeting sense of what I want to say or think, and hence of the thought that will come into being. If the thought that comes does not seem to accurately reflect the sense of meaning I first gleaned from the excerpt, I will "back up" and try to capture that meaning again. In other words, I may know when the thought I've just experienced is not consistent with the direction I had initially sensed in front of me. Much of the time I have a vague or not so vague sense of purpose that I'm pursuing while thinking. My thoughts either seem conducive to meeting that purpose or not.

The teleological phenomenology of thinking can be visually represented by the Slinky metaphor. When one end of the Slinky-thought hits the stair the other end is pulled forward and down by gravity. Heading toward its destination, the free end of the Slinky *pulls* the stationary end *along its path*. The awareness traveling this path feels itself expectantly moving toward a conclusion that seems somehow familiar or right, reflecting a phenomenology of teleology. In addition, inside a particular segment of the Slinky, each of which represents the immediate present, awareness can be compared to a dense and brightly glowing light. Just behind itself, in the immediate past, is where the light of awareness trails move diffusely. And just ahead, in the immediate future, the light of awareness radiates forth. As such, awareness fully embodies the meaning at hand, slightly embodies the meaning behind it, and premonitorily embodies the meaning just ahead.

### The Constraining Nature of Thought

Thinking can stand in place of and represent situational realities and contexts. When I think about certain situations (or read or hear about them), associations in the form of memory images, sounds, smells, feelings, tastes, and movements can rise into my awareness. In other words, thoughts which represent certain realities serve as constraints for the associations rising into conscious awareness. They constrain by way of placing limits on the associations that will likely rise in relation to them as a function of the specific situations they represent. Therefore, a field of potential associations is created as a function of the particular thought at hand.

In addition, when absorbed in and as the associations arising and co-occurring as thought unfolds, my awareness (which is illuminating and illuminated by these associations) is constrained by the extending framework of the thought at hand. This is an amazing phenomenal reality which most of us rarely if ever consider.

Metaphorically, imagine you are standing in an open field looking up into the night sky seeing the dome of stars above you. This experience can be compared to your awareness as well, which reflects the same qualities of openness and expansiveness as the entire universe above. Now, if I hand you a telescope and ask you to fix it on an object in the night sky, that telescope constrains and limits what you visually experience as you look through it. Quite suddenly, as a strict function of the presence of the telescope you're looking through, that celestial object is significantly altered or specified, thereby constraining the night sky. The entire universe gives way to the specific object on which you're focused as a function of the constraining nature of the tubular object pressed against you eye.

Looking through a telescope is much like thinking. The extension of a thought (over time) is like the extension of the telescope, through which your awareness seems to move and in which it is temporarily bound. Thus, every time you think, the open expansiveness of the limitless "field" of your awareness is suddenly constrained and limited by, fixed and focused on a specific object of attention to which you then directly react. In the act of thinking that specific thought, everything else, other than the attended-to-object at hand, disappears in your conscious awareness.

### William James and the Substantive and Transitive Aspects of Thought

William James (1950) described five properties of thought in his vast *Principles of Psychology*. This book was written over one hundred years ago and may represent one of the most insightful, thorough, elegant, and detailed descriptions of thought, in all its objective and subjective aspects, in Western history. James' insights, therefore, may serve as a philosophical foundation, potentially supporting the discoveries about thinking in this present work.

I will briefly touch on four of James' five properties of thought while extensively elaborating on the third. James' first property of thought is, "Thought tends to Personal Form": each individual's mind has thoughts solely its own and such thoughts assume the form of a personal consciousness.

"Thought is in constant change," says James (1950) of the second property. "The chain of consciousness is a succession of differents," he explains, and every thought of a given fact or object is therefore unique, even if such thoughts take the same fact or object as their focus:

> Experience is remoulding us every moment, and our mental reaction on every given thing is really a resultant of our experience of the whole world up to that date. (p. 234)

James (1950) spent much time discussing his third property of thought: "Within each personal consciousness, thought is sensibly continuous." In other words, the subjective sense of self-awareness is without breaches, cracks, or divisions. James says that this is true even when gaps of time occur wherein the sense of personal consciousness dissipates, during sleep, for example. Subjectively, the consciousness after the gap feels as if it belonged together with the consciousness before the gap, and experiences itself as the same self. Consciousness, according to James, does not seem to itself to be discontinuous. It flows like a river or stream, experiencing itself as a stream of thought or consciousness.

The thoughts of any given individual or the parts of any given thought, says James, may seem jointed or as consisting of separate parts due to the sudden contrasts in the quality of the contents in the stream of thought. Such contrasting contents lead one to believe that thought is subjectively discontinuous. James says that the things of which thoughts are aware, are, *in fact*, discrete or discontinuous. However, he adds, the transition between the thought of one object and the thought of another is no more a break in thought than a joint in a length of bamboo is a break in the wood.

James (1950) refers to the objects of our thoughts, the definite images of those objects, as "substantive parts." These substantive parts (excerpts) are known in a more restful and stable way than the "transitive parts," which reflect the experience of passage, relation, and transition between the substantive parts.

The pacing among the parts of consciousness (or stream of thoughts) James (1950) compared to a bird's life, which consists of alternating flights and perchings. Those perchings or resting places of thought are usually occupied by sensorial images, the substantive parts; and the places of flight consist of the relations between them, the transitive parts. These psychic transitions are always on the wing says James, and can be glimpsed only in flight. Their function is to lead from one set of images to another. As they pass, we feel both the waxing and the waning of their own (transitive) images to be quite different from the experience of the fuller presence of their substantive counterparts. Thus, the main goal of our thinking, says James, is to attain some substantive part other than the one from which we were just dislodged. The main function of the transitive parts is to lead us from one substantive conclusion to another.

To James (1950), the substantive qualities of the object of thought appear in the mind in a fringe of relations. The transitive parts of the stream of thought are more relevant to the relations rather than the object, and both the transitive and the substantive parts form one continuous stream. The only images intrinsically important to James are the halting places or the substantive conclusions of the thought. To that, I would add the starting points. Throughout the rest of the stream, says James, the feelings of relation, the psychic overtones, halos, suffusions, or fringes about the terms are everything.

Thus, lodged between the substantive elements of thought are the transitive elements (elaborative conceptual portion of thought). In addition, these substantive words and images are fringed throughout the thought, and hence, James (1950) argues, are not as discrete as they at first might seem:

> Every definite image of the mind is steeped and dyed in the free water that flows around it. With it goes the sense of its relations, near and remote, the dying echo of whence it came to us, the dawning sense of whither it is to lead. The significance, the value, of the image is all in this halo or penumbra that surrounds and escorts it,-or rather that is fused into one with it... (p. 255)

James elaborates on these transitive states:

> For the swift consciousness we have only those names of "transitive states" or "feelings of relation"...these consciousnesses melt into each other like dissolving views. Properly they are but one protracted consciousness, one unbroken stream. (pp. 247–48)

James (1950) discusses the transitive parts of thought very thoroughly because they are often disregarded by many philosophers, theorists, and laypeople. In part, this disregard is largely a function of the great difficulty of seeing them for what they are on an introspective basis. Because they are flights to a conclusion, trying to stop and look at them before the conclusion is reached "annihilates them." On the other hand, if we wait until the conclusion is reached, that conclusion "eclipses and swallows them up in its glare." He says that the rush of a thought is so headlong, we almost always end up at its conclusion before we can stop it, even as we attempt to snare its transitive aspects. And if we happen to be "nimble enough" to stop it, it ceases to be itself.

Each word in a sentence or thought has a felt meaning, according to James (1950), and we feel its meaning as it passes. Furthermore, the meaning of a word as it occurs dynamically or transitively in a thought may be quite different from its meaning when taken out of context. In James' understanding of language, there isn't a conjunction, preposition, adverbial phrase, syntactic form, or inflection of speech that does not express some shading or other of relation which we actually feel to exist between the larger, substantive objects of our thoughts.

Explaining the way felt meaning occurs during each unfolding segment of thought, James (1950) says that awareness of our own bodily position, attitude, and condition accompanies the thinking about every object in our focus. Our thinking is thus suffused through all of its parts with a particular "warmth and intimacy" that makes it ours.

We tend to minimize the importance of relational feelings in the transitive aspects of thought, James (1950) believes. During reflection, we name our thought simply by identifying the substantive object(s) that it's about. Of thought, he says,

> What each really knows is clearly the thing that it is named for, with dimly perhaps a thousand other things. It ought to be named for all of them but never is. (p. 241)

For example, he says that the object of the thought or sentence, "Columbus discovered America in 1492," is neither Columbus, nor America, nor its discovery. Instead, it is nothing short of the entire sentence, "Columbus-discovered-America-in-1492." If we want to speak of it substantively, we must write it with hyphens so we can capture it in all of its "delicate idiosyncrasy." If we want to feel that idiosyncrasy we must

> reproduce the thought exactly as it was uttered: …with every word fringed and the whole sentence bathed in that original halo of obscure relations, which, like an horizon, then spread about its meaning. (pp. 275–76)

James' (1950) fourth and fifth qualities of thought, on which I will not elaborate, are as follows, respectively: "Human thought appears to deal with objects independent of itself, that is, it is cognitive, or possesses the function of knowing," and, "It is always more interested in one part of its object than another, and welcomes and rejects or chooses, all the while it thinks."

Other than James (1950) and several other philosophers of his day, few have accounted for the "parts" and co-occurring phenomenologies of thought. In my opinion, James' substantive aspects of thought clearly parallel the reflective targets of thought: excerpts. For example, he identified the distinct word-parts of a particular thought with the numbers one through four. Preceding the onset of the thought was a zero, and following the thought, a zero prime. He then indicates that immediately after the zero, even before one has spoken the first word of the sentence, or thought the first word of the thought, the entire thought is present to one's mind in the form of the intention to utter it. He says this intention has no simple name. He believes it is a transitive state which is immediately displaced by the first word of the thought, and is a specific phase of thought "unlike anything else." Similarly, immediately before zero prime, after the last word of the sentence is spoken or the thought is thought, we're aware of its entire content upon realizing its completed deliverance. He makes a case that this final way of feeling the content of the thought is more full and rich than the initial way, at zero.

I believe that, in his explication of "zero," James is clearly touching upon the reality of excerpts as the substantive parts of thought that ground the end points of thought. I also believe that the transitive state "unlike anything else," immediately after James' zero, is that instant of time just after the appearance of the fully identified excerptive-clip, for example, of the "passing thought," which results in the entire thought being present to one's mind at the outset of the thought proper and which reflects the intention to utter it. In turn, the interplay between the excerptive-clip of the "passing thought" and the excerpt-found reaction of an unfolding reflective thought accounts for that sense of a fuller and richer awareness of the content of the "passing" thought, just before James' zero prime.

It is common to pursue a line of thought as a way to solve a problem, and hence to have a particular interest in the conclusion of each thought. This interest, James (1950) says, prompts attention to pounce upon it so that it may be treated in a substantive way. It's as if attention is just waiting to capture a certain conclusion that it will recognize as consistent, or not, with the problem or task being pursued.

The capturing aspect of a specifically inclined attention bears similarity to the reactive excerpt-found reaction at the outset of "RI of excerpts" (reflective form). Due to the prior instruction to pursue the problem at hand, this type of thinking moves toward an appearing excerpt looking for a potentially relevant answer to the problem. Because the reactive excerpt-found reaction is involved in identifying or recognizing the proactively identified excerpt, it is a lending hand to the subsequent reflective conceptual portion of the thought. This portion of the thought says, in essence, "That particular content is (or is not) relevant to the problem at hand."

Finally, James (1950) discusses the phenomenon of reflecting on and cognizing one's own thoughts. Because each thought dies or passes and is replaced by another, the newest thought is in a position to know its predecessor. Finding it "warm," the new can greet the old and identify it as being part of the same self. Each thought, says James, is born an owner and then dies being owned, transmitting whatever it realized to its proprietor. He compares each thought to a hook from which the chain of past thought-selves dangle:

> Anon the hook will itself drop into the past with all it carries, and then be treated as an object and appropriated by a new Thought in the new present which will serve as a living hook in turn. (p. 341)

Each new, present thought experiences itself as a living hook, treating and appropriating its predecessor as an object. Implied in this description is the experience of a powerful phenomenology of self, with many potential variations, depending on the development of the person at hand. For example, we can recognize elements of NCRT and CRT, the latter with its phenomenology of a past-self which is sacrificed and dies to a newborn self.

In sum, many of James' astute and insightful observations of thought are shared by and can be thoroughly accounted for by the theory of the microdynamics of thinking described herein. Therefore, the validity of this theory is given some support. However, by referring to your own mental experience as an introspective database, you can further establish its validity (or lack thereof) in an experientially compelling fashion.

Rarely prompting notice, thinking and self-awareness seem as natural as breathing. In this chapter, close inspection of elaborative and reflective thoughts has revealed their distinct phenomenal aspects. Elaborative thoughts are like minidreams, where the dreamer and dream seem nonexistent. Reflective thoughts are even more phenomenally complicated: like the eye blind to itself, we are unaware of mistaking the "passing thought" for our subjective presence (NCRT); at a level of greater complexity we are unaware that our self-sense is continually reborn in the present, relative to a version of self that is sacrificed to the "past" and dies (CRT). Ghostlike in their felt, yet unseen, presence, we've called these two types of self-awareness noncomparative and comparative reflective thinking, respectively. These two forms of reflective thinking bring our list of the types of thought to near completion. In addition, we've described the unique phenomenologies among the eight "parts" of thought. Last, we utilized the theory of the microdynamics of thinking and self-awareness outlined in chapters 1 and 2 to account for many of William James' introspective insights about thought.

Having finished the first three chapters, two of the major goals of this text have been completed: we have outlined a theory of the microdynamics of thinking and described how the "parts" and process aspects of thought engender a sense of self-awareness across various types of reflective thoughts. The insights and understandings stemming from this theory regarding the phenomenology of self-awareness strongly suggest that most forms of reflective thinking create illusory manifestations of self-awareness; the experience of self-awareness is erroneously personified in objectified thought-forms. Realizing this, you may be hard pressed to turn the page from here, for no insight could feel as important, and no deception could seem more relevant than the self-induced, thought-based perpetuator of mistaken identity. Exposed as an impostor, an entirely new version of self approaches while an old mirror lies shattered on the floor.

If you haven't yet grasped the thought-induced perpetuator of mistaken identity, chapter 8 explicitly describes and exposes the illusory manifestations of thought, based on the understanding of the "parts" and process aspects of thought among the various types of reflective thinking. Chapter 9 then outlines the negative consequences stemming from our attachment to and belief in the objectified sense of self, and some practices through which you can minimize such consequences. Ideally, the insights and understandings regarding the relationship between thinking and its illusory phenomenologies may help motivate you to consider pursuing such practices.

But we're a little ahead of ourselves because chapter 4 describes a wonderfully elegant model for conceiving the development of the sense of self across the human life span. Like a beautiful picture-puzzle with a few missing pieces, we can make some educated guesses about the developmental stages of the nine types of thought defined in the first two chapters (and one more to be addressed later), nearly completing the amazing panorama of the evolution of human consciousness and self-awareness.

# Chapter Four: The Development of Reflective Thinking

I N CHAPTERS 1 AND 2, we outlined eight potential "parts" of thought based on their phenomenal differences. We defined and distinguished two basic types of thinking: general elaborative and reflective. In all, nine types of thought were defined based on their respective component "parts." The structure and types of thinking are the foundation of a theory of the microdynamics of thinking and self-awareness. For example, I proposed that most adolescents and adults occasionally engage in NCRT, the experience of self-awareness embodied in the objectified "passing thought," where the self-as-object is mistaken as the self-as-subject. In other words, an understanding of the structure, phenomenology, and process aspects of thought helped us specify and expose the illusory nature of the thought-induced, objectively based experience of self-awareness.

We have also discussed the phenomenology of the different types of thinking while alluding to their developmental changes over the human life span. At this juncture I would like to present Ken Wilber's comprehensive, hierarchical model of human consciousness. After this brief overview, the theory of the structure, process, and phenomenology of thinking will allow us to make educated guesses about the placement of the different types of thought along this developmental hierarchy. Because each type of thought is associated with its own phenomenology and quality of self-awareness, we can discern the adequacy of their respective fits within this developmental progression, further establishing the potential utility of the theory of the microdynamics of thinking and self-awareness. In addition, with this theory incorporated into its makeup, Wilber's developmental model is further clarified.

## Ken Wilber's Full Spectrum Developmental
## Model of Consciousness

In a series of publications, including *The Atman Project: A Transpersonal View of Human Development*, Ken Wilber (1996a) has outlined human psychological development in his Full Spectrum Developmental Model of Human Consciousness. Wilber says that this model is developmental, structural, hierarchical, and systems oriented. In addition, it draws equally from Eastern and Western theorists, researchers, and philosophers as well as from the world's contemplative traditions, including Mahayana, Vedanta, Sufi, Kebalah, Christian mysticism, Platonism, and so on. For a thorough presentation of this model I suggest you read Wilber's other works. For our purposes, I plan to present some of his basic ideas along with a portion of his overall developmental model. It is in essence a master template constructed by combining the similarities of Eastern and Western religious, spiritual, and philosophical traditions.

In *Transformations of Consciousness: Conventional and Contemplative Perspectives on Development*, Wilber, Engler, and Brown (1986) divide structures of the human psyche into two basic types: the basic and transition structures. Basic mental structures are components of consciousness that emerge in stages and tend to remain as relatively autonomous units or subunits in the course of development. Transition structures are stage-specific and stage-temporary components of consciousness. The basic structures tend to be subsumed, included, or subordinated in subsequent development while transition structures tend to be negated, dissolved, or replaced as development proceeds.

Wilber (1986) indicates that a self-system, or one's subjective sense of self or "I," negotiates the structural, mental developments that unfold over time. He adds that there is no inherent self-sense in any of the basic structures of development. Instead, the self appropriates these basic structures or identifies with them.

What does this self consist of? William James (1950) believed that one's self-sense was based on the capacity to connect and organize this moment around the preceding one. For James, the innermost self consists of *the act of appropriating* the preceding moment by the succeeding one. Clearly the latter is a reflective phenomenon because the appropriating thought attends to passing thoughts as objects.

James (1950) indicates that the thought presently engaged in appropriating cannot appropriate itself or disown itself. Instead, it is the agent of appropriating and disowning. It is the Thought to whom various mental constituents are known. He says it appropriates *to* itself by being the living hook from which the chain of past (thought) selves dangle. He adds that the present moment of consciousness may feel its immediate existence, although nothing can actually be known about it until it is dead and gone.

It is clear that, as appropriator of the stream, the self must be constituted by functions other than the stream of its objects. Furthermore, its experience of self-awareness is, in large part, engendered by this process of reflective appropriation. In other words, one's self-awareness is engendered by objectifying and reflecting on the "passing thought." It's this action of reflective appropriating that gives rise to the particular experience of self-awareness I've referred to as NCRT.

In *Eye to Eye: The Quest for the New Paradigm*, Wilber (1996c) states that one characteristic of the self is the capacity to appropriate and organize the stream of psychological events in meaningful and coherent ways. Wilber cites Brandt (1980), indicating that the modern psychoanalytic view defines the self as the process of organizing. He says that it is the center and executor of psychological organization, integration, and coordination.

Similarly, Heinz Kohut (1977) defines the self as an independent center of initiative and perception. He says it is an organizing center of skills and talents, integrated with its central ambitions and ideals. The self experiences its body and mind as a unit in space and a continuum in time. Forever caught up in *being the center* of organizing, integrating, perceiving, and initiating, it is not knowable in its essence, but only in its psychological manifestations.

Wilber (1996c) states that the self is also the locus of identification and center of the sense of identity. By appropriating and organizing the stream of structural events, it creates for itself a selective identity in the midst of doing so. The self is also the locus of free choice, within the limits set by the basic structures at the present stage of development. It is the locus of defense mechanisms, of metabolism (e.g., of the assimilating of experience at each stage of development), and of navigation within a particular stage and between stages.

Thus, in the course of development, a self-system emerges that takes as its successive substrates the basic structures of consciousness. Wilber (1985) uses the metaphor of a ladder's rungs to represent the basic structures, upon which the self-system climbs and from which a new worldview is taken. Associated with the basic structure in which the self is identifying, it takes on a different view of the world, of other, and self-identity. It also takes on a different type of self-need, moral stance, cognitive capacity, and so on.

In *Sex, Ecology, Spirituality: The Spirit of Evolution,* Wilber (1995) uses Jean Piaget's (1977) developmental system of cognition as a general framework for discussing the evolution of the basic structures of consciousness in the human being. He might have used the developmental model of any one of a number of theorists as a general framework, but Piaget's is quite well known and draws from a great deal of empirical data. Generally, Wilber incorporates the research results and data from the myriad of other theorists' developmental models as a way to fill in the gaps of Piaget's model. Wilber (1997) does not equate the development of the basic structures of consciousness with the cognitive line of development per se, although there is a closer overlap with this line than with most of the others.

In Wilber's (1997) developmental model, the basic structures of consciousness serve as a type of skeletal frame. Through the basic structures there move at least a dozen different devel-

opmental lines, involving both enduring and transitional structures. These developmental lines include affective, cognitive,
moral, interpersonal, object-relations, self-identity, and special
skills, each of which develops in a quasi-independent fashion
through the basic structures of consciousness. Thus, there is no
single, monolithic line that governs all of those developments.

Individuals fluctuate up and down the basic levels of consciousness in different settings, says Wilber (1997), depending
on, for example, social triggers. Furthermore, in the same setting, components of a person's consciousness exist at different
levels. In the same social domain, and in a single transaction,
a person can, for example, be at a very high cognitive level of
development while simultaneously being at an extremely low
level of moral development.

Gardner (1983) indicates that much of what happens within
each developmental line proves to be unique to that line. Yet
there are parallels across development among particular lines.
The different developmental lines each progress through what
he calls waves. Gardner's research suggests that these waves are
universal, invariant, and based on deep biological constants.
Wilber (1997) says that both the streams (the different developmental lines) and the waves (the stagelike sequence common
to all the streams) show features that are largely universal. The
waves suggest that certain universal psychological processes may
occur across developmental lines.

Wilber (1997) indicates that the basic structures themselves,
which form the spectrum of consciousness, are the universal
waves through which the dozen or so developmental lines quasi-
independently proceed. The levels of the spectrum constitute
the waves of developmental unfolding of the basic structures.
The various lines are the different streams that move through
those waves. He says that the self-system is that which attempts
to traverse those quasi-independent streams with their cascad-
ing waves of development.

Wilber's stages of development reflect the evolution of consciousness in the manifest human being. Essentially, the form that consciousness takes at each stage is different, thereby providing a different foundation for one's subjective sense of self. The self identifies with each basic structure of consciousness, becoming embedded in or fused with it; it cannot truly see or experience itself as an object. In other words, the actual subjective structures of the self, at each given stage, are unconscious, and hence, form the embedded unconscious. They are part of the seer and thus cannot themselves be seen. Growth always involves a process of differentiation, of emergence from this embeddedness, where the new subjectivity can take aspects of its former self or vantage point as an object (Wilber, 1995).

Outlining a sequence of stages in his Full Spectrum Developmental Model of Consciousness (Wilber, 1995, 1996a), Wilber cites Piaget's (1977) research on cognitive development as a general framework. Piaget divided cognitive development into four general stages: the Sensorimotor (0–2 years), Preoperational (2–7 years), Concrete Operational (7–11 years), and Formal Operational (11+ years). At the outset of the Sensorimotor stage, the infant cannot distinguish between itself and the material world. From about the fifth to ninth months of life, the infant begins to differentiate itself as a physical bodyself from its physical surroundings. As Wilber states, the infant learns that when he bites his thumb, it hurts, and when he bites his blanket, it doesn't. With a newly formed bodyself, the infant reaches the first "fulcrum" or major differentiation in development. Here, consciousness (awareness) seats or grounds itself in the physical body, in contrast to being diffusely projected into the environment as well. Thus, it's during the Sensorimotor period (0–2 years) when the infant learns to differentiate its physical self from the physical environment.

At the outset of the stage of Preoperational thought (2–7 years), the infant's emotional self exists in a state of undifferentiation from other emotional objects, in particular, its mother. However, at around the age of eighteen months the infant learns to differentiate its feelings from the feelings of others. This is the second fulcrum or major differentiation in development, which Margaret Mahler (1975) calls the psychological birth of the infant.

Thus, by the age of three, if development has proceeded well, the child has a stable and coherent physical and emotional self. Subsequently, a new differentiation begins during the stage of Preoperations, as language starts to develop on the heels of newly emerging images and symbols. To the child, these images and symbols do not simply represent the objects to which they correspond: they are the things they represent (Piaget, 1977). In other words, images, symbols, and language are fused with or undifferentiated from the physical body and world. For instance, magical, felt connections exist between what the child imagines and thinks about the objects around him. Nevertheless, by the age of two or three, the child's emerging linguistic ability, culminating in a phenomenology of mind, results in an increasing ability to transcend his body. This transcendence, for example, is reflected by his ability to resist acting on bodily impulses and desires. This is the third major fulcrum or developmental differentiation: the one between mind and body.

As the child approaches the late Preoperational period (4–7 years), he is separate as a physical self from the environment, as an emotional self from others, and is developing a mind that is increasingly separate from his body and the environment. In addition, through continued interaction with the world, he learns that his thoughts do not control it. Instead, the child tends to believe that more powerful people (e.g., mom, dad, God, Superman, etc.) can control the world around him. In this way, remnants of a belief in causality, now between the minds of others and the world at large, continue (Wilber, 1997).

As the child reaches the age of seven or so and enters the stage of Concrete Operational thought, he has entered the world of other minds. He learns to take the role of other, which requires the ability to mentally reconstruct another person's perspective.

Less bound to his body and increasingly able to conceptually represent a wide range of phenomena, the Concrete Operational child is much more capable of taking the vantage point of others. In contrast, a child at and prior to Preoperations is so body-bound, he cannot step outside of himself to truly consider and understand someone else's vantage point. However, the child at Concrete Operations can take another's vantage point with less "contaminating" influence from his own (Wilber, 1997).

At the stage of Concrete Operations, the child also begins to experience himself as a unique persona or socially based role. Furthermore, this persona is experienced as his true self. As a result, his mind and body are experienced as lesser parts of the larger, persona-self. This is the forth major fulcrum of development, where the child is initially roleless in a society of people who have roles. As this stage progresses, the child learns and differentiates his role in relation to the roles of others, and then learns how to integrate that role in the society around him (Wilber, 1996a).

During the stage of Concrete Operations the child becomes increasingly adept at using concepts to represent his world. In addition, these conceptual representations become much less dominated by his emotions, impulses, needs, and desires. Again, prior to this stage, children are more of a body-self than a thinking-self because much of their experience of themselves and their world is influenced by their feelings, needs, desires, impulses, and the like. They are a body-consciousness. Their awareness is physically laden, and their minds are fused with their emotional-libidinal bodies. Their bodyminds are thus bound to naive sensory data; what they see, the *appearance* of things, dominates their interpretations of reality. In contrast, the interpretations of the Concrete Operational child are less bound to the realities of bodily existence and in turn to the realities of the environment. Moreover, because of an increasing facility with language, the seat of their consciousness is less body-based and more mind or thought-based. Thus, a child at this stage is more clearly a thinking-self than ever before (Wilber, 1996a).

As a clear thought-self, the Concrete Operational child is generally a prisoner of the beliefs and feelings engendered by being labeled and treated in particular ways by others. His thoughts about himself are generally consistent with the roles assigned to him by others (Wilber, 1996a). He can't readily take his "other-colored" thoughts as objects of attention, so he can't evaluate and challenge them. He has to rely on others to help him do so. Without the assistance of others, he's generally stuck with these "other-colored" thoughts and beliefs about himself (e.g., as per Eric Berne's [1972] concept of scripts).

As the child enters the stage of Formal Operational thought (11 years plus), he has a well-defined persona or set of roles distinguished from a society of others with roles. However, at the outset of Formal Operations, the self begins to emerge from its other-given social roles. Each social role will be seen as a facade or false appearance distinguished from what is experienced as a truer inner self (Wilber, 1997). This is the fifth fulcrum of development, differentiating an inner sense of self from the roles or social faces presented to others.

Wilber (1995) says that where Concrete Operations uses rules of thought to represent, operate on, and transcend the world, Formal Operations can operate on these rules. In addition, Formal Operations creates a space for considering possibilities that go beyond the obvious and the given. Where the Concrete Operational child remains tied to the appearances of objects, the formal Operational adolescent can *imagine* potential arrangements of the given. Formal Operations results in a type of awareness where the possible relationships among things can be held in the mind. It also results in an ability to hold different perspectives in the mind. Lastly, Formal Operational awareness is the first basic structure that is highly reflexive and introspective. For the first time, this introspective ability allows the adolescent to take his thoughts as explicit objects of attention.

By the end of the stage of Formal Operations, the adolescent is relatively adept at reflecting on his thoughts. Therefore, his attention and awareness are less bound to the realities of being a bodily presence in a physical world. In his mental world, he can reflect on, represent, manipulate, evaluate, and question thoughts, which in turn represent material, biological, interpersonal, and mental realities. He is capable of questioning his thoughts and beliefs via reflection, whereas before he was consumed in the experience of *being* his thoughts and beliefs. In addition, he is capable of representing, reflecting on, and questioning the beliefs, values, and judgments of others. He can question the roles assigned to him by others and hence can construe some of those roles as invalid and discard them (Wilber, 1996).

In sum, by the end of a child's second year of life, his consciousness exists as a separate bodyself. By the end of the third year, his consciousness exists as a separate, emotional, mind/bodyself. By the end of the seventh year, his consciousness takes the form of a separate thinking-self. By the end of the child's eleventh year, his consciousness is a thinking-self adhering to and identifying with various social roles. By the end of adolescence, the individual's consciousness is a thinking-self adhering to his personal beliefs versus an unquestioning adherence to the beliefs and expectations of others.

More generally, Wilber states that the evolution of consciousness develops from pre-egoic (body-based), to egoic (mind-based), to postegoic (witness-based). The post-postegoic stages will be addressed in the afterword.

Piaget (1977) did not explicate stages of cognitive development beyond the stage of Formal Operational Thought. However, others, including Loevinger (1976), Maslow (1968), Fromm (1941), and Broughton (1975) have looked beyond Formal Operations. In addition, Ken Wilber has done so in his Full Spectrum Developmental Model of Consciousness (Wilber, 1995, 1996a). Wilber refers to the next stage above and inclusive of Formal Operations as Vision-Logic (VL). Wilber says that VL reflects one's ability to look within the mind and operate on the rationality of Formal Operations itself. As a result, one is beginning to differentiate from rationality and can now integrate or embrace (and not just be) the mind.

Wilber (1995) indicates that where the rationality of Formal Operational Thought entails the ability to generate all possible perspectives (as reflected by thoughts that can stand for anything and be manipulated in a mental world space), VL adds them up in a totality. Where Formal Operational Thought establishes relationships, VL establishes networks of those relationships. He says VL can freely express itself in single ideas, but its most characteristic movement is a mass ideation, a system or totality of truth seeing at a single view. Such vision or panoramic logic apprehends a mass network of ideas, how they influence each other, and how they interrelate. It represents a higher order synthesizing capacity of making connections, relating truths, coordinating ideas, and integrating concepts. Wilber says it is dialectical, nonlinear, and weaves together incompatible notions into a new and higher whole, their partiality negated but their positive contributions preserved.

At the outset of VL, one has already become adept at taking thoughts as objects of attention and is beginning to move away from construing these thoughts as instances of self, as one does with NCRT. I believe that this transition away from NCRT is consistent with Wilber's sixth fulcrum of development, which begins with an undifferentiation or distinction between one's self as an always immediate awareness or witness and those *thought-objects* typically identified as instances of self. As VL progresses, one realizes that there is always a more immediate subjective awareness attending to any given thought-object at hand. Thus, at the stage of VL, a differentiation occurs between an always immediate, subjective awareness, or witness, and the thought-objects once identified as self. This differentiation is consistent with CRT. In my opinion, comparative reflective thinking is the likely hallmark for the onset of VL consciousness. By the end of this stage, one realizes that this ever-present, subjective aware-ness exists as it is, in its witnessing sameness, while all other objects of its experience pass, change, and are not-self.

At the stage of VL, says Wilber (1995), one's sense of self is established within a new, higher-order level of awareness. The self becomes aware of mind and body in their various experiential forms, as objects of attention. The self also learns that these experiential forms come and go, leaving an always present "field" of awareness (my words). Consequently, it is beginning to transcend both mind and body as forms *through* which to identify and experience itself. In other words, during the stage of VL, the self is beginning to objectify and "rise above" its own operation (primarily as a thought-self). The scaffolding of the human personality (in all of its tendencies) dissipates as awareness settles in its witnessing form. The habitual tendencies of thinking, believing, judging, and so on, lose their foothold as strictly subjective forms and become transitory *objects* recognized as not-self.

In *No Boundary,* Wilber (1979) refers to the self at the stage of VL as centauric (half-man, half-horse) because it can integrate mind and body in a new, wider embrace. The latter contrasts with Wilber's idea that Western man tends to ride his body like a horse. The horse, being separate from the rider, can be controlled and manipulated despite its physical needs. In addition, it's easier to ignore the horse's subjective experience because one is dissociated from what it feels. Similarly, below VL, the consciousness experienced as a thought-self tends to be cut off from the body. In contrast, the centauric self can integrate mind and body because the entire verbal-mental-egoic dimension, with its co-occurring manifestations becomes increasingly objective and is identified as not-self. Wilber (1995) says that where previously the verbal-mental-egoic self used these very structures (e.g., verbal-rational-egoic) as something with which or through which to view and cocreate the world (e.g., at Formal Operations), now these structures become objects of awareness and investigation by centauric consciousness. Thus, because awareness is beginning to differentiate itself from an exclusive identification with the body, persona, ego, and mind (thought), it can now integrate them in a unified fashion. The self as observer is increasingly distinguished from the self-concept as known, and from thought-objects once identified as self. An ever-present, witnessing self is distinguished from the objective forms of self (e.g., as in comparative reflective thinking).

## The Types of Thought and Their Stages of Development

Ken Wilber's consolidation of Eastern and Western religious and philosophical traditions into a unified model is an extremely important contribution with widespread ramifications and potential utilizations. For instance, it serves as a skeletal frame upon which the field of transpersonal psychology is largely based and validated. It is a developmental hierarchy of the human life span that extends beyond traditional Western paradigms; it incorporates Eastern religious and spiritual knowledge regarding the human potential for transformations to higher states of consciousness. It functions as a model for understanding "normal" human development, and pathology, relevant to specific stages and hurdles (Wilber, Engler, & Brown, 1986). As such, it can function as a diagnostic tool: with a little exploration, a person's negative symptomatology can be developmentally specified. As a result, a modality of psychological treatment consistent with that stage's role in the presenting symptom-picture can be identified and utilized to more effectively help the person at hand.

The structure and phenomenology of thought outlined by the theory of the microdynamics of thinking in chapters 1 and 2 was utilized to distinguish two types of elaborative thoughts, three types of reflective thoughts, and two additional types, each of which can be elaborative or reflective. The five types of reflective thoughts were detailed with regard to how they engender their own, unique experience of self-awareness. We can propose a placement of each type of thought along Wilber's developmental model of human consciousness based in part on what is already known about the stage-based abilities of children and adults, and the forms that their awareness and self-identity take along that progression. If our logical guesses and judgments are deemed adequate, we will have succeeded in further "rounding out" the picture of human development by incorporating the types of thought and their respective phenomenologies into that model. In addition, we will have clarified how the thought-induced experience of self-awareness is created across certain stages of development.

Since we know that all children from the late Sensorimotor stage and beyond are able to think, as reflected by their ability to form and speak sentences, it is safe to assume that they engage in the most basic type of thinking: general elaborative. Recall that general elaborative thoughts do not take excerptive-clips of "passing thoughts" as objects. In a series of general elaborative thoughts, one thought follows another in the same way that reaching for an apple is followed by picking it. One thought leads to an excerpt somehow related to it, which becomes the object of the next thought. If the thought, "I love strawberry ice cream" is followed by an excerptive memory of disliking the seeds in it, which is followed by the thought, "Nah, my favorite flavor is chocolate," the latter is a general elaborative thought.

Recall that IRI is a subtype of general elaborative thinking. If the thought "I love strawberry ice cream" is followed by an excerptive-clip of the image of disliking the seeds in it (where the seed image arose during the thought and was subsequently excerptively clipped), followed by the thought, "Nah, my favorite flavor is chocolate," the latter is an instance of IRI. By definition, because IRI is a reaction to an excerptive-clip of some experiential aspect of the "passing thought," it implicitly takes into account some meaning embodied in that thought more directly than does general elaborative thinking.

Pre- and concrete operational children are probably capable of IRI, although it is difficult to know for sure. Knowing whether one thought led to an excerpt which then became the object of a new thought (general elaborative thinking), or whether an image inherent to one thought was subsequently excerptively clipped and served as an object of a new thought (IRI), is an introspective talent that few people possess, let alone children at these ages. And since we cannot "see" into the minds of such children, we may never know for sure if they are engaging in IRI. Suffice it to say that as children get older across these stages of development, it is likely that they possess a greater ability to reflect on and excerptively clip an aspect of a "passing thought."

The introspective and reflective abilities of children at the stage of Formal Operations are well established, in contrast to their developmentally younger peers, who lack such abilities (Piaget, 1977). Thus, it is safe to say that, in general, younger children do not possess the ability to reflect on, excerpt, and explicitly identify "passing thoughts" (ERI).

Formal operational adolescents engaging in ERI are in a position to say, "I was just thinking about…." I believe that it is very unusual to hear a child at the stage of Concrete Operations say this. The Concrete Operational child is completely absorbed in the reaction *away from* their prior thought. Most of the time, ERI entails being explicitly aware of the identity of the "passing thought" and only implicitly aware of that thought as a presence per se. Typically, Formal Operational adolescents and adults are implicitly aware of the "passing thought" as a presence, but the emphasis of awareness is on the explicit identity of the thought. However, there are instances of ERI where one is explicitly aware of the presence of the thought per se.

At the outset of ERI, the excerpted thought is an explicit object of attention. Consequently, at the outset of ERI, I (at Formal Operations) tend to experience aspects of duality as a present, separate, observing awareness more vividly and distinctly than my cognitively less advanced peers, who are incapable of it. These aspects of duality include feeling as if I am outside of the reflected-upon thought, something more than it, and as if my present reaction to it is somehow a reflection of a truer self (see chapter 5 for more details). These phenomenal experiences are unconscious in that they aren't being taken as objects of attention per se; they are unattended-to-knowings. Nonetheless, they are a part of my subjective experience.

Explicit reflective identification requires the ability to at least be implicitly aware of the identity of a "passing thought." In other words, I can identify the "passing thought" as embodied in the excerptive-clip at hand and react to its identity without explicitly representing or acknowledging its identity. For instance, I can identify the "passing thought" of wanting to go out for pizza and react to it by thinking, "I think I'll go to Pizza Barn." Despite this implicit reaction to the content of the excerpt, the ability to reflect on and excerpt a "passing thought" is still required. If I was explicitly representing the excerpted "passing thought" in my reaction to it, I would think, "I was just thinking about going out for pizza." To explicitly represent a thought's identity, I must know about the presence of thoughts as experiential realities ("That's a thought about…"). Again, only Formal Operational adolescents and adults have the ability to experientially know, reflect on, and explicitly identify "passing thoughts" as objects.

As reflected in this breakdown of ERI, there are three potential levels of awareness in response to the excerpted identity embodied in the excerptive-clip of the "passing thought." There can be an implicit awareness of the excerptive-clip of the "passing thought's" identity as reflected in the reaction to it, that is not a direct representation of it. There can be an explicit awareness of that thought's identity as reflected by a reaction which is a direct representation of it, along with an implicit awareness of the thought as a presence per se. Last, there can be an explicit awareness of its identity *and presence* as a "passing thought," but this is less frequent.

"Reflective identification of excerpts" is a form of elaborative thinking and potentially of reflective thinking. Typically, the elaborative form of "RI of excerpts" embodies implicit conceptual reactions to the content of excerpts. In other words, awareness proactively discerns the content of the excerpt, but the reflective conceptual portion of thought is a reaction *to* that content, not an explicit representation *of* it. In addition, when an excerpt is presented to awareness, I am not aware of the presence of the excerpt per se; I'm proactively aware of its content, as an unattended-to-knowing, of which I'm quickly identifying and to which I'm reacting. For example, in response to the question posed to myself, "What year did Dave Waddle win the Olympic gold medal?" I might become aware of an excerpt-image of sitting on the couch with my mother watching him run. In response to this image I might think, "It was 1976."

The reflective form of "RI of excerpts" is embodied by a reactive excerpt-found reaction in response to the proactively identified appearing excerpt and subsequent explicit representation of that excerpted reaction in the form of the reflective conceptual portion of the thought. Typically, the reflective form of "RI of excerpts" entails the desire to answer a question, solve a problem, or access memories relevant to some content at hand. Therefore, my response to the excerpt-image prompted by the question about Dave Waddle could have been, "I just remembered sitting on the couch with my mom, so it must have been in 1976." This is the reflective form of "RI of excerpts" due to the explicit representation of the content of the identified excerpt in response to it.

Because the reflective form of "RI of excerpts" is prompted by a desire to answer a question, solve a problem, or access memories relevant to some context at hand, one is vigilant to the appearance of excerpts in awareness. This expectancy suggests that I have "stepped out of" some internal absorption in thought or activity and become aware of myself in relation to the task at hand: of me waiting for an answer. Consequently, "RI of excerpts" often includes the experience of GRO. In addition, the content embodied in the excerpt exists as a relatively prolonged object of attention from which awareness is separating and to which it is reacting. Consequently, experiential aspects of duality are occurring consistent with a subtle reflective phenomenology.

Elaborating on the differences between ERI and "RI of

excerpts" helps us place "RI of excerpts" along Wilber's developmental hierarchy. Because the elaborative form "RI of excerpts" requires the ability to implicitly represent the content of excerpts, in my opinion, all children who think, from the late Sensorimotor stage forward, engage in the elaborative form of "RI of excerpts." In other words, all "normal" children have the ability to identify and implicitly react to the content of excerpts that rise into awareness, whether such excerpts are prompted by questions posed to themselves or by others. For example, by the ages of eighteen months to two years of age children are already representing their world through mental images and are capable of object constancy; the ability to retain an image of an object in awareness despite the fact that it is no longer in sight. Thus, if I ask little Johnny where his yellow rattle is, an image of it and its location rises into his awareness and he goes and gets it.

In their respective forms (elaborative and reflective), "Reflective identification of excerptive-clips of external objects" is similar to "RI of excerpts." Typically, when I excerptively clip an external object and react to it in thought, I am only implicitly conceptualizing its content. Again, this content is an unattended-to-knowing. When I'm looking for my car keys and notice the bucket of soapy water outside, an excerptive memory of the keys on the top of the car pops into my awareness, which I then react to via the thought, "Now I remember where they are." The bucket of water was an excerptive-clip that prompted the excerptive memory of the keys on the car. My reactive recognition of the bucket of water was implicit and quickly led to the excerpt that followed it. When my awareness fixed on the object of the bucket, excerptively clipped it, and reacted to the excerptive-clip via a new excerpt, a very subtle duality of experiencing occurred. However, this duality is not so much engendered by the experience of a separating awareness being conscious of an object of attention; it is mostly a function of the general reality orientation of being aware of me looking for the car keys in relation to stimuli (the bucket) in my physical environment. The fact that the bucket was excerptively clipped suggests that it was significant enough to relate me to some other aspect of my environment. In general, I experienced a subtle awareness of me looking for the keys in relation to the bucket and to where it pointed me.

Like "RI of excerpts," "RI of excerptive-clips of external objects" can take on an elaborative or reflective form. It's elaborative if I identify the excerptive-clip through a proactive excerpt-found reaction and if my reaction to the proactively identified excerpt is implicit. For example, when Johnny sees a wheel of his toy truck by the couch, an image of the truck by the front porch enters his awareness and he yells for his mom to open the front door. The wheel served as an excerptive-clip and prompted an excerpt of the truck to rise into his awareness.

"Reflective identification of excerptive-clips of external objects" is a reflective type of thought if the reflective conceptual portion attends to the reactive excerpt-found reaction in response to the proactively identified excerptive-clip, thereby explicitly representing the identity and function of the clip in response to it: "I just saw that mitten on the floor and remembered that my catcher's glove is in my bedroom closet." Furthermore, the significance of the mitten is evidenced by a reactive excerpt-found reaction in response to its proactively excerpted appearance. In other words, that reaction reflects a prolonged attention to the excerpt so it can be explicitly represented. As a result, the experience of GRO during the reflective form of "RI of excerpts" is much more vivid than it is during its elaborative form.

I propose that all children from the late Sensorimotor stage forward are capable of the elaborative form of "RI of excerptive-clips of external objects." However, I believe that only adolescents and adults at the stage of Formal Operations and beyond are capable of it in its reflective form.

Noncomparative reflective thinking requires the ability to excerpt and explicitly identify the presence of thoughts as passing objects. Noncomparative reflective thinking is similar to ERI: the emphasis during ERI is to note the identity of a "passing thought," and the emphasis during NCRT is to note the presence of the thought per se while construing it as one's subjectivity in the form of a thinking-self. Therefore, only formal operational adolescents and adults (and beyond) are capable of NCRT.

When I become conscious of myself as a separating awareness in relation to my awareness of the excerpted "passing thought," I am engaged in CRT. Wilber indicates that at the onset of the stage of VL (1995), a person is learning to differentiate the witnessing self from those objects witnessed and once identified as self. Consequently, I propose that the ability to engage in CRT marks the onset of VL.

At the stage of VL, I believe that you become capable of attending to and recognizing the various forms of reflective thinking and their respective phenomenologies as they experientially "pass" before you. By attending to any one of them, you've turned what was an entirely subjective experience into an objective one. In the future, when you've been subjectively swept up in a thought's reflective phenomenology you may better recognize its experiential quality as it "passes," thereby releasing yourself from its phenomenal impact. I call the act of reflecting on, recognizing, and conceptually representing any one of these reflective thought-forms *transparent reflective identification* (TRI). I call it "transparent" because, at the stage of Vision-Logic, one is capable of taking these thought-forms as objects of attention and "seeing into," recognizing, and identifying their co-occurring phenomenologies. Because TRI is a type of reflective thought, attending to the excerptively clipped, just passing action of another reflective thought results in an awareness of experiencing another reflective act right now.

### The Acuity of Reflective Awareness

Detailing the structure of reflective thought helps us consider the degree and speed of reflective awareness at two junctures of its unfolding. I believe that the degree of awareness of the pro-actively identified content of the excerpt at the instant awareness meets, reflects on, and reacts to it via the reactive excerpt-found reaction (during reflective thoughts) is always the same acuity and longevity. The reactive excerpt-found reaction is equally fast (across all types of reflective thoughts) in response to the proactively appearing and identified excerpt. As a result, the degree of awareness of the proactively identified excerpt is the same across the various types of reflective thoughts. However, I believe that the degree of awareness at the outset of the reflective conceptual portion of thought, when awareness is released from the reactive excerpt-found reaction and reflects back on it, varies across the different types of thinking.

This difference in the degree of awareness when attention focuses on the reactive excerpt-found reactions at the outset of the reflective conceptual portions of various types of reflective thoughts can be clarified by a comparison to elaborative thoughts. Remember, general elaborative thoughts are always elaborations on prior reactions via excerpts *prompted* by their predecessors, with barely any reflective awareness of such excerpts and no *reflective* awareness of their thought-predecessors. Like all thoughts, general elaborative thoughts are always preceded by an excerpt, which is their object. However, general elaborative thoughts are never preceded by an excerptive-clip of a "passing thought." This is why there is no *reflective* awareness of the "passing thought" embodied in a general elaborative thought's reaction. Some of the "passing thought's" meaning is implicitly embodied in its reaction, but not because of any reflectivity on it.

Therefore, general elaborative thoughts take identified excerpts other than excerptive-clips as their objects. The degree of reflective awareness of the proactively identified content of these excerpts, embodied at the outset of the reflective conceptual portion across all elaborative thoughts, is always the same. I immediately turn away from that proactively identified content and react to it via the elaborative thought at hand. My only "agenda," so to speak, is to move into my reaction and away from the identified excerpt as fast as I can. Because my agenda is always the same, so too is the acuity of my initial, reflective awareness of that identified excerpt across all elaborative thoughts.

Implicit reflective identification (a subtype of general elaborative thinking) results in a degree of *reflective* awareness of an aspect of its thought-predecessor, whereas general elaborative thinking does not. During IRI, some meaningful aspect *of* that thought-predecessor is excerpted, resulting in some reflective awareness of it. In addition, the degree of awareness of some identified, excerpted meaning in the "passing thought" is a constant across all instance of IRI.

My awareness of the proactively identified excerpt of the "passing thought" intensifies and/or its longevity is greater at the outset of the reflective conceptual portion of ERI, as compared to that at the outset of IRI. Because my reflective awareness stays oriented *toward* the identified excerpt for a longer period of time, it allows for an explicit representation of the identity of the "passing thought" as the reflective conceptual portion of the present instance of ERI unfolds. This awareness is even more acute if one becomes explicitly aware of the thought as a presence per se, along with an explicit awareness of the thought's identity.

During an instance of NCRT, my awareness of the reflectively identified excerpt intensifies and/or its longevity increases at the outset of the reflective conceptual protion of thought, as compared to ERI. In this case, I'm attending to a reactively identified excerpt of a "passing thought" which is being explicitly identified, coupled with an awareness of the thought itself as a presence. In contrast to the typical instance of ERI, however, the emphasis of one's reaction during NCRT is on the thought as a presence, *and* as embodying one's subjectivity as a thinking-self. Now my awareness is subjectively more acute and prolonged because I'm *captivated* by the experience of self mirrored in the thought-object.

At the outset of the reflective conceptual portion of CRT,

I'm simultaneously aware of the reactively identified excerpt of the *act of observing* a passing instance of self in the form of the thought-object, of which I'm also aware. The emphasis of my awareness is on the action of *separating from and observing* that thought-object. Consequently, during CRT, I'm aware of *two* aspects of self-experiencing, as opposed to only being aware of the thought-object during NCRT. Because I'm aware of the actual separation and apparent movement away from that thought-object during CRT, this reflective moment seems more acute and prolonged than it does during NCRT; just like watching the clock seems to slow the passage of time.

Similarly, at the outset of TRI, as I reflect on an identified, excerpted reflective thought, I am even more acutely aware of the identity of the thought, of the thought as a presence, of separating from and observing that thought, and of that thought's phenomenal manifestations, as compared to CRT. My awareness of that thought, at the outset of the reflective conceptual portion, is more prolonged and acute than it is during CRT, contributing to an even greater awareness of further content.

Across IRI, ERI, NCRT, CRT, and TRI, the reflectivity on and awareness of each respective, reactively identified excerpt (excluding IRI because it consists of proactively identified excerptive-clips only) yields an awareness of more content and experience. The greater meaning embodied in each reactively identified excerpt across these thought-forms is more captivating to the reflective awareness reacting to them. This captivating phenomenology is *partly* responsible for the increase in the acuity and longevity of awareness across these thought-forms. For instance, during ERI I'm explicitly aware of a "passing thought's" identity, an aspect of which I was only implicitly aware during IRI. During ERI, if I'm also explicitly aware of the "passing thought" as a presence, I'm aware of more than when I was only explicitly aware of that thought's identity at the outset of the "lesser" form of ERI. During NCRT, I'm not only aware of the "passing thought's" identity and of its "presence" as a thought per se, I'm experiencing it as embodying my subjectivity. Comparative reflective thinking includes all of the contents of awareness of NCRT plus the conscious experience of being the *witness* of the thought-object. Transparent reflective identification includes all the contents of awareness that CRT possesses, plus an awareness of the phenomenal manifestations of the reflective thought-form being witnessed.

In sum, one's awareness is embodied in a proactively appearing and identified excerpt when attention first meets it. Then, as one reacts to the excerpt via the reactive excerpt-found reaction, the awareness of that excerpt is always the same acuity and longevity across all reflective thought types. Lastly, the acuity of awareness intensifies and/or is increasingly prolonged at the outset of the reflective conceptual portion of thought, in response to the reactively identified excerpt across ERI, NCRT, CRT, and TRI.

Below I provide a summary of the phenomenal, structural differences posited among the ten different kinds of elaborative and reflective thoughts, and of elaborative and reflective experiencing, in relation to their location in the hierarchy of human development.

### Elaborative Thinking (Being Thinking)

Individuals at the late *Sensorimotor* stage and beyond are capable of elaborative thinking. During this type of thinking, one is consumed in conceptual reactions to proactively identified excerpts, prompted by their respective thought-predecessors, with no awareness as a thinking-self in space and time.

### Implicit Reflective Identification (Thinking about…)

It is likely that individuals at, and certainly beyond the stage of *Preoperations,* are capable of the experience of implicit reflective identification, consisting of a very fleeting reflective awareness of an excerptive-clip of some content that occurred in the "passing thought." The conceptual reaction to the excerptive-clip makes up IRI and implicitly embodies some meaning reflected in that predecessor-thought.

### Reflective Identification of Excerpts
### (Elaborative or Reflective Type)

Individuals at the late *Sensorimotor* stage and beyond are capable of the elaborative form of "RI of excerpts," which is a reaction to the identified content of an excerpt presented to awareness in response to a problem, situation, or question. "Reflective identification of excerpts" is a form of elaborative thinking if the content of the arising excerpt is identified proactively and implicitly represented in the reaction to it. It is a form of reflective thinking if the content of the excerpt is identified reactively and explicitly represented in response to that excerpt. The reflective form entails a more vivid experience of GRO and duality, occurring at the outset of the reflective conceptual portion of thought in response to the reactively identified excerpt. The reflective form only occurs in adolescents and adults at the stage of *Formal Operations* and beyond.

### Reflective Identification of Excerptive-Clips of External Objects
### (Elaborative or Reflective Type)

Individuals at the late *Sensorimotor* stage and beyond are capable of the elaborative form of "RI of excerptive-clips of external objects," which is a reaction to an identified excerptive-clip of an external object. It's a type of elaborative thinking if the excerptive-clip of the external object is identified proactively and then implicitly represented in the reaction to it. It's a form of reflective thinking if the excerptive-clip is identified reactively and explicitly represented in response to that clip. In its reflective form, the experience of GRO and duality is more pronounced. The reflective form occurs only in adolescents and adults at the stage of *Formal Operations* and beyond.

### Explicit Reflective Identification (Thinking about...)

Individuals at and beyond the stage of *Formal Operations* are capable of the typical experience of explicit reflective identification, consisting of an excerptive-clip of the "passing thought," a reactive excerpt-found reaction in response to and embodying the explicit identity of that clip, and a conceptual reaction to the identified clip that explicitly represents that thought's identity, along with an implicit awareness of the thought as a presence per se. Despite one's potential, explicit awareness of the presence of the thought, the attentional emphasis is on the identity of that thought.

### Noncomparative Reflective Thinking

At the stage of *Formal Operations,* individuals become capable of excerptively clipping their "passing thoughts," and construing any given thought-object as an instance of self. They mistake that thought-object as their personal subjectivity, with no consciousness of the witnessing awareness attending to it. This is called noncomparative reflective thinking. The reaction they are having to the thought is an experiential awareness and explicit representation of it as self in objectified form. This type of reflective thinking results in a partial, internally-based general reality orientation.

### Comparative Reflective Thinking

When individuals at the stage of *Vision-Logic* excerptively clip the "passing thought," they can become aware of it, and of the act of attending to it. In other words, they experience and explicitly represent their awareness as a separating, witnessing self in relation to the objectified thought-self. As a result, the self is identified as this always present observing awareness, instead of as existing in the form of the thought-object at hand. This is called comparative reflective thinking. This type of reflective thinking results in an internally based general reality orientation, of identifying one-self as the reflective awareness and thought-self in relation to a thought-object, in both mental time and space. As a result, the phenomenology of a past thought-self juxtaposed in relation to a seemingly more present thinking-self is created.

### Transparent Reflective Identification

At the stage of *Vision-Logic,* individuals are capable of becoming aware of the reflective forms of thinking as mental processes by attending to them as excerptively clipped objects. This is called transparent reflective identification. As a result, they can understand their consequent phenomenologies of engendering a subtle dualism between a seemingly separate observing aware-ness that "has" seemingly separate, objectified thoughts as well as of the phenomenologies of "Something More," "The True Me," and "The Intending Self" (see chapter 5). Moreover, while attending to the excerpted, just "passing" action of the reflec-tive thought form in which they were just absorbed, they have a subtle awareness of experiencing the present reflective act, along with its co-occurring phenomenologies.

### Reflective Experiencing (Noticing Experiencing)

Individuals at the late Sensorimotor stage and above are capable of reflective experiencing. During this type of experiencing, they orient themselves to self based on their awareness of being a bodily presence in relationship to the activity at hand. They ori-ent to time and place by attending to external stimuli. This type of experiencing is synonymous with the externally based general reality orientation.

### Elaborative Experiencing (Being Experiencing)

Individuals at all stages of development are capable of elaborative experiencing. During this type of experiencing, they are consumed in the unfolding experiencing at hand with no awareness as a body-self in space and time.

### Reflective Experiencing in Comparative Reflective Thinking

There is a very important distinction between reflective thinking and experiencing that needs to be clarified. During the onset of reflective thinking, the instant I objectify the "passing thought" at hand, that thought is interrupted. In contrast, at the onset of reflective experiencing, the instant I objectify the experiencing at hand, that experiencing potentially continues, uninterrupted. For example, as a form of elaborative experiencing, I can be completely absorbed in playing tennis as I run to hit the ball. Then, during reflective experiencing, my attention shifts to the *action* of running itself. Shifting my attention to that action does not necessarily interrupt it.

Even though elaborative experiencing isn't necessarily interrupted once I reflect on it, its quality is negatively impacted. Remember, if I'm playing a musical instrument consistent with elaborative experiencing and then notice the act of playing, as per reflective experiencing, the quality of playing will deteriorate. Nevertheless, the playing itself can certainly continue despite my explicit awareness of it.

In sum, whereas reflecting on elaborative *thinking* seems to interrupt what was a flowing, progressive process, reflecting on elaborative *experiencing* does not necessarily interrupt it, although it's often negatively affected. This distinction has important phenomenal ramifications regarding the differences among the various types of thought.

During IRI, which is a form of elaborative thinking, I'm taking into account some excerpted aspect that occurred during the "passing thought" as I excerptively clip and conceptually react to it now. My present reaction reflects an implicit representation of the identified excerptive-clip. During ERI, which is a form of reflective thinking, my present reaction to an identified excerptive-clip of the "passing thought" embodies an explicit representation of its identity along with an implicit awareness of the thought as a "presence." In a sense, the thought as a presence is such a given, an explicit recognition of it is unnecessary. The experiential emphasis embodied in this reaction is on the explicit meaning or *identity*-of-the-thought. In contrast, during NCRT, another form of reflective thinking, my present reaction embodies an explicit awareness of the excerptively clipped identity and presence of the "passing thought." The experiential emphasis embodied in this reaction is on the presence of the thought, or identity-of-the-*thought*.

In contrast to the forms of thinking noted in the last paragraph, CRT and TRI attend to the *action* of the separating awareness in relation to "passing thoughts," along with the meaningful contents therein. Embodied in their reactions to the thought-object is an awareness of the identity-of-the-passing-thought-in-relation-to-*the-observing-separating-awareness*-reacting-to-it, with the emphasis on the experience of an observing, separating awareness.

During the outset of the reflective conceptual portions of CRT or TRI, as I become explicitly aware of the excerptively clipped identity and presence of the "passing thought," I have the experience of being an observing, separating awareness. Thus, during CRT and TRI, *reflective experiencing* is also occurring. In other words, while objectifying or excerptively clipping a "passing thought" and reacting to it at the outset of the reflective conceptual portion of the present thought, I'm observing the separating, reactive *experiencing* (in response to that thought-object) as it's occurring (reflective experiencing). Because I'm engaged in a form of reflective thinking, I've seemingly interrupted and captured the "passing thought" by objectifying it. However, attention to the separating and stretching of awareness from that thought (reflective experiencing) does not interrupt the present flow despite the phenomenal awareness of it.

Reflective experiencing can occur in relation to any physical activity at hand, thereby creating a sense of self-awareness. Similarly, reflective thinking can occur in relation to any thought-object at hand, thereby creating a sense of self-awareness. However, in the realm of thoughts, reflective experiencing engenders an explicit sense of self-awareness when it occurs during the outset of the reflective conceptual portions of CRT or TRI in response to excerpted thought-objects. Only when awareness is momentarily free from its absorption in the identified excerptive-clip of the "passing thought" can a duality of experiencing occur as it feels itself separate from and observes the excerptive-clip of that thought-object. In other words, during CRT and TRI there is an extremely small "window" of time where reflective experiencing and thinking can combine to create this powerful and unique phenomenology of self-awareness.

### A Holarchical Developmental Pattern

A hierarchical pattern can be discerned among the different types of thinking, and across the stages of development discussed thus far. Ken Wilber (1995) discusses this hierarchical developmental pattern at length in *Sex, Ecology, Spirituality: The Spirit of Evolution.* He shows us that this hierarchy is reflected across all aspects of reality: material, biological, mental, and spiritual. More specifically, Wilber borrows Arthur Koestler's (1976) term "holon," which refers to an entity that is itself a whole and a part of some other whole. Wilber indicates that every domain of reality consists of holons, and that there is no whole that isn't also a part of some other whole. In addition, Koestler's term "holarchy" is a hierarchy or order of increasing wholeness. He says that all evolutionary and developmental systems proceed in increasing orders of wholeness and inclusion, a rank-ordering of holons. Each higher holon unites and links what would otherwise be separate, conflicting, and isolated parts into a coherent unity, where the parts come together in a common wholeness. Furthermore, each holon transcends and includes its predecessor(s), leaving us with a pattern in evolution where holons transcend and include, indefinitely and unendingly.

I believe that a holarchical pattern can be discerned across general elaborative thinking, IRI, ERI, NCRT, CRT, and TRI; where the developing individual uses the meaningful experience of one thought as a springboard to an excerpt in response to which a new thought reacts (general elaborative thinking), or becomes implicitly aware of some excerpted meaningful aspect that occurred during the "passing thought" (IRI), or explicitly aware of the identity of the excerpted, "passing thought' (along with an implicit awareness of the thought per se) (ERI), or explicitly aware of the excerpted presence of the "passing thought" (while construing it as embodying one's subjectivity as a thinking-self) (NCRT), or explicitly aware of an excerpted "passing thought" (construed as a prior instance of subjectivity in relation to the awareness witnessing it) (CRT), or explicitly aware of an excerpted "passing thought" (construed as a prior instance of subjectivity in relation to the awareness witnessing it, while also being aware of the reflective phenomenology occurring then and now) (TRI). The awareness embodying each new type of thought is subjectively less bound to its developmentally less advanced predecessor given its respective capacity to objectify some aspect of its predecessor. Thus, the subjectivity embodied in the earlier thought-type can step out of and objectify some aspect of that thought-type in its new found embeddedness in a subsequently new and developmentally more advanced thought-type.

In other words, a general elaborative thought reacts to an excerpt prompted by its predecessor-thought, IRI excerpts and reacts to some aspect of its predecessor-thought, ERI excerpts and reacts to the identity of its predecessor-thought, NCRT excerpts and reacts to the presence of its predecessor-thought, CRT becomes aware of the witness of the excerpted presence of the predecessor-thought, and TRI becomes aware of the phenomenology engendered by the predecessor thought. Again, the subjectivity embodied in the earlier thought-form steps out of and objectifies some aspect of that thought-type in its embeddedness in a subsequently new thought-type.

A holarchical pattern of increasingly less attachment to one worldview, coupled with greater perspective and awareness through a new worldview, can also be posited regarding the GRO across cognitive developmental stages. At the Sensorimotor stage and beyond, children become aware of themselves by attending to some objectified physical experiencing in the moment in relation to their surroundings (E-GRO). Then at Formal Operations, children are increasingly capable of becoming aware of themselves as thinking selves; they take the passing thought-object as an instance of their present subjectivity (partially-based I-GRO or NCRT). Thus, they become aware of themselves as a mental and physical self. At the stage of VL, I've suggested that individuals become self-aware as a witnessing self in relation to the objectified "passing thought" (I-GRO or CRT). In addition, individuals at the stage of VL become capable of taking the experience of I-GRO itself as an object of attention. Thus, evolving individuals traversing E-GRO, partially based I-GRO, and I-GRO are less bound to the prior forms of self-awareness in relation to their world (although they're still capable of it), and increasingly conscious of other realities that broaden self-awareness.

In this chapter, a portion of Ken Wilber's developmental model of consciousness was presented. Understanding the abilities of children and adults, and the forms that their awareness and self-identities take at different stages of development, helped us make educated guesses about the placement of ten different types of thought along this evolutionary progression. This placement, in turn, helps us better understand the phenomenology of their experience and further "rounds out" the picture of human development.

Consistent with the understanding that all evolutionary systems form a hierarchy or holarchy of increasing wholeness and integration, we hypothesized that the types of thought reflect the same developmental pattern. The fundamental distinctions regarding the structure and types of thought allowed us to specify their hierarchical nature. However, the implications of this holarchy of thought-types can be easily overlooked. For instance, prior to reading the first three chapters of this book, you reacted to the contents of appearing excerpts thousands of times a day without any explicit awareness of their existence per se. Thus, for the first time in your life you are in a position to *experientially* recognize their presence. Similarly, prior to Formal Operations, and on a daily basis, your consciousness was embedded in thousands of general elaborative thoughts, with little-to-no conscious awareness of their existence. Upon entering the stage of Formal Operations, however, you became increasingly capable of objectifying, excerpting, and recognizing them as objects of experience per se.

Within the hierarchical pattern of thinking outlined in this chapter, aspects of the type of thinking in which awareness is embedded at one stage of development can be objectified, witnessed, and recognized by a new type of thought at the next stage of development. As a result, awareness may learn to free itself from the confines of lower types of thought and from the phenomenal manifestations dictating how you experience yourself in relation to the world around you. For example, at the highest developmental level we've discussed, the stage of VL, we saw that the repetitive experience of NCRT gave way to the realization that thought-objects construed as self were finally recognized as not-self (CRT). Instead, the experience of a witnessing self unfolding in relation to objectified "passing thoughts" was realized to always be the case: "I'm not the thought witnessed, I'm always the witness of thoughts and of all other objects of awareness!"

Wilber says that at each higher stage of development, the self, with its embeddedness in certain experiential forms, becomes conscious of objects and aspects of experience that did not exist in its reality at the prior stage. In other words, at each higher stage of development, the self takes on an entirely different worldview, where objects and aspects of experience seem to materialize out of nowhere. In the realm of thought, for example, the self, embedded in *being* general elaborative thoughts, suddenly becomes aware of the existence of them as objects, in its newfound embeddedness in ERI or NCRT, at the next stage of development. The release of awareness from its embeddedness in thought-types typical of an earlier stage of development allows for an awareness of them as objects, and potentially frees it from the impact of phenomenal manifestations unique to those types.

Realize this: at the next stage beyond and inclusive of VL, a new insight about the nature of awareness and self takes root due to the holarchical patterning of the evolution of consciousness across the human life span. But this insight is not a mere intellectual one: it results in permanent experiential changes in the forms your awareness takes in relation to the world at large. Aren't the implications of this holarchy of human development unbelievable?!

In chapter 5, we will discuss four different phenomenologies created by reflective thinking. Like a mental earthquake, an understanding of these manifestations and of how they are engendered, shakes them from their embeddedness as unquestioned givens of our experience. Loosened and thrown from this foundation, we can observe, recognize, and move into other forms of awareness, no longer at the mercy of their impact.

## *Chapter Five:* More Me

AMONG THE TEN TYPES of thought outlined in the prior chapters, six types of reflective thinking were identified. Awareness, at the outset of the reflective conceptual portion of each type of reflective thought, embodies the reactively identified excerpt, and then stretches away from and looks at it. This stretching of awareness, while only milliseconds in duration, is just long enough to engender the experience of separation (whether implicitly or explicitly represented), and the recognition of difference between here and there. Awareness feels itself to be a single identity, but only recognizes itself as such given its contrasting conceptual "shapes." And this recognition occurs only during that briefest of reflective moments, as awareness, in its "new" form, feels different and separate from the one it just took, the one being observed now.

The most significant phenomenal differences among the six types of reflective thinking concern the degree of awareness and distinctive interpretive construal of this experience of a separating, observing self (at the outset of the reflective conceptual portion of the occurrent reflective thought in response to the reactively identified excerpt of the "passing thought"). In other words, this experience of the separation of awareness from a prior mental, conceptual thought-form exists across all six types of reflective thinking. However, the degree of consciousness and interpretive distinctiveness of self-awareness varies among them.

Across the reflective types of thought, the degree and distinctive interpretation of the intermittent consciousness of a separating awareness varies. Despite such differences among reflective thoughts, the phenomenology *while* this experience occurs is very similar and quite pervasive. In fact, there exist several interpretive, phenomenal variations as this separating happens which can occur at the onset of all types of reflective thoughts.

### Something More

Many forms of reflective thinking can engender an experience of self-awareness that has a very significant quality of egoism or narcissism in relation to the just passing, objectified thought-self. This experience has a better-than or something-more-than quality. It occurs because this present, reflective, thinking-self recognizes and knows everything the now objectified "passing thought-self" knew, plus something more. The reflective-self has the present, and hence, a new, different, and additional vantage point, in comparison with that now objectified thought-self. Thus, my present experiencing is one of superseding, of being more than or greater than.

Throughout much of our day-to-day experience, most adults have intermittent experiences of noticing thinking. When I acknowledge to myself or someone else that, "I was just *thinking about...*," I'm engaged in explicit reflective identification. During ERI, where the content of the excerpt being reflected on is of a "passing" *thought about...*, I experience a sense of, "I'm something more and better than you." This experience occurs at the outset of the reflective conceptual portion of the present, unfolding thought, taking the reactively identified, excerptively clipped "passing thought" as its object. This *something more* experience is a function of representing that excerpted thought at a level of abstraction one-step removed from it; that excerpted thought is being observed in its entirety and identified as a whole. I become the context within which that thought is now contained by virtue of seeing it as an identified whole from this different and more encompassing vantage point. Therefore, for the first time, it is explicitly seen and experienced in its entirety. In addition, however, it is simultaneously experienced as a part because it seems to exist as a separate object within the larger framework of the awareness observing it now.

Thus, during moments of ERI, for example, it always seems as if there's this greater and more present thinking-self bring-

ing greater meaning, significance, or value to bear in relation to
what that last subjective thought-self (which is now objectified)
had to offer. This present, unfolding self sees its "prior" self as
less adequate because it now knows something about that self
which that self hadn't known. And this present self remembers
what that "prior" self knew because it just embodied that prior
self's reaction to the object *it was knowing*. As a result, it recognizes that "prior" self's reaction as familiar and accurate. In other
words, from here I can be aware of it as "that thought about the
scene from my favorite movie," for example, while also being
aware that, when I was that thought, I wasn't aware of it as such.
Instead, when I was that thought, I was only aware of that scene
from my favorite movie. Therefore, I can be aware of the identity
of that particular thought now as a whole, while also recognizing
that I wasn't aware of it as such then when I was being it.

It's as if this always more-than, reflective-self is always necessary. It seems as if I always need this best or most important
me to reflect on thinking so to bring something more to my
experiencing. The reflective self is always in the position of
identifying "passing thoughts," and hence, is convinced that
without itself something is being missed, which in a sense, is
true. Nevertheless, the reflective self doesn't want to miss anything important about what I'm thinking or of the fact that I'm
thinking. From reflective thinking's vantage point, a thought
that's not captured or reflected on is a thought which doesn't
exist. Therefore, reflective thinking sees itself as the discoverer
of thoughts. To reflective thinking, thoughts exist or really matter only when they're reflected on, noticed, and identified. As a
result, it experiences itself as having greater significance or value
than the "passing thoughts" it captures. It feels better and more
important than any one thought when it notices and identifies
it because it knows something more than it; it has something
over on it. Reflective thinking convinces itself of being a necessary and important figure by discovering a particular, *Thought
about...*, which it thinks that thought should have known about

itself but somehow didn't.

It's almost as if the reflective thinking-self is a fossil collector who looks for and finds specimens, which he then identifies. He realizes that (at best), without him, these fossils would exist in and of themselves but would somehow be of no real significance because neither themselves nor their identity (which only he can bring to them) would ever be "discovered."

In sum, there's a seemingly greater me (potentially) born in each reflective, self-awareness-engendering moment; a me-be-yond-me. This greater me appears to be a necessity because it's a me that brings something more. It's a more-me that always seems to know more than the less-me on which it's reflecting.

### *The True Me*

Much of thinking involves making judgments, evaluations, and decisions. Such judgments and decisions often occur in relation to one's thoughts. However, thinking about one's thoughts requires reflective thinking ability (e.g., ERI) so one can take the mean-ingful content of thoughts, as well as the thoughts themselves as objects of attention. Remember, by reflecting on the last thought it can be excerpted or meaningfully identified, and hence, reacted to as an object of attention. The identity of the "passing thought" is embodied in an excerpt which is in the embrace of awareness taking the form of an unfolding reflective thought.

Similar to the phenomenology of "Something More" is that of "the True Me" experience. The True Me phenomenology can also takes place at the outset of the reflective conceptual portion of the unfolding reflective thought, which is taking the "passing," reactively identified, excerpted thought as its object. The act of judging the "prior" thought (which might be a thought-judgment or decision itself) lends itself to the phenomenology of "The True Me" experience. "The True Me" experience occurs as it corrects, falsifies, or validates the passing thought-judgment/decision. For example, let's say that I'm at work and my boss does yet another rude thing to me. Later, when I recall this rudeness, I think, "Man, do I hate him!" Then, as I reflect on this thought, thereby excerpting and meaningfully identifying it, I think, "Ah, hate's too strong a word. He just makes me so mad!"

Following the act of excerpting and meaningfully identifying the thought about hating my boss, and during the reflective conceptual portion of the thought that followed it, I had the subtle experience of *this* judgment/decision feeling like the truest, smartest, best, and most personally meaningful, valid, and relevant one. The most recent thought experiences itself as more meaningful and significant than its excerpted predecessor-thought. Here, the reflective thought-self does more than just subsume its predecessor on the basis of seemingly having its predecessor's vantage point *plus* its own more comparatively holistic one. The reflective thought-self also embodies greater meaning and significance than its predecessor on a logical, personally valued, and meaningful basis. The reflective thought-moment has its predecessor's meaningful, personal position in its grasp, plus its own, which adds some personally meaningful elaboration. This meaningful elaboration could simply reflect some minor clarification or reaffirmation of the former thought, but it is still tantamount to the experience of bringing greater personal and meaningful significance to it.

Thus, almost every time I reflect on and react to a passing thought, this moment's reflective judgment/decision (in relation to it) feels like the truest, smartest, best, and most personally meaningful and relevant one (this experience, however, is unconscious because it's not the object of attention). In my reaction to an excerpted and meaningfully identified thought, I'm the judger and it is merely the judgee. I'm the Superior Judge who always overrules its predecessor. I literally experience my *present* reaction to the former one as the truest me and as more valued than that objectified me-reaction. In each reflective moment the "real" me is reestablishing and reexperiencing the importance of its existence by bringing more validity to what was just experienced as the real, most valid me. In this moment the "real" me stands up by replacing a less real me that was only moments ago the one who was standing or doing the replacing. My phenomenology is one of, "Ah, here I really am, this is what I truly stand for, this is the real me, the best me (not that)." In other words, "This moment rules!" In this moment's reaction, "I am the man!"

### *The Intending Self*

I believe that the experiences of intending, choosing, controlling, directing, or deciding are actions synonymous with our sense of being autonomous, free-willing creatures. It is these experiences that seem to be living proof that, as human beings, we determine our fates. What do these experiences of controlling, choosing, deciding, directing, and intending consist of? How do they occur? When do they occur?

In my opinion, the experience of being a free willing, deciding, controlling, intending presence occurs only during the reflective conceptual portion at the outset of a given reflective thought. It's only during this portion of every reflective thought that a duality of experiencing between a present, separating, reflecting awareness in relation to a seemingly present, separate, mental object of attention occurs. Thus, to experience one's self as free-willing, one has to have the experience of being a separate or freestanding entity (in relation to another object), and it's only during the reflective conceptual portion of a given reflective thought that this occurs. Let's take an example.

Leaving the house one morning, I noticed that the front steps were icy. At that instant, an excerptive reminder of the salt I bought yesterday (that I had intended but forgot to sprinkle on the steps) popped into my awareness as a flash-image. This excerpt embodied a reminder of that earlier decision to sprinkle salt on the steps after buying it. The reflective conceptual portion of the thought, in response to this recognized, meaning-laden excerptive reminder might be, "Oh, I need to salt the steps before I leave for work."

Considering this experience about the icy steps, as I reacted to the recognized excerptive reminder of having decided to sprinkle salt on the front steps yesterday I was having the experience of intending. Even though the intending experience itself is unconscious (as an unattended-to-knowing), in that I'm not explicitly aware **of** my experience of intending as it's occurring, I am (implicitly) experiencing it nonetheless. The act of intentionality consists of a reflective, conceptual, reactive-decision to a recognized excerpt, where that reactively identified excerpt somehow embodies either a reminder of a "prior" decision or a piece of meaning-laden ground of decision-influencing potential.

In the example above, you are seemingly an intending, reflecting awareness in the form of a reaction to an excerptive reminder of a "prior" decision. You are experiencing a subjective, reactive decision in response to an objectified excerpt that meaningfully embodies that decision. That excerpt embodies a reminder of your "prior" intention to act in a particular way, and you, as a seemingly separate entity, move away from while reflecting on and reacting to it. You react to it as the self who intends to act accordingly (or not). You unfold as the intending self, as if saying, "Yes, I'll do this (in view of that)." The phrase in parentheses represents the fact that the unfolding self isn't explicitly conscious of the content embodied in the excerpt as an object of attention per se. Instead, that self is conscious of the content embodied in the excerpt, but is entirely absorbed in reacting *to it.*

The reactive, deciding self takes credit for the entire decision-making or intending act, instead of realizing it has a partner in a transaction. In other words, this decision-making process is a dual affair: the excerpt at hand embodies a decision and the reflective reaction arising from it embodies a superseding directive (whether in agreement with it or not). Thus, once you're released from the confines of that excerpting moment, you seem to be free or separate from it and can choose to follow the decision-influencing meaning embodied in it or not. In a very real sense, the recognized excerpt is supplying some meaningful information from which you, the reflecting awareness, get the benefit.

Here's another example. After work one day, while driving home, I came to an intersection where I normally turn left. To my right, I noticed the gas station across from the video store and suddenly experienced an excerptive reminder of the following as a totality: the videotape under my seat that I had decided to return to the video store earlier in the day. I then had the thought-reaction in response to this excerpt, "I need to return this video before it's overdue." Instead of turning left, as I usually do, I went straight and headed off to the video store.

As an awareness absorbed in a reactive decision to the excerpt at hand, I experience a subtle sense of being a separate, intending self. This separate sense of self is engendered only in relation to a seemingly separate, observed, excerpt-object, "containing," in the example above, a reminder regarding some "prior" decision of the self. The decision-making at hand owns the present, and is meaningfully and experientially "more than" the object of "prior" self-experiencing to which it's attending. My experience then, is one of being the decision-maker as a seemingly separate, superseding, observing entity in relation to the decision embodied in the seemingly separate, recognized excerpt at hand.

As an initial reaction to a reactively recognized excerpt at the outset of reflective thoughts, I briefly experience being a present, separating, reflecting awareness that suddenly seems to be free-floating and observing another objectified form of self-experiencing. It is only during this moment of freedom from the recognized excerpt, where the interplay between it and my seemingly contrasting, reactive, self-experiencing as a separate entity, can occur. Thus, the only way I can have an experience as a separate entity (in "mind-space") is when there's a contrasting object at hand that I can experience being separate from. As this seemingly separate, reflecting awareness begins to react to this excerpt-object embodying a potential course of action, it becomes a contrasting experiencing that seems other to, more than, and yet identified with that excerpt, as its own. This identification is a function of recognizing that the content of the excerpt is evidence of a certain "prior" self-experiencing. This unfolding, contrasting, comparative, reactive, decision-making process, coupled with the free-floating sense of being a reflecting, observing awareness, results in the experience of being a separate decision-maker. And my sense of being a separate, free-willing, or intending self can occur only during this moment of seeming freedom from a meaningfully recognized, excerpted object during the outset of the reflective conceptual portion of the reflective thought at hand.

Again, the act of intending consists of a reflective, conceptual, reactive-decision to a recognized excerpt, where that excerpt embodies either a memory of a "prior" decision or a piece of meaning-laden ground of decision-influencing potential. Having detailed an example of intending based on an excerptive reminder of a prior decision, let's look at an example of an excerpt that embodies a piece of meaning-laden ground of decision-influencing potential.

In my example of driving home from work, I came to the intersection where I usually turn left, only to experience a flash-excerpt-recognition, as a totality, of the video under my seat I had earlier resolved to return to the video store. Let's say that my thought-reaction rising out of this recognized excerpt was, "I don't want to return the video today." Then, the latter thought prompted an excerptive memory of my girlfriend being angry with me due to my history of paying two-dollar late fees. As I react to this recognized excerpt, I have the thought, "I'd better return this video now or I'll be in hot water!" The recognized excerpt of my girlfriend's anger about my late fees is an example of an excerpt with decision-influencing potential. In other words, in any context where one is caught up in a decision-making process, excerpts can come to mind that embody decision-influencing potential. Again, in response to such excerpts, I experience my self as a separate entity who is intending.

### Having Thoughts versus Being Thoughts

Explicit reflective identification involves the intention to acknowledge to myself or another person my experience of *thinking about* something in particular. During ERI, I'm reflecting on the "passing thought" and identifying its particular, excerptively clipped content. Therefore, the reflective conceptual portion of the thought at the outset of ERI reflects on and reacts to a reactively identified and excerpted "passing thought." The excerptive-clip of that prior thought brought a "formal" end to it. Subsequently, for the first time, it is *explicitly* recognized in its entirety as a discrete, conceptually identified entity.

The "formal" endings of thoughts that are the objects of ERI contrast to the "informal" endings that occur to the predecessor-thoughts of general elaborative thinking. At the outset of general elaborative thinking, the only "evidence" that a given, prior thought existed is reflected by its influence on the present thought. The present thought implicitly embodies (more or less) the meaning-based influence of the prior one as a function of the excerpt lying between them and related to both. But that prior thought dies, in essence, with no "formal" acknowledgment whatsoever.

During ERI, reflecting on and identifying the "passing thought" creates or transforms it into a discrete, meaningful thought-object, "seen" as a whole. Upon reflection, it is given an explicit identity, and hence, "formal" acknowledgement. As a "passing" elaborative thought, it would have had the benefit of reflective awareness, and therefore, no chance of recognition that it even existed. But as a result of ERI, that "prior" thinking dies as an unfolding, elaborative process and is born (to awareness) as a discrete, meaningfully identified, mentally solidified, and holistically objectified "thought" about something in particular.

During general elaborative thinking, my awareness embodies every part-reaction in that elaborative process. No part of that elaborative process is consciously available to me because I'm not orienting my attention to any part of it as an object per se. However, the instant I reflect on a "passing thought" as an object of attention (ERI), I have the experience of being an observer (as an unattended-to-knowing), separate from that excerpted, objectified, and identified thought, the content of which I'm now explicitly aware. Moreover, I often equate this experience with the actual experience of *the thinking* of that objectified thought. To this reflective and seemingly separate observer, there is often (at that instant) no acknowledgment of the actual act of thinking that went on just prior to the observation of that thought now as an object of attention. In other words, as I reflect on that "passing thought" as an object, I'm typically not reflecting on the reality of having just been absorbed in it. Consequently, I experience the observing of this meaningfully identified thought-object as the actual experience of the thinking of it. Thus, I experience myself as "having" thoughts, as if I'm always a separate noticer or thinker of thoughts as objects. After all, I have just created (without realizing it) a meaningfully identified and objectified thought at the *instant* of looking at it. In other words, very suddenly, I seem to have a finished product right in front of me. I identify it as *"My thought about…,"* and I experience seeing it now as "my" experience of thinking it. Therefore, I experience myself as a present, separate, observing self who thinks thoughts by finding and seeing thoughts as present, fully formed, identified, and separate objects. The greater reality, however, is that I first live out (think) a thought as an unconscious, elaborative reaction to an excerpted object of attention. Only at that thought's completion, once I reflect on it, do I seemingly become a separate, observing awareness who is conscious of it as a seemingly separate thought-object (about whatever) which I "have."

In sum, during ERI, in my attempt to be aware of what I'm *thinking about*, a "passing thought" must be excerpted and identified. The instant I respond to that reactively identified excerpt, it exists as a fully formed and identified thought. My phenomenology is often one of being a present, separate observer who seems to look for and find a present, fully formed thought-object as an already finished product. I'm the observer who seemingly found this fully formed thought "over there." It's "my" thought because I just found it in "my" mind. Therefore, it seems like I have thoughts, as if there's a separate "I" or self-experiencer that "has," as objects, separate thoughts or self-experiences. I seem to find those thoughts as objects, fully formed and meaningfully identified "inside" my mind. Consequently, I usually equate this action of "finding" these fully formed, identified, and meaningfully "holified" thoughts as *the* experience of "thinking" them.

The four phenomenal experiences highlighted in this chapter are experienced separately or in some combination throughout each and every day. Throw in the various phenomenologies engendered by the separating of awareness from its excerpted "passing thought" (NCRT and CRT, as examples), and we're tasting a buffet of flavors of self. Every one of these is derived from the same basic ingredients but with slightly different recipes. Take an excerpt here and an excerpt there, throw in the outset of the reflective conceptual portion of a reflective thought in response, a particular experiential construal, and "Voila!"—our ego-based masterpiece is rising! In the same way eggs, water, flour, and sugar result in many amazingly different and tantalizing eatables, so too are these personally treasured experiences of self the product of a few basic ingredients.

As a result of delineating a structure of thinking based upon the phenomenal differences occurring within the unfolding of thought, we have thus far identified ten types of thinking. Although we experience these parts and types of thought every day, we are conscious of very few of them. Consequently, there are ghosts among us. Present but unseen, their influence is more profound than one could imagine. The "ghosts of consciousness" exert tremendous effect on the way we experience ourselves and the world: elaborative thoughts, pervasive in their presence and impact, are like minidreams, ghostlike, ephemeral, and rarely noticed or identified; reflective thoughts create intermittent experiences of a separate self-sense at different intensities of awareness, based on different interpretive construals of various excerpts in relation to feeling separate from them; the phenomenologies of reflective thoughts consist of bringing something more to and feeling truer than their thought-predecessors, being the author of all observed thoughts, and the controller, intender, chooser, and decider of actions.

The fleeting thought-based experiences reinforcing the separate existence of self create a belief in one's central importance as the "I" around which all experiences orbit. Supposedly, I am not experience, *I "have" experiences.* In the awareness of myself, I alone exist (to me) as an entity of utmost importance (to me). The experiences I "have" exist as separate from me, and are judged according to their value in furthering or hindering causes relevant to my needs. In chapters 7, 8, and 9, the falseness of this belief of the separateness of self—reinforced by erroneous interpretations occurring in response to that experiential juncture of the stretching of awareness from an observed excerpt—will be exposed. The exposure of the illusory nature of the separate self-sense may loosen one's attachment to and belief in that self. As a result, strong and pervasive tendencies supporting the motives and actions meant to foster pleasure and avoid/minimize pain, discomfort, and frustration may be weakened and less frequently engaged. The freedom resulting from such changes has been thoroughly documented by Eastern religious and philosophical traditions, as introduced in chapter 9.

The central culprit engendering a large number of problematic manifestations related to the illusory self-sense is the excerpt. Excerpts represent the most significant ghost-figure among all the types of "ghosts of consciousness." Chapter 6 explores and describes those factors influencing the presence, quality, and nature of excerpts rising into awareness.

# Chapter Six: Say "Thank You" To Your Ghosts

THERE'S AN IMPROVISATIONAL COMEDY show on television called *Whose Line Is It Anyway?*. The moderator of the show creates the contexts in which the comedians are to respond. During one segment, two of the comedians act out directions given by the moderator. In one instance, the moderator gave the direction, "Beetles on the reef." Upon hearing this, I paid attention to my internal/mental experience. I noticed myself experiencing a vague, fleeting excerpt-image of little bugs on a rocky reef. I then watched the actors and heard one of them say to the other, "Nice to see you, Ringo!" In response, I experienced a flash-image of the drum player, Ringo Starr. This flash-image was another proactively identified excerpt. As I reflected on this excerpt I had the thought, "Yes, he was a Beatle." Almost immediately, I "flashed" on the excerpt of the initial direction given, "Beetles on the reef," recognizing it as a contrast to the latter. I quickly reflected upon and reacted to this excerpted recognition by way of laughing, which is similar to the reflective conceptual portion of a thought.

In another example, the moderator gave the direction, "A blind date." As soon as I heard this, I flashed on an image of a man and woman meeting, as I watched the comedians walk toward one another. Staring straight ahead, the man bumped into the woman and said, "Excuse me." I experienced the flash-image and subsequent recognition of the man as blind, followed by the thought, "The man is blind." I then flashed on an excerpt of the initial direction and experienced it as a contrast to the blind man. In response to this excerpted recognition, I laughed.

These internal reactions to jokes reflect an important reality about the nature of thinking per se, and hence, about much of our waking experience. The excerpt-image of Ringo, for example, is given to me out of the "depths" of my subconscious mind. I am certainly not responsible for it. I didn't intend this specific, image-based, excerpt-reaction. It arose into awareness as a response to the stimulus sentence, "Nice to see you, Ringo!" In turn, the initial reaction to this excerpt-image, whether a verbal identification of that excerpt, "Yes, he was a Beatle," or some other personal reaction to it, is given to me, so to speak. It spontaneously arises in and as my awareness in response to the recognized excerpt.

Our spontaneous, unintended reactions to jokes stand in contrast to the general belief that we control and determine everything we think and do. We typically see ourselves as the deliberate authors of all of our thoughts, decisions, actions, and reactions.

When you pose a question to yourself and an answer is forthcoming, you typically believe that you authored its content. While making a decision in response to the content of an excerptive reminder of a prior decision, for example, you experience yourself as intending your actions as an independent entity. When becoming aware of a "passing thought," you often believe that you are the separate self who thinks and "has" thoughts as objects. In all of these instances, the conscious experience of self is, to varying degrees, manifested as awareness stretches away from the content of a reactively identified, excerpted object. Therefore, this self believes that it is the independent author and owner of that content. Because the conscious self knows *only* the experience of itself, it can't be aware of those times when it doesn't know itself. Therefore, it's aware of itself in relation to making a decision, arriving at an answer, "thinking" a thought, and not aware of itself when such activities occur in its absence (such as during elaborative thoughts). Thus, the manifesting self-sense is not necessary for those activities to take place. But it believes that it is because it's only aware of itself when it's aware of itself (in relation to an excerpted decision, answer, thought, etc.).

Because the manifesting self-sense is aware of itself only when it's aware of itself, it believes that it is present at all times, and hence is the independent author of all of "its" observed activities. It even provides reasons, in retrospect, for why a particular action was taken, even if it played no intending role in the action taken at that time. It constantly narrates explanations for behavior because it believes that it controls, directs, and determines all of it.

In addition, the manifesting self-sense often has no awareness of the "parts" of thoughts. Therefore, it certainly has no control or authoring role of such "parts." Its sense of control and deliberateness is far from the case. Instead, various "ghosts of consciousness" play a major role in thinking, intending, and behaving. The most prominent "ghost" in this regard is the excerpt. The conscious, manifesting self-sense in the form of a separating awareness in response to the content of an excerpt has no awareness of the excerpt per se. In addition, excerpts rise into awareness automatically and in response to a number of factors unrelated to any determining influence of the conscious self.

Julian Jaynes (1976) discusses the phenomenon of solutions automatically rising into awareness when he describes an experiment by H. J. Watt (1905) performed around 1905. In this experiment, nouns printed on cards were shown to subjects who were to offer a reply by uttering an associative word as quickly as they could. However, the associations were "partially constrained" in that subjects could be asked to give a superordinate association to the stimulus noun (e.g., oak-tree), a coordinate association (e.g., oak-elm), or a subordinate association (e.g., oak-beam). The nature of this task made it possible to divide consciousness of it into four periods: 1. The period during the instructions as to which of the constraints were to be used; 2. The period during the presentation of the stimulus noun; 3. The period during the search for the appropriate association; 4. The period during the spoken reply. The subjects were asked to be introspective observers of their internal experience and to confine themselves to introspecting on one of the four periods at a time, across a series of trials.

It was expected that the subjects' consciousness of the act of thinking, defined as arriving at a solution, would be found in the third period of searching for the word that would suit the particular instruction or constraint offered. What Watt found, however, was that it was during this third period that subjects were "introspectively blank." What seemed to be happening was that "thinking" was automatic and subjects weren't conscious of it once an instruction had been given and the stimulus-word was presented. Instead, it appeared that their "thinking" was done on a level of which they weren't conscious.

Jaynes says that the important part of this task was the instruction or constraint which allowed the whole process of "thinking" to go off automatically. Naming this conceptual constraint, Jaynes coined the term "struction" to connote both meanings reflected by the words "instruction" and "construction." The word "construction" suggests a conceptually based and created context that represents a specific set of defining characteristics, and hence, limits or constraints. The word "instruction" refers to a conceptual representation of a task one is to complete. Jaynes (1976) says of thinking,

> Thinking, then is not conscious. Rather, it is an automatic process following a struction and the materials on which the struction is to operate. (p. 39)

He gives another example by presenting a series of figures similar to the following: $ # $ # $ # $ #. He then asks, "What is the next figure in the series?" Jaynes says if you introspect on the process by which you came up with the answer, all you would be conscious of is the struction, the figures on the page, and then the solution. Your awareness is capable of taking each as an object of attention as they unfold in sequence. But you wouldn't be conscious of the action of "going in" for the solution. He concludes that what we call "thinking" is not conscious at all. Instead, only its preparation, materials, and end result are consciously experienced.

One phenomenon frequently referred to in introductory psychology texts is that of "incubation" (Zimbardo, 1980). Jaynes (1976) indirectly refers to this phenomenon as well, noting that some of Albert Einstein's greatest ideas came to him very suddenly while, for example, shaving in the morning. Jaynes says that there are several stages to this kind of creative thinking. First, there is a stage of preparation during which the problem is consciously worked. Second, there is a period much like incubation during which the problem is forgotten. Third, is the illumination or solution period during which the answer seems to pop into one's conscious awareness out of nowhere.

To Jaynes, the period of preparation is essentially the setting up of a complex struction, along with one's conscious attention to the materials upon which the struction is to operate. Oftentimes, one isn't conscious of the process of working out the solution. In fact, it's almost as if the problem had to be forgotten in order to be solved!

Returning to the discussion of the thinking process, it would appear that many of our thoughts function as instructions to ourselves and that these thoughts simultaneously embody the "materials" and context (or constraint [s]) from which an excerpt-answer is generated. For example, if I think to myself, "I want to remember the events from my vacation at the Cape last summer," the statement itself is an instruction and a stimulus-context from which answers are generated. After thinking this to myself I was presented with an image of my family on the beach and thought, "We spent a lot of time on the beach." Reflecting on the latter, I was presented with an image of a seashell and thought, "We collected a lot of shells." Then I noticed that no other images were presented to me so I thought, "What else did we do?"

Impressively, the struction serves as a stimulus-prompt and contextual constraint influencing the excerpt-searching reaction, the proactive excerpt-found reaction and appearing excerpt. Thus, the process of arriving at answers to questions, for example, involves the presentation of a struction or stimulus-prompt followed by an excerpt-searching reaction, the subsequent pro-active excerpt-found reaction, and excerpting instant. Moreover, following the presentation of the struction, these subsequent reactions occur automatically, without any conscious awareness of them as reactions per se. Therefore, one's conscious self can't be responsible for or the author of, these reactions because it isn't even aware of them as they occur.

We just discovered another type of ghost in our heads. If they secretly lived in our homes instead, upon asking for some-thing, it would magically appear before us. Moreover, we'd prob-ably believe it was ourselves who had the magic power. After all, every time we ask for something, there it is, *poof.* I think the ghosts would be rather angry though, giving and giving without receiving any credit for it.

Well, it seems to be this way in thought, too. Many of our excerpt-solutions seem to be given to us, as if by ghosts, from the "depths" of the unconscious mind. Moreover, we take credit for the delivered solutions to questions or problems posed. After all, a given solution showed up "in my head" in response to my stated desire for it to come. In addition, we're typically not conscious of the "arrival" of the excerpt-solution because we're so focused on its content. As a result, it's even less likely we'll give credit to this particular ghost of consciousness.

I was able to tell you about some of my internal experience above, once I posed the question to myself about what my fam-ily did on our last vacation, because I had given myself the prior instruction to introspect on the process as it unfolded. As already stated, with much of thinking there is little-to-no consciousness of any part of the process. Moreover, each part-reaction along the way is automatically given to me. If I hadn't given myself the instruction to introspect on the thought process as it unfolded, the only point where I might have become conscious of part of it was when I noticed that nothing else came to me after I thought, "We collected a lot of shells." Subsequently, I facilitated the task by re-prompting myself: "What else did we do?" In other words,

I posed a struction upon noticing that nothing more came to mind as a way to prompt an association, excerpt, or memory-image. In essence, I became reoriented to myself and to the task at hand (GRO).

### *Waking the Ghosts*

What are the factors that influence the nature of the excerpts rising into our awareness from this subconscious ground of response potential, given the fact that we don't consciously control, author, or direct them? One such factor just touched on is the instruction or struction a given thought represents.

Recall that when I asked myself—"What did we do on our family vacation last summer?"—a mental representation of a particular situation or context came into existence. In response to that representation, meaningful and thematically consistent excerpt-associations rose in relation to it. In addition, this thought is simultaneously an instruction reflecting my intention to allow an unconscious search for associations that I intuitively recognize as response potential. Thus, thoughts play a significant role in determining the potential excerpts rising into conscious awareness out of the subconscious ground of response potential.

Thoughts, by their very nature place limits or constraints on the contents that rise into awareness as a response to them. Thoughts can stand in place of and represent situational realities and contexts. When I think about certain situations (or read or hear about them), associations from my subconscious mind in the form of memory images, sounds, smells, feelings, tastes, and movements rise into my awareness in direct relationship to the represented situation reflected in the thought at hand. In other words, the thought serves as a constraint for what I will likely experience regarding the associations rising into my conscious awareness. It constrains by way of placing a kind of limit on the associations that will likely rise in relation to it. A field of potential associations is created as a function of the particular thought at hand.

As a brief aside, thought also constrains awareness itself. When I am absorbed in and as the associations arising and co-occurring as thought unfolds, my awareness (which is illuminating and illuminated by these associations) is constrained by the extending conceptual framework of the thought at hand. This is an amazing phenomenal reality that most of us rarely, if ever, consider. Remember our discussion in chapter 3 about the constraining nature of thoughts? I asked you to imagine standing in a wide open field seeing the night sky and the entire dome of stars above you. If you look through a telescope, however, and fix it on an object in the night sky, that telescope constrains and limits what you visually experience. Quite suddenly, as a strict function of the presence of the telescope you're looking through, that celestial object is significantly altered or specified, thereby constraining the night sky. The entire universe gives way to the specific object being focused on as a function of the constraining nature of the tubular object pressed against your eye.

Looking through a telescope is much like thinking. The extension of a thought (over time) is like the extension of the telescope, which your awareness seems to move into and through. Thus, every time you think, the open expansiveness of the limitless "field" of your awareness is suddenly constrained, limited, fixed, and focused on a specific object of attention to which you then directly react. In the act of thinking that specific thought, everything else, other than the attended-to-object at hand, disappears in your conscious awareness.

Following the appearance of a meaningfully recognized, reactively identified excerpt, you are immersed in the reflective conceptual portion of the thought in reaction to it. Your awareness of the excerpted content wanes as you are then swept into the elaborative conceptual portion of the thought. Your awareness then surfaces from the elaborative portion of the thought, reacting to meaningful nuances therein. Subsequently, awareness "dives" into the subconscious depths of mind or toward some other internal or external stimulus. In either case, you're (unconsciously) expecting an excerpt-association to be presented to you. Thus, during thinking, another factor influencing the nature of excerpt-associations presented to your conscious awareness following a specific thought is the meaningful nuances your awareness embodies at the tail end of that thought. These meaningful nuances, for whatever personally and situationally based reasons, trigger specific associations (excerpts) from the subconscious depths, for example, toward which your attention is directed.

Another major factor influencing the nature of excerpts rising out of the subconscious depths of awareness is the historically based emotional significance regarding a given thing. In other words, the physical surroundings or some anticipated situation activate some historically based emotional concern of mine. For example, if I have had one or more humiliating experiences in public speaking contexts, I may retain a remembered emotional concern about being humiliated again in a similar context. Anxiety about this possibility, embodied in appearing excerpts of these experiences, becomes a source of potential humiliation because it hampers my speaking performance. As a result, as I find myself in a meeting waiting for a turn to speak, my attention looks for signs of anxiety, which become excerptive-clips embodying that humiliating history. I'm hypervigilant about signs of anxiety because of my "background" emotional concern about feeling anxious and humiliated in this situation.

This emotional concern is similar to fearing that the mythic Medusa herself is in the audience. The intensity of my concern compels me to look for her even while recognizing that it's not in my best interest to do so. Of course, I inevitably find her and am turned to stone! In other words, I'm sure to find some sign of anxiety due to the presence of my fearful concern. An excerpted fearful symptom embodies meaning related to my history of humiliation in public speaking. For you, noticing some slight tension in your breathing may, at most, result in the reaction, "Oh, I guess I'm feeling a little anxious." Whereas for me that excerpted tension meaningfully embodies an imagined prelude to the extreme of humiliation, as if my entire history of humiliating experiences in similar contexts exists within it. As a result, my reaction to it might be, "Oh no! Here it comes again, I have to get out of here!" Thus, the present or anticipated situation is associated in my mind with a history of emotionally loaded experiences occurring within similar contexts. This, coupled with my self-protective emotional concern, influences the objects toward which my attention searches, and hence, likely finds. In addition, my emotional concern determines, in part, the reactions I have to those objects.

My biologically based experience is another determining factor in the nature and excerpted objects of my reactions. For example, on a given day at work I may have had eight enjoyable and productive hours, a nice lunch with friends, and a good commute home. However, when I arrive home, I am feeling very tired, hungry, and grouchy. When my girlfriend asks me about my day, I don't even excerpt pleasant memories from it. Instead, those excerpts from my day are tainted by how I feel right now so I tell her it was lousy. My reactions are contaminated simply as a function of the way I feel right now. I don't want to respond to my day in such negative terms but I find myself doing so anyway.

The realities of and relationships between language, experience, and meaning influence the nature of the excerpt-associations rising into conscious awareness, as well. Ken Wilber (1995) draws on F. Saussure's (1966) work related to language and meaning to help us understand the realities of each. Saussure discusses the concept of a sign, of something that points to something else, as a word does. Saussure says that all linguistic signs have two components: a signifier, which is the material component of the sign (the written or spoken symbol or sound, said aloud to one's self as in thought), and the signified, what comes to mind when you see, hear, or think the signifier.

Both the signifier and the signified are to be distinguished from the actual referent, whatever it is toward which the sign is pointing, whether interior or exterior. Saussure pointed out that the signified is not the same as the referent because, "What comes to mind" depends on a host of factors other than the referent.

A sign cannot be understood as an isolated entity because, in and of itself, the sign is meaningless. The signifiers and signifieds exist as a structure of contexts within contexts (Wilber, 1995). Thus, meaning itself is context-bound. If you change the context of a sign you elicit a different meaning for it. In other words, meaning is not found in the word alone but in all levels or aspects of the context co-occurring with the word. For example, Wilber states that the word-signifier "bark" has a totally different meaning depending on the context within which it is used.

Wilber (1995) indicates that the word "dog" has a shared meaning to you and me because the sign exists in a shared linguistic structure and cultural background of social and interpretive practices. But what if you'd never seen a real dog or anything like it? Wilber says that he could describe one to you, but without some points of shared experience nothing will come to mind in the way of a signified. In other words, the word "dog" will be meaningless to you. Thus, another basic factor influencing what "comes to mind" from the subconscious depths of response potential, in response to a specific word or thought, is my history of "stored" personal and cultural experiences in relation to language and the referent for which the signifier stands.

It seems common sense to conclude that our biological and physical nature play an important role in determining the contents rising into awareness. Yet, because our physical reality is such a given, it is easy to take it for granted as playing a major role in the nature and contents of our conscious experience. Consequently, it might be helpful to take a closer look at this reality now.

One researcher at the forefront of cognitive neuroscience over the past five decades is Michael Gazzaniga. In Gazzaniga's book (1985) *The Social Brain*, he discusses the relationships between subconscious and conscious regions and functions of the brain. Gazzaniga states:

> The normal person does not possess a unitary conscious mechanism in which the conscious system is privy to the sources of all of his or her actions...The

> normal brain is organized into modules and… most
> of these modules are capable of actions, moods, and
> responses. All except one work in nonverbal ways
> such that their modes of expression are solely through
> overt behaviors or more covert actions. (p. 74)

Gazzaniga (1985) indicates that clusters of neurons in the brain function as largely autonomous modules that operate outside of conscious awareness. He says that these modules can "compute, remember, feel emotion, and act." He goes on to say that the brain's single verbal module is an intricate component of the conscious self because it is

> …committed to the task of interpreting our overt be-
> havior as well as the more covert emotional responses
> produced by these separate mental modules of the
> brain. It constructs theories of why these behaviors
> occurred and does so because of the brain system's
> need to maintain a sense of consistency for all our
> behaviors. It is a uniquely human endeavor. (p. 80)

In other words, the verbal module is often involved in generating conscious explanations for behaviors generated by the nonverbal modules operating outside of awareness.

The psychotherapists Bruce Ecker and Laurel Hulley (1996) indicate that cognitive science has explicated an understanding of the synthesis of emotion and cognition in what is called an emotion scheme (Neisser, 1976). Ecker and Hulley state that an emotion scheme is

> …a module of experiential knowledge consisting of
> a multilevel integration of stored sensory, emotional,
> and cognitive information regarding a particular type
> of situation or theme of meaning. The activation of
> an emotion scheme by a perceptual cue generates the
> felt meaning of the situation as well as a predesigned
> response to it. (p. 119)

Thus, neuroscience research indicates that there is a vast array of autonomously functioning brain modules, including modules of experiential knowledge, existing outside of one's conscious awareness. Furthermore, given specific external or internal conditions or contexts, contents of any one of these modules can be activated, becoming part of one's experience, and potentially, of one's conscious awareness. In other words, given the right set of stimuli in the right context, one may have a strong, unconscious potential to respond in a particular way. This response potential can result in certain reactions and experiences that arise from subconsciousness and into one's conscious awareness.

To help us better understand the relationship between brain physiology and conscious experiencing, I would like to summarize Jenny Wade's (1996) discussion of the neurology of consciousness in her amazingly thorough and scholarly book *Changes of Mind*. According to Wade, researchers such as Paul MacLean (1973, 1990) indicate that the human brain is organized into distinct parts. Across the evolution of the human species, older parts of the brain were retained but overlaid by newer ones. The oldest brain structure of the human species is the innermost and lowest part of our neurological system. It is also the one most fully developed before a child is born and which begins functioning first. In addition, this brain structure bio-chemically and anatomically resembles the basic brain of reptiles, serving the same function in humans as the reptile's brain. This "reptilian brain" functions to preserve the individual and species through the regulation of innate behavioral patterns. MacLean refers to this part of the brain in humans as the R-complex. It is hardwired, meaning, the responses for which it is responsible are automatic or involuntary. It is the dominant force accounting for the quality of consciousness in infancy and earlier childhood.

The next brain structure to develop in the evolutionary progression of the human species MacLean calls the paleomammalian brain or limbic system (MacLean, 1973, 1990). It caps the R-complex and is also concerned with individual and species preservation. It functions by mediating messages between the internal state of the body and stimuli from the outside world impinging on the senses. It also mediates survival by distinguishing between pleasure and pain, thereby providing an emotional basis for motivating the organism to feed, fight, flee, and mate.

The evolution of mammals (especially in primates) added the third layer to the human brain, the neocortex (MacLean, 1973, 1990). With its addition, the paleomammalian brain now acts as a relay center between the R-complex and the neocortex. The neocortex is concerned with events in the external world, allowing for language, reflective thought, "civilized" morality, and for much of what we experience as uniquely human.

Last, the most recent evolutionary advance in the human brain resulted in its "split" into halves, the left and right hemispheres, each of which has its own kind of consciousness. The left and right hemispheres, as with the other evolutionary, anatomically, and functionally distinct brain structures, have also been referred to as "small minds" (Ornstein, 1986). Each small mind has its own unique sense of time and space, intelligence, subjectivity, and chemistry (MacLean, 1973, 1990). Each reacts differently to the same stimulus, out of its own unique type of awareness (MacLean, 1990). In addition, each one is active and aware at all times, but together they culminate in the phenomenology of a single, whole, or unbroken awareness (Gazzaniga, 1985).

The first three small minds send messages to the others so to form a "triune brain" that operates as a whole. Research indicates, however, that each small mind dominates awareness depending on the circumstances at hand, one small mind at a time. Thus, even though simultaneous awareness by the different small minds is occurring, the flow of consciousness is dominated by one small mind at any given instant.

The speech center of the left hemisphere is responsible for the task of interpreting and reporting on the forms of consciousness arising from the various small minds. It is a narrator, reporting on events rising into awareness at any given moment

(Gazzaniga, 1985; Ornstein, 1986; Eccles, 1989). The small mind that predominates consciousness from moment to moment, habitually reacting to various kinds of stimuli of concern to it, results in well-worn neural pathways (Gazzaniga, 1985). The more frequently the small minds are engaged, the more they reinforce a chronic set of responses, in part, due to these well-worn paths. In essence, the small minds perpetuate themselves by creating and maintaining their potential predominance, resulting in a type of awareness unique to the predominate one (Restak, 1979; Gazzaniga, 1985; Ornstein, 1986).

As stated earlier, the R-complex is the small mind dominating awareness during early childhood. Research indicates that adults who spent their early lives in static or less "enriching" environments may retain neurological patterns reflecting greater reliance on lower brain centers. In addition, researchers have observed cognitive patterns in fully functioning adults which are consistent with those more commonly seen in children (Harvey, Hunt, & Schroder, 1961; Lunberg, 1974; Luria, 1976). As with children, it would appear that such adults experience a form of consciousness *dominated by the activity of lower brain centers.* Although such adults have greater neocortical activity than children, the neocortex is more frequently engaged in interpreting information from the lower brain centers. This contrasts with the fact that, in older adults, the *neocortex often dominates* or suppresses inputs from the lower small minds (Loevinger, 1976; Hughes & Flowers, 1978; Werner, 1980; Levy-Bruhl, 1985).

It seems clear that neurophysiology plays a significant role in determining the particular quality and contents of one's consciousness. Genetic, situational, and historical factors, resulting in a particular neuronal circuitry and relationship pattern among the small minds of one's brain, can dictate the quality of one's awareness. The latter is reflected by the experiential contents that one characteristically attends to, the nature of one's typical responses to such contents, and the quality of those responses.

In sum, it seems incredible that any one excerpt-association rising into conscious awareness is a function of so many inter-related factors. The particular thought at hand, reflecting a particular struction, representing a particular context, coupled with a particular, historically based emotional concern as I enter this situation, along with my particular biological/emotional experiencing of the moment, within a genetically and developmentally determined neuronal circuitry among the small minds of my brain, all occurring within the larger, culturally and personally determined linguistic realities (among others) of my past and present, come together all at once to determine the specific excerpt-associations rising into my conscious awareness at this instant. Wow!

### *Hypnosis, Trance, Dissociation, Amnesia, and the Ideodynamic Principle*

The theoretical underpinnings of Ericksonian hypnosis represent common sense, everyday understandings of human functioning. A basic summary of this unique type of hypnosis can help us highlight the relationship between conscious and unconscious functioning and what we do and do not control among our thoughts, emotions, and behaviors.

Clinical hypnosis has been revolutionized over the last twenty years or so. The understandings of the human mind are much more common-sense-based in the theory and practice of a great number of contemporary hypnotherapists than ever before. The one man most responsible for this revolution in hypnosis is Milton Erickson.

While alive, Dr. Erickson acquired a great following of treatment providers who became extremely impressed with his understandings of human nature, his expertise in the practice of hypnosis, and with the amazing results he helped others achieve in their work with him. Before Dr. Erickson died, a number of his followers, especially Ernest Rossi, worked extremely hard to help him explicate his understandings of human beings and his theory and practice of hypnotherapy.

Generally, for Erickson and most other hypnotists, helping the client experience a trance state is a prerequisite to helping him or her hypnotherapeutically. In addition, Erickson (1985) believed a trance is not unique to hypnosis as an altered state of awareness. Instead, he believed that all of us experience a "common everyday trance" intermittently throughout any given day.

According to Rossi (Erickson, Rossi, & Rossi, 1976), Erickson understands trance to be a "normal experience of everyday life that occurs naturally whenever a person becomes deeply absorbed in some internal or external reality." However, he primarily saw trance as a state of deep *internal* absorption. He defined a trance state as those intermittent periods throughout the day when we "take a break and let our minds wander" (Erickson, Rossi, & Ryan, 1985). Erickson (1976) says of trance:

> A basic aspect of trance is allowing mental processes to take place by themselves...This autonomous flow of undirected experience is a simple way of defining trance. (p. 23)

He also says (Erickson, Rossi, & Rossi, 1976), "Going into trance is like going away because you're going distant from external reality" (p. 97). Rossi (Erickson, Rossi, & Rossi, 1976) adds:

> In trance there is a reduction of the patient's foci of attention to a few inner realities; consciousness has been fixated and focused to a relatively narrow frame of attention versus being diffused over a broad area, as in the more general reality orientation...(p. 247)

Rossi says that in everyday life, consciousness is in a constant state of flux between the GRO and the momentary microdynamics of trance. Rossi adds that we are usually amnestic for these daily, intermittent, light trance periods.

Regarding the relationship between conscious and unconscious functioning and trance, Erickson (1976) states:

...Consciousness is always focal and thus limited to what is within momentary focus. It can't possibly deal with everything at once; at every moment in our lives we are dependent upon unconscious processes (to regulate everything from our blood chemistry to our next verbal association)....(p. 233)

Rossi (Erickson, Rossi, & Rossi, 1976) elaborates on this relationship as it functions in hypnosis:

Therapeutic trance can be understood as a state in which unconscious work is to some extent freed from the limiting focus and sets of consciousness. Once the unconscious has done its work, the conscious mind can receive and focus it in the various moments and circumstances of life. (p. 233)

Erickson (1976) says that when a patient in a trance tries to observe and understand by using the reflective, directing, and controlling tendencies of the conscious mind, there is interference with the process of learning by the experience of just letting things happen. In trance it is necessary to learn by experiencing versus intellectualizing. He says that "not knowing," of not having to understand and be aware of the experiencing at hand, is compatible with the essence of trance:

...which is to allow more autonomous, spontaneous responses to take place without the habitual sets of consciousness structures directing and controlling them. (p. 241)

Similarly, Rossi (Erickson, Rossi, & Rossi, 1976) states:

Trance is an active process wherein the unconscious is active but not directed by the conscious mind...In a trance state you've released the unconscious to do its own work without interference from consciousness. (pp. 138–39)

Regarding the concept and experience of hypnosis per se, Erickson (1985) defines it as a "...state of special awareness characterized by a receptiveness to ideas." He says that in the hypnotic trance:

> ...you would listen to me; and you would merely listen to the ideas that I presented...you would give your full, conscious attention solely and simply to the ideas being presented. (p. 225)

He adds:

> ...it is a state of special awareness, of special receptiveness to ideas, of special willingness to examine ideas for their inherent values. (p. 224)

Erickson (1976) believed that all hypnotic techniques are centered primarily around directing the patient's attention to within himself. Consistent with this, Rossi says the purpose of trance induction is to reduce the foci of attention to a few inner realities. It also facilitates alterations in subjects' habitual patterns of direction and control, while facilitating receptivity to their own inner associations and mental skills, which can then be integrated into therapeutic responses. This is accomplished, he says, when Erickson tells a patient to sit a certain way, focus on a spot, and remain quiet while he talks. He then embarks on a train of associations that will help the patient focus attention inward on memories, feelings, associations, developmental patterns, and learning experiences. In this, Rossi states, Erickson is not so much suggesting (as in putting something in a patient's mind) as he is evoking. The effectiveness of his words is in their calculated design to evoke preexisting patterns of association and natural mental processes.

This evoking of pre-existing patterns of association and natural mental processes relates to Erickson's (1976) *ideodynamic principle* of hypnosis. In essence, this principle reflects the reality that a verbal description of a life situation tends to evoke some psycho-neuro-physiological experience of it inside the person attentively listening to that description. This principle is very tied to Gazzaniga's research, which indicates that given the right set of physical stimuli in the right context, one may have a strong, unconscious potential to respond in a particular way. This is a function of "autonomously functioning brain modules of experiential knowledge" that are activated by such contextual stimuli.

I've indicated that a thought can represent or stand for a specific context representing a specific, interrelated set of stimuli. Consequently, such a thought has the potential to evoke certain associated reactions from the depths of one's subconscious mind because it stands for particular, real-life contexts. It can activate an autonomous, unconscious module of stored experiential knowledge relevant to particular stimuli, settings, or contexts represented by the thought. For example, if a good friend is earnestly describing a sexual encounter she once had, you might find yourself becoming sexually aroused in response. To become aroused, certain experientially based memory associations (embodied in excerpts) must have been activated inside of you as a strict function of your own history of sexual encounters. As another example, if Erickson wanted to help a tense person relax, he might allude to the experiences of warmth, comfort, and coziness, because doing so automatically and unconsciously activates associated, relaxing, mind-body memories and experiences within that person. If Erickson wanted to help a person lessen their chronic pain experience, he might share an anecdote about the experience of losing a toothache on the way to the dentist's office. He trusted that components of the described experience would be activated within the person at hand and could be utilized in a helpful manner.

Another frequently discussed experiential concept in hypnotherapeutic circles is that of *dissociation*. In general terms, dissociation reflects where one's conscious awareness is and is not. When a hypnotic subject allows his awareness to focus away from, and hence, to temporarily "forget" his surroundings and what he's doing in favor of responding to internal, imaginal/conceptual realities, he is dissociated from the external realities in favor of the internal ones. Similarly, if a woman is so absorbed in an exciting movie that she is no longer aware of her chronic pain, she is dissociated from that pain. In addition, if a person consciously believes he is not feeling angry when, in fact, his teeth are clenched, his face is red, and his fists are tight, he is dissociated from his feelings of anger. And, as we've already seen, if I ask a friend a question during a conversation, he will unconsciously engage in an extremely fast internal search so to respond to it, as reflected externally by eye-accessing cues, such as a quick darting of the eyes up and to the left (the excerpting instant). During this brief accessing period, he is literally dissociated from me and his surroundings without even knowing it. Thus, there are many instances of dissociation occurring throughout the course of each day, leaving us unaware of certain aspects of experience in favor of other, just as present aspects of experience.

An experience and hypnotherapeutic concept that is often a function of dissociation is that of *amnesia*. Following a hypnotic trance experience, the subject is often amnestic for much of what he or she experienced during the trance. Amnesia is basically a function of the relative absence of a reflecting awareness during trance, which might otherwise be taking some of the experiential flow at hand as an object of attention. In other words, during hypnosis, the subject is so absorbed in the experiential (elaborative) flow, that he or she will likely be amnestic for much of it.

Erickson had a number of methods for facilitating amnesia so the limiting biases and beliefs of one's reflective, conscious mind wouldn't undo, doubt, or somehow interfere with the unconscious trance experiencing during the hypnotic encounter. For example, as soon as the person reoriented to herself and her surroundings following a trance, he might immediately ask her what she had for breakfast that morning as a way to prevent her from reflecting on the trance experience that just unfolded.

Like dissociation, Erickson saw amnesia as a common, everyday human experience which is a function of typical states of consciousness that simply preclude a reflective kind of experiencing. I have called such states elaborative thinking and experiencing.

In general then, trance, hypnosis, dissociation, and amnesia are very overlapping conceptual and experiential realities. All four involve the manipulation of the direction of one's attention to particular objects or aspects of experience. In addition, their experiential character hinges on the depth of one's absorption and responsiveness to the objects of attention at hand. Last, Erickson views these experiential realities as not unique to the hypnotic context per se, but as a part of day-to-day functioning.

Having defined and discussed some core concepts and experiential realities of hypnosis, and hence, of everyday living, I would like to note that the trance experience is synonymous with the experiences of elaborative experiencing and thinking. Thus, during trance or during elaborative experiencing and thinking, you are completely absorbed in the images, sounds, feelings, and thoughts that are unfolding as a simultaneous whole in each successive instant. Your consciousness embodies those stimuli in each given instant. There is no experience of a reflective attention at work, resulting in a consciousness of you in relation to your present experiencing.

In contrast to unconscious or trance experiencing (elaborative experiencing and thinking) is conscious experiencing (reflective experiencing and thinking). Regarding the relationship between trance and conscious experiencing Rossi (Erickson, Rossi, & Ryan, 1985) states:

> the conscious mind is usually present with varying degrees of focus and continuity as a calm witness to some of the inner experiences that are taking place during trance. (p. 247)

Thus, consistent with Erickson's belief that hypnotic states are part of our day-to-day states of consciousness is his belief that our conscious mind is present with varying degrees of focus and continuity during hypnosis and moments of our daily experiencing.

In relation to hypnosis, Erickson (1976) believed that the more the conscious mind is present, focused on, and observing the trance experiencing at hand, the more interference it causes in the natural course the unfolding experiencing might otherwise take. As a result, Erickson utilized a number of hypnotic techniques to help get the hypnotic subject's conscious mind out of the way so that its controlling and directing tendencies wouldn't interfere with the trance experiencing at hand. If he succeeded in this task, the activities of the subject's conscious mind gave way to complete absorption into and as the natural, unfolding, internal, experiential flow at hand.

Likewise, it's common for your reflecting awareness to interfere with or interrupt your performance during elaborative experiencing, while deeply absorbed in playing a sport or a musical instrument, for example. This interference is consistent with the fact that reflective experiencing/thinking and elaborative experiencing/thinking mutually exclude one another phenomenally. In other words, when one is phenomenally "on," the other is phenomenally "off." There is little-to-no phenomenal access between these two sets of experiential realities in their extreme forms. Thus, during trance, I can be so elaboratively absorbed in the experiencing at hand, I'm dissociated from (not attending to) all other potential objects and aspects of awareness, including the experiencing itself. In addition, following such a trance, I am amnestic to much of it because the elaborative phenomenology therein precluded the reflective phenomenology that would have allowed me to objectify that experiencing so as to be able to recall much of it later. In other words, there are few if any excerpts of it for me to access.

Erickson's ideodynamic principle reflects, in part, the experiential reality that Gazzaniga finds research support for neurologically: certain physical contexts stimulate unconscious and autonomously functioning brain modules "carrying" stored emotional and experiential knowledge associated with those contexts. Erickson's ideodynamic principle also reflects the fact that language, or our ability to conceptually represent any situation, can serve as a potent stimulus for recall of memories (excerpts) associated with a given situation.

Much like Erickson's description and comparison of a dream to a trance experience, one's experience of an elaboratively connected series of thoughts might be like walking down a long corridor with ceilings and walls covered with paintings in which I become completely absorbed. Likewise, my elaboratively connected thoughts serve as contextual and experientially based constraints for what I will experience as I am fully absorbed in their unfolding elaborative flow. In contrast, to reflect on the fact that I am thinking about something just now is tantamount to instantly interrupting, on a phenomenal basis, that natural, absorbing, elaborative, experiential flow.

This general discussion about the parallels between hypnotic states of consciousness and those occurring in the course of our lives further clarifies the fact that we consciously control and determine very little of our daily mental experience. In addition, highlighting the experiential concepts of trance, hypnosis, the conscious mind, dissociation, amnesia, and the ideodynamic principle helps us better understand the experiential realities and relationships between the elaborative and reflective forms of experiencing and thinking.

### *Lightning and Thought*

To end this chapter, I would like to take another, more global look at the action of thinking by comparing it to a lightning bolt. This lightning bolt metaphor holds fascinating parallels to certain realities of the thinking process discussed thus far.

As you may already know, clouds are formed as water evaporates from lakes, rivers, oceans, and the like. Once in the air, tiny water droplets begin to collect or condense, thereby forming clouds. As a function of air currents, pressure, and temperature variables, a cloud can billow or rise, causing water droplets within it at the higher, cooler levels of the atmosphere to turn into ice. As this occurs, rising ice crystals within the cloud collide with heavier, falling hailstones. These hailstones strip electrons from the ice crystals. Consequently, the top of the cloud becomes positively charged while the bottom of the cloud becomes negatively charged. This negative charge at the lower portion of the cloud induces a positively charged region on the earth below. The interplay between the charges of the lower cloud and the ground below causes a buildup of static electricity. From this buildup, a negative spark or "step-leader," consisting of a negative stream of electrons, is launched from the lower part of the cloud. This descending spark creates jagged, branched channels, which then triggers an upward positive spark sprouting like a weed from the ground. When the downward and upward streamers meet, their paths form a channel for the lightning bolt we see. The bolt itself spreads in both directions along the channel, superheating the air around it and creating shock waves that produce thunder. As the bolt ends, discharges in the cloud called streamers, sometimes reach toward the channel, initiating a second "return" bolt, accounting for the flashes of lightning we sometimes see in the same place (William, 1993).

The interesting thing about the formation of lightning is that we cannot see most of the action leading up to the visible lightning bolt itself. To us, it seems as if lightning is a single event of a visible bolt darting to the ground. In reality though, there's an invisible, negative electron stream moving out of the clouds as well as an invisible, positive electron stream rising from the ground. Both are preludes to a visible lightning bolt when they meet and spread in both directions, up and down the channel.

There are a number of metaphorical parallels between how a particular lightning bolt occurs and how a particular thought occurs. For one, the physical conditions producing the cloud itself are a necessary prelude to the potential occurrence of a particular lightning bolt. In the same way, there are certain necessary conditions of my physical/emotional self in relation to the particular situation at hand which serve as a prelude to the potential occurrence of a particular thought. In each case, the conditions have to be very specific before a particular manifestation of those conditions can occur. As stated above, the negatively charged lower part of the cloud induces an associated, positively charged region on the earth below. Similarly, the struction or thought at hand represents a particular stimulus situation that activates a subconscious region of response potential related to the thought. The struction or thought is like an attention-headed "step-leader" striking out, as if searching for some potential excerpt-association, which, like a positive streamer, is rising toward it from the subconscious region below. In the same way that I can't see the negative or positive streamers as a prelude to a lightning bolt, I can't see or am not conscious of the initial action of attention searching for an excerpt (excerpt-searching reaction), or the action of attention finding that excerpt (the excerpting instant).

Moreover, in the same way the lightning bolt becomes visible as the positive and negative streamers meet and spread across the entire channel, so too does a reactively identified excerpt become visible to my awareness once my attention moves away from it while reflectively reacting to it (the reflective conceptual portion of the thought).

Last, as a result of and following the lightning bolt, there are streamer discharges in the cloud that can reach toward the remaining electron channel, initiating a second "return" bolt. Similarly, following the end of a particular thought, the meaningful nuances of that thought (coupled with "background" factors) can prompt attention to move toward a related excerpt-association, thereby initiating a "return" or thematically related thought.

In this chapter, we addressed the fact that the conscious self-sense believes that it is responsible and present for all choices, decisions, actions, and thoughts. These activities occur in relation to the contents of excerpted objects, from which awareness stretches and looks toward, thereby experiencing itself as the separate author of them. Yet, this self-sense knows only the experience of existing to itself, thereby assuming that it is the always present, independent author and determiner of all of "its" activities. But it isn't conscious of the times when these activities are occurring in its absence. In addition, it only exists (to itself) at that juncture where awareness is separating from the content of an excerpted object. It's unaware of every other part of the thought process, and during every elaborative thought and experience. Thus, this self-sense is not responsible for all of these activities because they can occur in its absence. It's not even responsible for or the owner of the only "part" of the stream of mental events of which it is ever aware: the content of the excerpted object. Instead, as this chapter delineated, many factors play a responsible role in the arrival and nature of the excerpt-associations rising into awareness.

At the end of the present chapter, our discussion of Ericksonian hypnosis highlighted the nature of the relationship between the conscious self and all of the unconsciously determined contents of awareness that come into the view of that self. Last, the metaphor of the physics of a lightning bolt helped clarify the relationship between conscious and unconscious processes and phenomenologies embodied in thoughts.

In chapter 7, we begin to challenge the illusion that an independent self can be separate from experiences and objects. The foundation of this challenge will be based on the elaborative character of all experience. The reality of an elaborative phenomenology inherent to reflective thoughts will then be generalized to our relationship to objects in the environment. Do you think it's possible that you are never experientially separate from any of your surroundings? Chapter Seven addresses this insight, perhaps one of the most profound of your life.

# Chapter Seven: The Embodiments of Consciousness

I N THIS CHAPTER WE explore the reality that reflective thinking is also elaborative thinking. You may feel confused by this
statement, given all of the effort to establish their differences
thus far. Hopefully, with further discussion, the confusion will
dissipate, clearing the way to important ramifications regarding
the illusory nature of the thought-induced, separate self-sense
split off from experience.

Understanding that reflective thinking embodies reflective
and elaborative phenomenologies is, for example, consistent with
the structure of thinking outlined earlier: specifically, reflective
thoughts consist of both *proactive* and reactive excerpt-found reactions. In other words, because proactive excerpt-found reactions
largely determine the phenomenology of elaborative thoughts,
their presence in reflective thoughts partly determine the elaborative phenomenology therein.

In the remainder of this chapter, the reality that reflective
thinking is also elaborative is extended to the illusory experience of being a separate entity in relation to your surroundings.
The impact of this insight may be so profound that the way you
experience yourself and the world will change forever. But first,
to facilitate a discussion regarding the differences and similarities
between elaborative and reflective thoughts we need to better understand the relationship between the contents of consciousness
and awareness of consciousness.

What does one's consciousness consist of experientially? In
other words, what does one's general, mental experiencing consist of in any given instant. David Chalmers' distinction between
awareness and consciousness can help us think about consciousness in its general, experiential sense. In his book *The Conscious
Mind: In Search of a Fundamental Theory,* Chalmers (1996)

defines consciousness as the subjective quality of experience. It is the internal aspect regarding what it is like to be a knowing agent. He says that a mental state exists in consciousness if it has a qualitative or subjective feel. Such subjective qualities of mind are synonymous with one's phenomenology. For example, there is a specific experiential quality or phenomenology regarding what it's like to think. That phenomenology exists in consciousness. In addition, there is a unique experiential quality to visual, auditory, olfactory, gustatory, kinesthetic, mental, and emotional experiences.

In contrast to the general, experiential aspects of consciousness, Chalmers indicates that someone is conscious of something when they are paying attention to it. Attention is a particularly high degree of awareness of an object or event and is accompanied by a phenomenal component as well. Attention can be defined in functional terms whereby a significant portion of one's cognitive resources is directed to a specific object

Chalmers equates the experience of awareness with consciousness. He defines awareness as the functional equivalent of consciousness. In other words, awareness is the psychological or functional correlate of consciousness where some information is directly accessible and available for deliberate control of behavior and verbal report. We are aware of some information when that information is directly available for a wide range of behavioral processes which serve a functional purpose. In contrast, consciousness is considered as the phenomenological aspect of awareness, rather than serving a potentially functional role.

Chalmers says that the *contents* of awareness consist of *first-order phenomenal registrations* that are directly available for use in directing behavior. For example, when we hear a musical note there is an accompanying psychological state concerning that musical note. That state can also be characterized as a content-bearing cognitive state, a state of contents that are implicit, phenomenal "knowings." Chalmers says that during the sensory-perceptual experience of a red book, for example, there is a corresponding first-order phenomenal registration of the red book.

These first-order phenomenal registrations are states represented in awareness that, for example, correspond to every detail in an experienced visual field. There is some kind of cognitive state carrying the relevant visual information, evidenced by the fact that the information is at least available to the purpose at hand because he or she can verbalize it, for example. However, a first-order phenomenal registration need not be conceptualized or verbalized by the person. Nevertheless, it is a content-laden mental state that is potentially available to that person.

According to Chalmers, first-order phenomenal registrations are the contents of perceptual states. For example, my visual experience of a glass on the table is accompanied by a functional perception of the glass. Optical stimulation is processed and transformed by my perceptual system which *registers* that object. Each detail of what is experienced is represented in awareness as some form of knowing. To see that each detail must be so represented is evidenced by my ability to comment on those details and direct my behavior in ways that depend on them. I can point to appropriate parts of the glass. Such systematic availability of information implies the existence of an *internal state carrying that content*. This mental state is a first-order phenomenal registration.

Sogyal Rinpoche (1993) says that consciousness has the capacity to reflect in precise detail whatever comes before it. Buddhist spiritual teachers sometimes compare consciousness to a mirror. In this sense, all things reflected in the mirror of consciousness at any given moment are first-order phenomenal registrations.

In contrast to first-order phenomenal registrations *second-order phenomenal registrations* are *about* consciousness. Chalmers says that when I have a sensation of redness, I sometimes *notice* that I am *experiencing* that sensation. If I have an itch, sometimes I notice that I'm *experiencing* the itch. For any object or aspect of experience represented in consciousness, I have the capacity to become conscious *of* the experience. Chalmers says that although we have the ability to notice our experiences, most of the time we notice only the *contents* of the experience.

Similar to the differences between first-order and second-order phenomenal registrations, is the distinction between unattended-to-knowings and attended-to-knowings. Bruce Ecker and Laurel Hulley (1996) indicate that Bateson's (Bateson, 1972, 1979) and Maturana's (1980) biological theories emphasize that all activity of the psyche is epistemological or a "whole-being embodiment of knowing." They say that all human psychological activity reflects an experience of knowing that occurs with or without the involvement of the conscious "I." In their view, these changing experiential knowings, when left unattended to by the conscious "I," are called unattended-to-knowings. Furthermore, such unattended-to-knowings proceed autonomously. In addition, to say that an emotional, cognitive, or somatic item is unconscious means that the knowing constituted by this item is present in consciousness without the metalevel awareness or the conscious, verbal "I" attending to it. Such unattended-to-knowings are essentially equivalent to first-order phenomenal registrations. In contrast, to say that one is conscious *of* an item means that the person knows the knowing constituted by the item. This is a metaknowing. In other words, she has attended to the *experience* of a particular knowing, transforming it into an attended-to-knowing or second-order phenomenal registration.

### Reflective Phenomenology Overlays Elaborative Phenomenology

The distinctions between first and second-order phenomenal registrations, and their respective counterparts, unattended-to and attended-to-knowings, help clarify a very complicated relationship between elaborative and reflective experiencing and thinking, respectively, and hence between unconscious and conscious phenomenologies, respectively. Remember, during elaborative phenomenology, you lack an awareness of yourself as a seemingly freestanding entity because your awareness combines with the experiencing at hand, resulting in a phenomenology that is much like dreaming. Whereas during reflective phenomenology, you experience (more or less) being a self-experiencer who "has" self-experiences as separate objects. Very suddenly then, during reflective thinking and experiencing, there's an actor on the stage being conscious of himself acting. Hence, there seem to be two actors. Whereas, during elaborative thinking and experiencing, the actor isn't at all self-conscious; he simply lives the part he is playing as a single experiential entity without any self-awareness.

During elaborative experiencing, my consciousness is the embodiment of some experiential knowing: the knowing illuminating and illuminated by my awareness. For example, the red book I attend to is the knowing illuminating and illuminated by my awareness (first-order phenomenal registration or unattended-to-knowing). During reflective experiencing, my consciousness is the embodiment of knowing *about* some experiential knowing. I'm aware of my experience of seeing the red book (second-order phenomenal registration or an attended-to-knowing).

During the various types of reflective thinking, my consciousness is the embodiment of a separating awareness and unfolding thought-self that is being more (CRT) or less (ERI) aware of itself as such, in relationship to an apparently present, separate, objectified thought-self, of which it is also aware. My experience of being a separating, knowing self occurs as a function of this duality of awareness between two apparently present forms of self-experiencing. My sense of self-awareness as a witnessing self (implicit or explicit) is created by the action of a present, separating, subjective, knowing-self, which is experiencing itself in relation to an objectified, excerpted thought about something else. The subjective thinking-self experiences itself as both separate from, and yet, identified with the *object* of itself as another apparent form of self-experiencing.

Despite the apparent distinctiveness between elaborative and reflective experiencing and thinking, I believe that reflective experiencing and thinking are also elaborative because one cannot be conscious *of* them in the immediacy of their occurrence. For example, the inherent elaborativeness of all experiencing exists because as soon as I turn my attention to some aspect of it to become conscious *of* it, there's the experience of doing just this of which I am presently not conscious. For instance, when I reflect on and become aware of the "passing thought" about my date tonight, I cannot be conscious of the *act* of that awareness in the same instant. During any attempt to become conscious of something, it must be objectified, and the very act of attending to that object precludes objectification of the act itself. Thus, during any attempt to become objectively aware of the present moment, one loses sight of the *act* of that objectification. The witnessing instant, bound to the absolute present, is forever elusive and unconscious because the witness that attempts to capture or *objectify* itself still needs itself to do that witnessing. Therefore, the immediate actions of elaborative and reflective thinking and experiencing are always unconscious in this sense because the absolute present cannot be captured by being *objectified.*

Thus, when taking thought as an object of attention, as in reflective thinking, one experiences a phenomenology of being conscious of it. And yet, there's the experience of doing just this of which one isn't *presently* conscious. Therefore, all thinking and experiencing has an unconscious (or elaborative) character in that one cannot be conscious *of* its witnessing aspect in the immediacy of its occurrence. Consequently, during reflective thinking and experiencing, an inherent elaborative phenomenology is overlapped or dominated by a reflective phenomenology.

This unconscious, elaborative aspect of reflective thinking seems to belie your experience as a separate entity split off from observed experiences (of self). The truth embodied in this elaborative aspect is that the phenomenology of a duality of experiencing is actually a single experience. Your awareness of two sets of experiences is really one experience. In other words, when you're construing yourself as a separate experiencer "having" an observed experience, you're unaware of being absorbed in *this* single experience while it's occurring (especially prior to the stage of VL). Therefore, you as an experiencer are never separate from any experience, even though it may seem this way given that you feel separate from the object of attention at hand. At bottom, the experience, "I'm separate from that," is one experience.

Metaphorically, during elaborative thinking and experiencing it's as if the object of your attention is a light on which the light of your awareness also shines. The emanating and lluminating lights from you and the object combine, becoming one, in the immediacy of your awareness. The combined oneness of the illuminating lights constitute the experiential form the object takes "in" your awareness, whereas during reflective thinking and experiencing, it's as if *the object* of your shining attention is a light *and* a mirror. Thus, in the act of attending to the object, you witness yourself mirrored in it, resulting in an awareness of yourself in a seemingly separate relationship to it, creating a duality of experiencing. However, the illuminating lights from you and the object, resulting in the phenomenology of a duality of experiencing, are still combining, becoming one in the immediacy of your awareness. Thus, that emergent phenomenology of a seeming duality, which occurs during reflective thinking and experiencing, is actually one experience, consistent with an elaborative phenomenology. Nonetheless, that emergent, reflective, duality of experiencing phenomenally overlays and dominates the elaborative one.

One brief aside: earlier we discussed the fact that CRT and TRI are forms of reflective thinking *and* experiencing. During the onset of the reflective conceptual portions of CRT and TRI, as I become explicitly *aware* of the excerptively clipped identity and presence *of the "passing thought,"* I'm also *aware of* being *an observing, separating awareness.* Thus, during these forms of reflective thinking, where the phenomenology of duality is at hand, reflective *experiencing* is also occurring. As I'm objectifying the "passing thought," I fleetingly observe the separating, witnessing *experiencing* as it's occurring. In other words, for an instant, I am witnessing the witness. Can this be possible? After all, we just acknowledged that whenever the witness tries to see itself (in a certain form), it always remains elusively outside that reality of objectification. Well, in the same way that I can witness and become explicitly aware of running backward from a specific object of which I'm also aware without interrupting the running, I can fleetingly witness and become explicitly aware of *separating* from a thought-object of which I'm also aware without interrupting the separating. Thus, during CRT and TRI, we're fleetingly attending to, and hence, *aware of* being a separating witness (of a "passing thought-object"). And yes, because we can't objectify this (italicized) act of witnessing in that instant, the always immediate witness continues to elude us, but barely. We're about as *objectively* close to the subjective and immediately-bound witness as we're going to get, and we're damn close! In truth, however, the witness can only be experienced as subjectively lived.

In chapter 2, it was indicated that the most prominent, defining structural feature of elaborative thoughts is the proactive excerpt-found reaction. By definition, the proactive excerpt-found reaction results in implicitly knowing the identity of an excerpt at the instant it appears to awareness (as an unattended-to-knowing) at the onset of thought. The meaningful nuances at the tail-end of one thought give rise to the excerpt, which awareness embodies as it appears in its entirety. The evolution and identity of the excerpt is fully available to awareness at the instant of its appearance because awareness assumes its "preceived," then "infantile," and then fully matured forms.

The fact that awareness embodies the proactively identified excerpt throughout its evolution explains why its meaningful significance is accounted for by the elaborative thought stemming from it: awareness knows its identity as lived and takes into account the excerpt's meaningful significance. That elaborative thought is a reaction and implicit response *to* the excerpt's content. Consequently, the proactive excerpt-found reaction largely determines the forward moving, progressive nature and elaborative phenomenology of elaborative thoughts. In other words, without proactively generated excerpts, general elaborative thoughts would not exist because they could not proceed in a relatively autonomous and progressive fashion.

In chapter 2, elaborative thoughts were said to consist of proactive excerpt-found reactions, while reflective thoughts consist of both proactive and reactive excerpt-found reactions. The present chapter has so far revealed that reflective thoughts are also elaborative, although an emergent reflective phenomenology overlays and obscures the elaborative one. This revelation is based on the observation that all experience is inherently elaborative in nature because the witnessing awareness can't successfully and completely objectify itself; it can't really split itself in two.

Regarding its "parts," the emergent reflective phenomenology of a reflective thought is initially engendered when a reactive excerpt-found reaction attends to the *proactively identified, appearing excerpt*. The reactive excerpt-found reaction results in a prolonged attention to and unfolding explicit awareness of the proactively apparent identity of the excerpt. The proactively identified excerpt is initially an unattended-to-knowing embodying implicit content. Whereas, the reactive excerpt-found reaction embodies an *unfolding* knowing of that knowing (an attended-to-knowing); awareness stretches away from, reacts to, and knows the content of that initial, implicit, proactively excerpted and idnetified embodiment of knowing. Thus, the reactive excerpt-found reaction is *manifesting* itself as a second, more explicit knowing. Then, when attention objectifies that reactive excerpt-found reaction at the outset of the reflective conceptual portion of the reflective thought, a second excerpt is established, a reactively identified one which embodies *explicit* content. During this portion of the thought, an objectified, explicit knowledge exists to awareness, in response to which the thought proper unfolds, rendering the experience of an attended-to-knowing. That thought is a reaction *about* and response to the excerpt's explicitly identified content.

Thus, the reactive excerpt-found reactions facilitate the ability to "look back on" and identify "passing thoughts," contributing to the reflective phenomenologies of temporarily stopping thinking (or so it seems), of looking backwards (so it seems), and of self-awareness (so it seems). And now that we have revisited the "parts" of elaborative and reflective thoughts, we can highlight the fact that general elaborative thoughts could not occur without the proactively identified excerpts, which literally determine and facilitate the forward moving progression and elaboration of thought. Moreover, even though the reactively identified excerptive-clip of the "passing thought" engenders (at the outset of reflective thoughts) the phenomenology of a duality of experience, of looking backwards, and of temporarily stopping thought, *that reactively identified excerpt emerged "out" of, but still includes, a proactively identified one*, the nature of which yields a forward moving, progressive elaboration of thought.

In other words, the reactively identified excerpt embodies reflective phenomenologies which dominate, obscure, and distort the elaborative phenomenology of its essence as a proactively-based excerpt. Thus, the second "reason" why reflective thoughts are partly elaborative in nature is because they embody proactively generated and identified excerpts (the hallmark of general elaborative thoughts), from which emerge reactively identified excerpts.

### Human-Laden Reality

For centuries there has been a philosophical debate as to the existence of a world that is independent of the mind. In general, those who believe in an independent world are "realists" and the opposite are "idealists." In the purely idealist school, things are believed to exist only when perceived and dissolve when they are not. A less absolute version of idealism posits the existence of a world independent from mind, but suggests that the mind determines its perceptual particularities (Paranjpe, 1998). This moderate form of idealism is represented in the beliefs described below.

I believe that the inherent elaborativeness of all mental experiencing holds true in your experience of external objects as well. Yet, your experience of duality, of experiencing yourself as separate from the objects *around you*, seems to be an absolute truth of existence. I believe, however, that during all *experience*, by attending to an object, that object combines with your literal presence as a human being. Awareness brings form, color, texture, taste, and sound to that object as a strict function of your unique physical-sensory-perceptual presence. In other words, all of what you attend to in the world is literally human-laden. It doesn't exist in and of itself *as you experience it*. Instead, via your awareness, it manifests itself through your living, physical presence. Experientially, you transform all of reality into human form. Thus, whenever you're focusing on a particular object, *experientially*, you are "in" that object as much as that object is "in" you. It is as much a part of you as you are a part of it. You become that object as much as it becomes you. In a very real sense, that object is enlivened through your biological presence. It is manifested through you. Thus, during all *experiencing*, you and the object of your attention become each other as one *experience*, which is only occurring exactly where *you* are. No attended-to-object is ever separate from your *experience* of it.

For instance, I only know intellectually that the tree I see over there is an entirely separate entity from me. But, in my literal experiencing of the tree, I am never separate from it. The light reflected off the tree is entering my eyes and accounts for, in part, my experience of the tree. The tree light is here, *on* and *in* me. Thus, my experience of the tree (whether through sight, sound, touch, smell, or taste) is occurring right here with me, at the boundary of my skin and below. Experientially there is never any "over there" to the tree. The tree (or tree light) is only over here with and as me. This is true for my every experience, of everything, at every time.

Similarly, the bird I hear singing on the fence outside is causing the air around it to vibrate at a certain frequency. Those air vibrations entering my ears are being transformed into electro-chemical impulses which are then interpreted and experienced as sound in the temporal lobes of my brain. The bird's song and my experience of that song are combining as one form, right here, with and as me. Because I experience everything through my eyes, ears, nose, tongue, and skin, which manifest in my awareness or consciousness, all of it is right here with me. See K. Wilber (1979), Da Free John (1983), and S. Rinpoche (1993) for similar discussions.

It's amazing that when I stand outside and feel the warmth of the sun on my face, it's literally *part* of the sun *on* my face. When I glance at the sun, the sun I see is the light from the "older" sun that's hitting my face and eyes at this instant. The light leaving the surface of the "truer" sun right now is actually 8.3 minutes away. Thus, the "old" sun I see right now is literally on my eyes and its light is transduced into perceptual information in my brain, resulting in the appearance of the sun I presently see.

This reality about the sun holds true for the stars and gal-axies in the outer reaches of the universe. The Hubble Space Telescope has allowed us to see stars that are billions of years old (Newcott, 1977). The light from a given star hitting the telescope's lens left its surface, for example, 10 billion years ago. It is old light hitting the telescope, and hence, the observer is seeing that star as it looked 10 billion years ago. If we wanted to see that star as it appears now, we'd have to wait 10 billion more years for the light presently leaving its surface to reach us.

Consistent with this reality about stars and galaxies, the light being reflected off of all the objects in the landscape around me is responsible for, in part, my visual experience of them. It's "old" light reflected from those objects around me reaching my eyes. I'm experiencing some visual reflection or reverberation of the object's "essence" as a function of certain physical light-related properties of the object which I then register.

Furthermore, I can't ever experience any object in its (hypothetical) essence because I can't keep myself out of the equation in my experience of it. For example, it's not that there is a blue flower over there that I can then experience as a blue flower from over here. Aspects of the flower reflected in physical stimuli moving away from it land on me, and I transform that stimuli into the *living experience of seeing* a blue flower.

Thus, we're never seeing things the way they supposedly "are"; the way we see them is partly a function of the way we are. The object, the light reflected off of it, and my physical-sensory-perceptual presence in relationship to them, combine and interact at the boundary of my skin and below, resulting in my visual experience of the object.

These physical-sensory-perceptual descriptions of experience seem quite consistent with a portion of S. N. Dasgutpa's (1975) overview of the Sankara school of Advaita Vedanta. According to Paranjpe (1998), Dasgutpa says that the mind reaches out to objects in the environment through the senses and becomes transformed into their shapes. It tries to know them by being transformed into them. The mind, as pure consciousness, illuminates and is illuminated by the world of objects.

In sum, whether you're gazing at stars or your mother's morning glories, it's old light from them penetrating your eyes. As objects, they are manifested and enlivened through and as your living experience. Your experience of any object is a function of your unique presence as a living creature and of the physical properties of the object, which result in some physical stimuli directly related to the object impinging on and in you. The hypothetical "actual" object, in its hypothetical entirety, is absolutely unattainable to you. Yet, somehow you think of an object as having its own preordained, particular, and inherent experiential reality. Somehow you're supposed to have an experience of it that exactly matches its so-called, particular, inherent, experiential reality, in your so-called, entirely separate relationship from it. In actuality, you can't ever separate yourself out of the equation in your relationship to the object. You can never know it as it is to itself because you're imbuing it with who you are. In turn, your experience of any given object is, in part, a function of the physical stimuli somehow related to the object landing on you. Thus, yours is always a single experience despite the apparent reality of the seeming duality of separateness between you, the self-experiencer, and it, the object of experiencing.

The metaphor of a mirror for consciousness is elegant, but it is misleading in one major respect. The notion that consciousness has the capacity to reflect whatever comes before it suggests that an inherent reality exists regarding the appearance of things that consciousness then reflects perfectly. This belief in an inherent reality in our surroundings is what most of us assume to be true. As stated above, however, this belief, in my opinion, underestimates the role of consciousness in the appearance of reality.

It may be more accurate to think of the physical-sensory-perceptual body-mind as a film projector and the physical stimuli from the surroundings as the film. In essence, these physical stimuli enter into and run through you much like film into a projector. The visual display in front of you is literally the projection of your consciousness. The physical stimuli are now human-laden and take the experiential form of the projected display wherever you direct your gaze. As the film projector, you are turning on, creating, and largely responsible for the visual appearance in front of you. If you were the last person on earth who died, the particular human (experiential) form that the world took would also die, forever. The world would be left to appear as it does for elephants, mice, dogs, birds, cats, ants, and cockroaches.

Thus, during thought and interactions with the sensory world, there is never a moment of being separate from any experience. Sometimes, during reflective thinking, the awareness observing and stretching away from an excerpted thought remembers its experience as reflected there, while recognizing its present experience is no longer that. The contrast between here and there engenders the sense of being an independent entity that "has" separate experiences. This witness of the excerpted thought is aware only of the apparent splitting of experience, and cannot observe, in the same instant, that this splitting is the embodiment of one, whole unbroken experience. The witnessing act cannot be aware of itself *as one experience* while observing the apparent splitting of experience.

Similarly, intellectually I know that I am separate from the birds I see in the yard, but experientially, I am never separate from them. I am the experience of hearing and seeing them. I cannot separate the experience of me over here from the experience of them over there. We are one experience.

The fact that you are always the embodiment of all that you experience is a profound insight, one that intimately connects you with all stimulus forms. Such forms combine with and are enlivened through you as function of your sentient presence. No more you apart from everything else, experientially. There is nothing untouched and undetermined by you in your experience of it. You and any "it" are always one experience. The ramifications of this insight are many and will be outlined in chapter 9.

In sum, this chapter has revealed that the contents of awareness consist of first-order phenomenal registrations. Such registrations are typically content-bearing perceptual states that represent implicit phenomenal knowings. In other words, they represent the contents of awareness, say of a red book, for example. In contrast, second-order phenomenal registrations represent the *experience* of the contents of awareness. For instance, I'm aware of looking at the red book. Similarly, unattended-to-knowings are contents present in awareness and hence are synonymous with first-order phenomenal registrations. In turn, attended-to-knowings represent an awareness of the contents of consciousness and are synonymous with second-order phenomenal registrations.

These concepts regarding the different types of knowings helped us better understand the nature of elaborative and reflective experiencing and thinking. During elaborative experiencing and thinking, awareness consists of particular contents, but one is not conscious of what they are because there is no attention to, and hence, awareness of presently experiencing them; awareness simply embodies those contents as unattended-to-knowings.

In addition, this chapter specified that there is an elaborative aspect to all experience because one cannot be conscious of the witnessing awareness in the absolute immediacy of its occurrence through attempts to objectify it. In other words, when experience itself (in the form of particular contents) is the object of awareness, that experience is an attended-to-knowing. However, the witness doing that attending cannot itself be witnessed *in that instant*, thereby highlighting the elaborative aspect of all experiencing. Moreover, when the experience being attended to is that of the separating of awareness from its object, the belief in the splitting of experience occurs; there's the apparent experience of being a witness who "has" separate experiences.

However, because the witness is focusing on the apparent splitting of experience, it cannot, in that instant, also be aware of the fact that this is, itself, one experience. The single, whole, unbroken experience of this moment is being dominated by the phenomenology of experience being split in two. Nonetheless, the elaborative nature of all experiencing exists whether it is reflective or not. This actuality was further extended to the experience of ourselves in relation to external realities.

Lastly, in this chapter we discussed the fact that reflective thinking is partly determined by the presence of the proactive excerpt-found reactions, which are the central defining components of elaborative thinking. Therefore, an elaborative phenomenology exists during reflective thoughts because reactively identified excerpts emerge out of proactively identified excerpts, and therefore embody the phenomenology inherent to the nature and function of proactively generated excerpts: to facilitate the forward moving progression of thinking. However, reactive excerpt-found reactions, which are the defining component of reflective thoughts, result in reflective phenomenologies which dominate, distort, and obscure the elaborative ones.

In chapter 8, we will define and challenge eleven illusions engendered by reflective thoughts based on what we know about their structures and phenomenologies. Specifically, the experience of being a separate entity split off from "its" experience will be exposed as an illusion. In chapter 7 it has been shown that this experience of duality is an illusion because a co-occurring elaborative phenomenology is as existent during reflective thinking as it is during all forms of experiencing; in any given instant, awareness is the embodiment of certain contents as one, unbroken experience. In chapter 8, however, the duality of a separate self split off from "its" experience is challenged as an illusion based on what we know about the component "parts" of reflective thinking. In essence, the excerpt will be exposed as the biggest culprit in this ghostly trickery of consciousness.

# Chapter Eight: Eleven Ghostly Illusions

T HE GHOSTS OF CONSCIOUSNESS are slippery, elusive, and practically invisible. They interact with us throughout the day, are an intrinsic part of our experiences, yet leave us with no awareness of their presence. They're unseen partners in our decision-making and we alone take all the credit. They're secret librarians researching the answers to questions, and in arrogant self-delusion, we pose as near geniuses.

The ghosts are mischievous, too. They love convincing us that what we witness in them is the essence of who we are, or some passing version thereof. They're the ones responsible for the illusory forms of self that we experience. They're even responsible for our belief in a unique form of time, where one self can seemingly die into a past while giving birth to a newer and better self in the present. What a bag of tricks they have!

In chapter 7, the thinking-based, illusory phenomenology of an independent self split off from "its" experience was exposed based on the understanding that all experience has an inherent elaborative character. In other words, the awareness of a splitting of experience is itself one unbroken experience. In this chapter, the phenomenology of duality is further challenged based on our knowledge of the "parts" and process aspects of thinking. In addition, we will explore how the different types of reflective thinking create illusions related to time, an objectified thought-self, a perpetual presence of self, and all the phenomenologies outlined in chapter 5, with challenges based on the structure and unfolding of thought.

The reader should note that some of the illusions addressed here are overlapping or related and that this list is not meant to be exhaustive. In addition, even though I frequently focus on ERI and CRT as examples of reflective thinking that engender specific illusions, please remember that all of the forms of reflective thought share, to various degrees and at various times, aspects of these illusory phenomenologies.

### 1. The observed thought is not the actual thought, and therefore its presence is illusory.

Because of your ability to mentally represent objects and react to them in thought, you develop the capacity to represent any given "passing thought." However, you are not turning that thought into a solidified object, like the mythic Medusa turning a living person into stone. You are creating a mental representation of thought into the form of an excerpt or snap-shot imge, and are experiencing another thought in response to it. Nevertheless, you tend to believe that you are reacting to the actual thought itself, as if capturing it alive in the grasp of your mental hand. In reality, the actual thought is gone; you have only represented it in a mental form that stands for it. By excerpting that thought, attention seems to have temporarily kept alive a thought that is dead and gone. Consequently, you, the reflecting-self, tend to construe it as an actual thought in its original form.

The "passing thought" of which we are now consciously aware exists only as an excerpt. This is the experiential form the act of thinking takes for us during reflection. In other words, we are not consciously aware of thinking in any other way. We consciously experience a thought in retrospect by reflectively transforming it into a stable (albeit brief) mental form. We experience it as a stagnant, fully formed thought-object that can be observed, but its actual presence as such is illusory.

### 2. During noncomparative reflective thinking, the thought-object being reflected on is construed as one's self, but this is an illusion.

During NCRT, while reflecting on a "passing thought," you literally construe it as the truest instance of your subjectivity. This type of reflective thinking results in an explicit, conscious awareness of self embodied in the thought-object at hand. In actuality, however, this thought is an objectified aspect of a more immediate subjective awareness subsuming it.

In NCRT, attempting to capture your subjective presence is so compelling, the thought-object and your construal of it totally dominate awareness. That thought-object fills and illuminates awareness so completely, nothing else exists for you at that time. As a result, you experience a conscious awareness of self as embodied in that thought-object, which you're conceptually reacting to and construing as a present instance of subjectivity.

However, the thought-object isn't an actual, presently occurring thought; it is an excerpt (or memory snapshot) of a thought that is now gone. Therefore, that "thought" can't embody your subjectivity (as a true thought) because it is only an objectified excerpt. Moreover, there is a reflecting awareness taking that object as its focus. But that so-called thought so dominates phenomenal experience with its presence, you are blind to the reflecting awareness taking it as its object. This reflecting, witnessing awareness is your true subjectivity, but it cannot be observed, captured, and objectified in its entirety.

### 3. Reflective thinking creates the illusory experience of a self-sense that always seems to be "on" or present.

From the vantage point of the reflecting, self or "The self who knows the self," it is always "on," here, or present. This is the self-sense engendered by reflective thinking. It always seems to be "on" because, during elaborative thinking, when "the self who knows the self" is "off," no self exists to realize it's "off." Consequently, to the reflective-thinking-engendered-self, it's "on" all the time. *It knows no other experience other than being "on."* Thus, to "the self who knows the self," it's always "on." Therefore, it would be more apt to call it "the self who knows *only* the self."

Another way of thinking about this illusion is to say that

elaborative and reflective thinking mutually exclude one another phenomenally. In other words, neither tends to know the other on a subjective, phenomenal basis. From the vantage point of the self-sense engendered by reflective thinking, there is no awareness of elaborative thinking, of thought existing as an unfolding process. It is generally only aware of thoughts as objects it seems to witness. Similarly, from the vantage point of elaborative thinking, there is no awareness of self. Such a self-sense is engendered by taking the closest thought at hand as an explicit object of attention. Since elaborative thinking never takes itself as an explicit object of attention, it doesn't even exist to itself. It simply exists as the embodiment of various contents of awareness. Thus, generally, with these two types of thinking, when one is phenomenally "on" the other is phenomenally "off."

Julian Jaynes (1976) also indicates that the seeming continuity (or perpetual on-ness) of consciousness is an illusion. Using the analogy of a flashlight, he says that the flashlight would be conscious of being on only when it's on. It can't be conscious of times when it's off when it's not conscious of such times. Therefore, at those times when it's on, it would seem to the flashlight itself that its light had been continuously on, even if long periods of being off had occurred.

Similarly, Jaynes says that because one cannot be conscious of things of which one isn't conscious, consciousness seems to be a much bigger part of mental life than it actually is. In this regard, consciousness is like that flashlight searching around a dark room for something that doesn't have any light shining on it. The flashlight, he says, would have to conclude, since there is light in whatever direction it turns, that there is light everywhere. Thus, consciousness can seem to pervade all mentality when, in actuality, it does not.

We addressed this illusion of the perpetual "on-ness" of self-consciousness when we discussed a series of connected thoughts in Figure 4 of chapter 2. Remember, the solid lines in the diagram represent those portions of a thought where one is aware of being a separate identity while conscious of a seemingly separate object of attention. Whereas, the dotted lines represent those periods where no duality of experiencing occurs, and hence, when no sense of being a separate self in relation to a separate object occurs. As a result, the reflective-self isn't even aware of these dotted-lined periods. Thus, "the self who knows the self" experiences itself only during the solid-lined periods, without knowing about the dotted-lined periods. Therefore, it erroneously believes that its experiencing accounts for the entire act of thinking, and that it is "on" all the time.

### 4. During explicit reflective identification and comparative reflective thinking, the observed thought is not in a "past."

During ERI, one explicitly identifies the content of a thought and acknowledges the awareness of it. One experiences (as an unattended-to-knowing) being a separate observer who "has" objectified thoughts that are construed as *present*, separate thought-objects. Sometimes, however, one experiences the phenomenology of "the thought" as if it's moving away into a *past*.

It may seem contradictory to suggest that, during ERI, one could either experience the so-called observed thought as present or as moving into a past. Sometimes, however, a person (at Formal Operations or beyond) may experience a fleeting recogniion of *just having been* immersed in the thought that is now being reflected on and identified. Consequently, one seems to "capture" that thought through the process of reflectively objectifying, excerpting, and identifying it (ERI). In so doing, one may experience that thought as if it's exiting the doorway of the present and entering the "room" of the past. It's as if one is capturing that thought by reflectively taking a picture of its backside as it enters that "room." In this case, one is subtly recognizing having just been absorbed in that objectified thought as an unfolding form of experiencing which is now passing.

The illusory nature of experiencing a reflected-upon thought as passing or past during ERI is very similar to one's experiencing during CRT. During CRT, however, one is more consciously aware of this phenomenology of a "passing" form of self-experiencing because one is attending to aspects of it quite explicitly. Due to their similar phenomenology, I will discuss why a thought, existing in a so-called past, is illusory for CRT. This discussion is also applicable to ERI and the reflective forms of RI.

If and when one begins to move beyond the stage of Formal Operational Thought and into the stage of Vision-Logic, one may recognize that, by trying to capture their subjectivity as a thinking-self, the thought-object being reflected on is not the actual, present self. Instead, one may interpret it as a "passing" or "past" instance of self. In addition, one may experience a present, witnessing awareness and subsequent thinking-self unfolding in relation to that "past," objectified thought-self (CRT). This stretching of awareness and subsequent thought, arising out of one's attention to a "snapshot" of an objectified thought, is essentially one of "I was once there but now I'm over here." It's this juxtaposition of an objectified "once-there"-thought, coupled with an unfolding, "now-here" thought, which literally generates one's experience of an objectified version of self that is more dead in comparison to one that is more alive. Both co-create each others' meaningful significance. This juxtaposition of the two creates an experience of space, distance, meaning-laden difference, and hence of a past-me alongside a present-me.

When one's reflective awareness consists of the latter, the experience of an existing "past" which thoughts can move into, or of thoughts that can be "past," is seemingly more real than at any other time. And yet, this is an illusory experience because thoughts cannot and do not exist as or in a past. Reflecting on a thought results in a "mentafied" excerpt of it. Therefore, thoughts never exist in a past because the excerpt of a thought isn't a real, presently occurring thought.

Another reason why thoughts seem to exist in a past is due to the comparative phenomenology occurring during CRT, for example. In my comparative reaction to that excerpted thought,

I *remember* having just been absorbed in it as a reaction to something else while simultaneously recognizing that my reaction to it now is different. Consequently, I interpret it as a past thought while my more present awareness unfolds in meaning-laden contrast to the excerpted identification of it. Because of this experiential, memory-based comparative process, a past thought seems to exist alongside a more present one as a contrast to it. Two experiential realities, one past and one present, can seemingly exist side-by-side in the same space and paradoxically in the present moment. So now, thoughts can seemingly be past or passing ones, not just present ones, and can be witnessed in the present as well! I can seemingly witness something in the present that is moving into a past. But that thought never exists in a past or as past. It doesn't exist as past in any way other than in my creative construal of it as past, given my comparatively contrasting, memory-based vantage point as I seemingly witness it from here.

Also of note is the fact that many of our representations and conceptions are of objects existing in our surroundings. Indeed, many objects are concretely and tangibly there to be perceived and conceived by us. Yet, we may be so accustomed to this reality that the understanding of objects that exist only as creations in mental "space," and not as external, perceptual referents, is foreign to us. As a result of the more common construal of a to-be-conceived concrete reality, the act of representing and conceiving of a past implies that there is an actual referent, or existing thing or place "out" or "in" there called a past. We experience this past as if always existing "there," as potential, somewhere behind the present moment, to be found whenever we choose to look for it. But as we've seen, the past exists only as a mental, psychological, and experiential creation.

### 5. The distinctions of time, engendered by explicit reflective identification and comparative reflective thinking, are illusory.

Given what was said in #4, by fooling myself into believing that there is a real past I can observe thoughts moving into, as if at a distance, I also believe that a version of my always present subjectivity can go into that past. I believe that my subjectivity can be something other than always immediately present. As stated earlier, it's ironic that the experience engendered by ERI (potentially) and CRT is tantamount to killing off an objectified version of myself that I essentially bury in a past, so I can be a seemingly more alive and present self in relation to it. Again, this experience is an unattended-to-knowing, and hence it's more subtle and vague during ERI as compared to CRT, where one attends to, reacts to, and conceptually represents this experience (thereby rendering it an unattended-to-knowing). Thus, as a function of ERI and CRT, temporal distinctions regarding the thinking-self are created, and hence my immediateness as a subjective-self seemingly becomes relative in time. In other words, when my reactive awareness compares itself to and distinguishes itself from an identified thought, distinctions of time regarding one's *experience of self* are created.

Even if the identified thought was "over there" in an observable "place," it isn't a discrete instance of my subjective presence. At most, if it was actually "there," it would simply be an object of one's always immediate, subjective awareness that illuminates and is illuminated by it. But this comparative reflective phenomenology results in distinctions of time that so dominate experience, the phenomenology of my always immediate subjective experiencing is obscured and misconstrued. Thus, the truest actuality is that each and every thought is always and only, now here, now here, and now here.

Moreover, that thought-object is actually a mentally based representation or image of a "passing thought," which is then conceptually identified as a *thought about....* In other words, it's not even an actual thought "over there." Thus, that thought-object isn't over there at all; an excerpted representation of that thought is "there." Consequently, the distinctions of time, based on a so-called past thought-self in relation to a more present one, crumble altogether, leaving the foundation of the always immediate present.

### 6. During explicit reflective identification and comparative reflective thinking, as you reflect on a thought, you are not "outside" of it.

During ERI and CRT, one is seemingly a separating, witnessing awareness outside of a separate thought-object being observed. Again, this duality of self-experiencing is much less conscious during ERI than during CRT, but it is experientially present nonetheless, existing as an unattended-to-knowing. During CRT, however, one is explicitly caught up in comparing the thought-object-self-over-there against the experience of the unfolding thought-self-over-here. In so doing, one is aware of being a separate entity, witnessing a thought-object as a whole, as if at a distance. As such, it seems as if, at the instant one's awareness "moves out of" that "passing thought," it's freed from and hence seemingly outside of it as well. The experience of being outside of this thought suggests again that there is a real object over there, that thought, which I was just inside.

The phenomenology during CRT suggests that there is this separate entity, "over-here," that is inside a given thought at one moment and outside of that same thought at another! It's as if a thought is an object in and of itself, simply passing through me in one instant and which I can then observe unchanged in another instant. However, as stated in the section under illusion #2, the excerpt of the thought is not the thought itself. The thought-moment itself is gone, period. Thus, I'm never outside of a given, objectified thought because the once the occurrent thought itself has disappeared only the excerpt standing-in for the thought is present as a fleeting object of awareness.

Most often, the phenomenology during ERI usually doesn't include the sense of just having been inside the thought and now outside of it as I reflect on it (as in CRT). More typically, the phenomenology is one of experiencing myself as a separating, witnessing entity who "has" thoughts as separate objects. In other words, During ERI, I often equate the act of thinking with seeing the objectified thought, as if I'm *always* outside of and separate from thoughts. Therefore, the illusion is frequently one of always being outside of thoughts because I experience myself as an always separate entity who "has" separate thoughts as objects.

During ERI, as I reflect on a thought to identify what I was thinking about, I too can experience myself as a separate, observing entity in relation to a seemingly separate thought of which I take ownership. I seem to "have" a thought as a separate object which is conceptually distinct from my reactive, conceptual experiencing. To observe that so-called thought as a particular *thought about...*, often leaves me feeling somehow outside of it. When ERI includes a sense of just having been inside the observed thought (which is, in a sense, a more accurate construal), I feel outside of it as I explicitly identify it. This phenomenology is an implicit or unattended-to-knowing. But again, I'm never outside of a given thought because the thought itself must be present in order to be outside of it. And because the thought is actually an excerpt, this experience of being outside of it is an illusion.

### 7. During explicit reflective identification and comparative reflective thinking, as you reflect on a thought you experience freedom from, you are not free from thought.

True freedom from a "passing thought," for most of us, is a very short-lived experience indeed. The instant awareness is released from its absorption in one thought, it is momentarily free from thinking. As stated earlier though, every thought consists of an excerpt followed by a meaningfully discrete conceptual reaction to it. Thus, the instant this "free" awareness takes an excerpted, "passing thought" as its object, a new thought is being initiated.

During ERI, at the instant of excerption, my awareness is essentially "inside" the beginning of a new thought while potentially experiencing being free from thought. During ERI, I don't know I'm the living embodiment of a new thought because

I'm too busy attending and reacting to the objectified thought at hand. Consequently, the actual freedom from thinking is very short-lived.

In contrast to ERI and one's potential to feel free from thought, the experience of freedom during CRT seems longer or more acutely intense. One's experience of a contrasting separateness and freedom from thought during CRT engenders a strong sense of a separate self, and consequently, of self-awareness. This is a function of a prolonged attention to and conscious representation of this freedom, as reflected by one's awareness of the excerpted thought at hand. However, during CRT, one is less likely to be fooled by the illusion of being free from thought (as compared to ERI) because one is more aware of the always immediate, reflecting awareness taking that thought as its object, and hence, of being absorbed in a new thought.

### 8. During explicit reflective identification and comparative reflective thinking, the experience of missing something during the last moment's thinking is an illusory one.

During the reflective reaction to a thought-object, where I acknowledge my experience of "*Thinking about...*" (ERI), my identification of the observed thought can seem so familiar and accurate I can't believe I wasn't aware of it while I was absorbed in it. Consequently, I believe I am aware of something more now that I wasn't aware of then, but seemingly should have been. After all, I'm seeing it clearly now so it must have been there before. How could I have missed it!? The answer to this question is that the current reflective vantage point is having trouble recognizing that the vantage point then didn't have access to the object of awareness it has access to now. The current vantage point has access to the identity or gist of the prior vantage point's reaction. Therefore, the last thought couldn't have been aware of its own content because it was reacting to an altogether different object. It's only from here, from this subjective vantage point right now, as I reflect on my last thought, that I have the experience of seeing what it was about, and hence of having seemingly missed something about it when I first lived it. But it's *only* "from here" that the so-called blindness "over there" exists. I'm creating what was missed "over there" by simultaneously finding it from "here" as I look "over there." This simultaneous finding from "over here" what was supposedly missing "over there" (during both ERI and CRT) is a function of having more information available to me from the current vantage point than I did when I was experiencing the prior one. From there, I was focused on a certain object of attention and was absorbed in a conceptual reaction to it. Whereas from here, I reflect on the latter as a whole, thereby recognizing it for all that it *was* (I know all that it knew), while also knowing something more about it now than it even knew itself. From here, I have created an object out of something that exists only as subject. It's as if I'm looking out of my eye from here to my eye over there and I'm seeing what my eye saw then plus the eye itself.

In his *Principles of Psychology*, William James (1950) discussed the illusory belief that the passing thought should have been conscious of itself in the same way that the reflecting awareness is conscious of it now. He called this illusion the Psychologist's Fallacy. He saw this fallacy as a confusion of one's standpoint with the thought one is considering.

One slight variation of the Psychologist's fallacy is the assumption that the mental state being studied was conscious of itself in the same way the person is conscious of it now. James reminds us, however, that the mental state is aware of itself only from within, grasping its own content and nothing more:

> What the thought sees is only its own object; what the Psychologist sees is the thought's object, plus the thought itself, plus possibly all the rest of the world. (p. 197)

The psychologist's fallacy, as engendered by reflective thinking (ERI and CRT), is parallel in many respects to another common human experience. Most of us have had the experience of making a decision regarding a plan of action only to regret it later based on how it turned out. Oftentimes our regret takes the form of a self-berating, "Man, was I stupid!" In the vast majority of cases, to blame ourselves for that decision is illogical because we didn't have the information then that we do now, hence the cliché, "Hindsight is 20-20." Somehow we fail to recognize this basic fact. We're simply too caught up in our present, more informed vantage point to recognize the nature of our prior, less informed one.

### 9. Explicit reflective identification and comparative reflective thinking engender the illusory experience of a separate, subjective self in relation to a seemingly separate self-object.

The phenomenology of being a separate entity during ERI and CRT is illusory (whether this is an attended-to or unattended-to-knowing). The experience of being a separating, witnessing awareness occurs at the outset of the reflective conceptual portion of the thought. One then conceives of this experience during the remainder of the reflective conceptual portion of the thought. During CRT, the experience of separation from the excerpted thought-object being attended to is engendered by a conceptually based comparative process. The awareness stretching away from the excerpted thought-object recognizes the conceptual difference between itself and the "passing" thought-object, and this *literally creates* the experience of a separate self-sense. This experience is essentially one of "I'm separate from that now because I recognize that my meaningful experience over here is different from what my meaningful experience was over there." During CRT, as I reflect on that thought-object, I remember it for all that it was as a conceptual experience because a moment ago I "was" it. I know all that it knew. At the same time, I recognize that I know something more about it now, and hence that I am different from it. I identify with it by recognizing having been it while experiencing myself as more than and other to it. The reflective self relates to that thought-object as if it's a distinct conceptual mold of its "prior" subjectivity.

In CRT, I remember what my thought was a reaction to while also seeing that reaction as a meaningful totality from here. In addition, I remember what my thought was not: it was not what I'm construing of it now. Hence, *the experiential recognition of difference between meaningful conceptual forms which are construed as two versions of the same subjective awareness engenders the experience of separation, movement, change, time, and hence of a witnessing self that seems to own the present and embody the life force of subjectivity.* Thus, in this meaning-laden, unfolding instant, I'm caught up in a conceptual and memory-based comparative process between two supposed forms of self, one currently unfolding in relation to the objectified other. Within the "field" of this always present subjective awareness, I'm having the conceptually and comparatively generated experience of separation, of one form of self against another, of a present self-experiencer observing its present self-experiencing (which is construed as past or passing). This duality of self-experiencer as a witness of a contrasting form of self-experiencing totally dominates my phenomenology at this moment.

In essence, these dual self-experiences co-occur. One has a subjective flavor in relation to the other which has an objective flavor. One is the self-experiencer and the other, is self-experiencing. These dual entities are subjectively experienced as separate from one another in the same instant. They are experienced as separate sets of co-occurring experiences, as if I, the separate subject, "have" experiences as separate objects. But this duality of self-experiencing is occurring and exists as one experience. A single experience underlies this *phenomenology* of a duality of self-experiencing in this very instant. Therefore, the experience of a subjective-self in relation to the experience of a seemingly separate self-object is illusory.

During ERI, as I reflectively react to the meaningfully recognized content that the excerpted thought at hand embodies, I experience an unconscious sense of being an awareness that is separate from and observing an identified, *thought about*.... I seem to be a self-experiencer observing a separate form of self-experiencing. As with CRT, this separateness from that apparent thought-object is illusory. Instead, my awareness embodies and subsumes this entity observing a seemingly separate thought-object. There is one experience within which two separate experiences seem to be occurring.

Please note that a person capable of NCRT is already accustomed to identifying specific thoughts as explicit objects because of his or her frequent experience of ERI. As a result, that person is accustomed to experiencing the various aspects of duality that occur during ERI, including the unattended-to-knowing of seemingly being a separate thinking-self that "has" separate thoughts as objects. Thus, when one seems to capture that thinking-self as a thought-object during NCRT, one is convinced that it's the ultimate evidence of one's present, subjective awareness which has been implicitly experienced over and over during ERI: "There it is!" As we've already indicated however, this is an illusion (see Illusion #2).

### 10. Explicit reflective identification and comparative reflective thinking engender the illusory experience of a separate self who "has" thoughts.

During ERI and CRT, at the instant of reflection upon the excerpted "passing thought," one's experience of being a separate entity standing apart from that thought is either an implicit unattended-to-knowing (ERI), or an explicit attended-to-knowing (CRT). In addition, various phenomenal forms of duality are unconsciously experienced during ERI and consciously experienced during CRT. This reflective phenomenon of being a seemingly separate witness of an objectified thought accounts for why many of us experience ourselves as "having" thoughts versus being thoughts.

When I speak of just having "had" a thought, I'm generally referring to my internal, reflective experience of just having noticed it, as an object "over there." When I notice that objectified, identified thought, I construe myself as thinking it.

For example, an unfolding thought is taking what Sue said to me at lunch today as its excerpted object. Then a second thought takes as its object this thought about lunch with Sue. It's at the outset of this second thought that I have the conscious experience of thinking the thought about Sue. This second thought is an instance of ERI. During ERI, by excerpting the former thought, it seems like I'm cutting out a slice of my experience with the knife of conceptual representation. Consequently, the thought about Sue seems to be a slice of experience that I'm witnessing in front of me. Thus I seem to split the whole of my immediate experience in half so that part of itself can look at another part of itself! I cut it into a witnessing part and an observed part. So now there's an immediate self-experiencer that can "have," as an object, another (so-called) form of immediate self-experiencing. But in actuality, the first thinking about Sue had already occurred; it's over and done.

On the other hand, when awareness breaks out of a sequence of elaborative thoughts and reflects on a given "passing thought," you're typically not representing the experience of having been lost to yourself and entirely consumed in the thought on which you're now reflecting. As a result, when you reflect on a "passing thought" and thereby excerpt, objectify, and identify it, you often react to it as the one that you, as a separate, observing awareness are "having" right now, as if for the first time. The reflecting self is generally too unfamiliar with the existence of elaborative thinking to construe thought in any other way than by how it's objectively experienced. The greater reality is that you already experienced *thinking* when you were immersed in its elaborative flow. Thus, the first and actual thinking of a thought consists of your awareness embodying a conceptual reaction to an object of attention. The second thinking of the thought, which for most of us is our only (known about) experience of thinking, occurs during reflection, when you objectify that "passing thought," interpret it as an actual thought, and as *the* act of thinking.

Because thoughts *consciously* exist only in retrospect, the reflective-self construes the thought-object as its creation. To that self, it feels as if the thought-object came into existence at the instant of reflective contact with it. As stated, the reflective-self often ignores the fact of having just been absorbed in that thought prior to reflective contact with it. It's too consumed in its own vantage point to attend to this reality. Furthermore, elaborative thoughts can't know themselves and exist only as "fossilized" specimens that the reflective-self finds. Despite the influence of these misconstruals and oversights that contribute to the illusion of "having" thoughts, every thought exists *only* as a subjective, elaborative process; thoughts never know themselves as they really are. Thoughts never exist in retrospect and are never separate from the subjectivity that embodies them. Therefore, the experience of a separate self who "has" thoughts is illusory.

### 11. The experience of being a lone participant during the act of intention is illusory.

Earlier I stated that the acts of intending, deciding, directing, and so on consist of a reflective, conceptual, reactive-decision to a recognized excerpt, where that excerpt embodies either a reminder of a "prior" decision or a piece of meaning-laden ground of decision-influencing potential. Experiencing a reflective, conceptual reactive-decision to either of these excerpts creates the sense of being a separate, intending awareness or entity. The intending, deciding, choosing act is real; one is making a decision in relation to an excerpt of meaning-laden, decision-influencing information. However, the phenomenal experience of being a lone participant in this decision-making process is illusory.

There is always an inherent duality to each and every thought because thought consists of two players: a fleetingly stagnant, objectified, represented experience, in response to which an unfolding, subjective, reactive experiencing arises. Therefore, the witnessing awareness rising out of the recognized excerpt initially "receives" the information from its excerpt-informant via the excerpt-found reaction. It takes into account that information in the reaction it has to it. But almost as soon as this reactive-self begins to conceptually respond to the excerpt-informant, it totally "forgets" or loses sight of the fact that this informant even existed. This is similar to running the final leg in a two-man relay race, taking credit for the success of the entire race because you've forgotten you had a racing partner who just handed you the baton! In this regard, the excerpt is like a dream, perhaps the most fleeting dream state known to the human species.

In this chapter, we have described and challenged eleven illusions engendered by the various types of reflective thought. Some of these challenges may seem a bit complicated, but in reality the existence, nature, and role of excerpts alone successfully exposes and undermines nine of the eleven illusions. The fact that the excerpted "passing thought" is not an actual thought is the central factor disclosing the illusory phenomenologies of reflective thinking in these nine cases. No more need have been said to successfully challenge them.

The illusory phenomenologies of seemingly missing something during the reflected upon thought and the sense of self that seems to be perpetually "on" needed more explanation than that of the nature of excerpts alone. To successfully challenge that self which seems to be perpetually "on" required all that we know about the structure and process aspects of thought.

Those illusions regarding the experiences of time, freedom, being outside of thought, and "having" thoughts all relate to the phenomenology of duality, of experience being split in two. These illusions of duality were challenged based on the nature of excerpts, the elaborative character of all experience, and the comparative, memory-based, and excerptively based processes occurring between the awareness stretching away from and looking toward "its" excerpted thought-object.

By now you are intellectually, and ideally, experientially aware of the existence of excerpts. This knowledge alone could help you see through the illusory phenomenologies of reflective thinking as you experience and notice them. In fact, the descriptions of the phenomenologies, and hence, "parts" of reflective thoughts, put you in a better position to notice them. Before reading this book, they were most likely unattended-to-knowings.

With an understanding of the structures, phenomenologies, types of reflective thoughts, and challenges to their illusory natures, you are in a position to discredit and disempower your experience of being an independent self split off from experience. Like challenging your tendency to "guilt-trip" yourself by noticing it and invoking more "rational beliefs," you can also notice and challenge concrete, experiential instances of duality. Regularly applying such challenges can profoundly change the way you experience yourself and the world. Such changes, addressed in chapter 9, represent shifts in emotions, motivations, aversions, thoughts, and behaviors. Moreover, your consciousness can change by no longer identifying who you are with your thoughts. By de*personalizing* your thoughts, awareness and self-identity expand to incorporate more of your experience. For example, as chapter 7 suggested, you may come to realize that you, the clouds, and the beautiful gold horizon are one experience; they are as much you as any thought you "have." So go on, turn the page, and open yourself to the possibilities ahead.

# Chapter Nine: The King and I

WHAT IS THE RELEVANCE of introducing a theory of the microdynamics of thinking based on a phenomenally based structure and typology of thought? In this chapter, we address this question as we consider having *become* the tool of thinking. We are so habitually attached to our thoughts as the most personal embodiments of self that we are at the mercy of their problematic manifestations. Many of the negative consequences of thinking are so automatic and inherent to the thought process that we don't give them any notice; we endure their impact on our lives without question. As a result, we don't even realize that they can be eliminated or minimized. The negative consequences of thinking are profound in their significance, impact, and pervasiveness. This chapter discusses the ways we can reduce the negative consequences of thinking, with ramifications as far-reaching as changing the way we experience ourselves and the world at large.

In earlier chapters, we discussed the phenomenologies engendered by elaborative and reflective thoughts. One subjective reality of thinking not yet acknowledged is that of talking to ourselves. This internal dialogue takes the form of thoughts "spoken" silently in "mind-space." The structure and various phenomenologies engendered by the different types of thought helps us clarify and better understand certain subjective realities of this internal conversation, as if between twin-selves.

The phrase "talking to yourself" refers to a basic reality of being a modern human. Within each one of us an internal dialogue is occurring, as if between two participants, closer and more alike than twins could ever be. In Western society, talking aloud to one's self is frowned upon, as if it's a sign of mental illness. Yet a silent internal dialogue is going on all the time (Berne, 1972) and is not much different than talking with any other person, only more intimate and knowing.

As the listener during *natural* conversation I must attend to and excerpt the gist of the speaker's words in order to formulate a response to her message. During *internal* conversation, however, the gist of the speaker's words need not be attended to and excerpted in order to formulate a response. I'll explain why this is the case shortly. Similarly, during internal conversation I'm the speaker and the listener simultaneously. In other words, as the speaker I behave as if sending a message to a listener, but I'm so intimately connected to the message, I need not consider it as fully as a listener during natural conversation. Consequently, during internal dialogue it's as if the listener is super-fast in formulating his or her responses.

After completing a spoken thought during natural conversation, I don't know what the listener is going to say. In addition, I may have to wait for her to respond. During internal conversation, however, I have a preliminary sense of the response to a particular thought, and hence, its occurrence is very fast. Consequently, internal dialogue can be much faster than that during natural conversation. In addition, the two "participants" of internal dialogue seem to know each other extremely well, as if reading eachother's minds.

The theory of the microdynamics of thinking helps us better understand the subjective realities of the ongoing dialogue inside each one of us. Generally, because internal dialogue is in the form of thoughts, it consists of general elaborative thoughts, IRI, RI (in all of its forms), ERI, and to a lesser extent, all the other forms of reflective thinking. Therefore, the quality of that dialogue will vary depending on the types of thought making it up. Generally, I believe that the bulk of internal dialogue consists of general elaborative thoughts.

I believe that general elaborative thoughts embody a clairvoyant quality of dialogue more than any other type of thought. Remember, general elaborative thoughts do not involve any re-

flection on or excerption of their predecessor thoughts. In a series of general elaborative thoughts, the content of one thought
is usually an elaboration on its predecessor, albeit indirectly because the latter thought is a response to an excerpt prompted by
its predecessor. Yet, the following thought is typically a natural
extension of or elaboration on it. Because my awareness subjectively embodied the predecessor thought, it already knows
its content as lived, thereby creating a clairvoyant sense of the
following elaborative thought knowing its predecessor. The
predecessor thought need not be directly considered for another
thought to follow it, as a result.

There are other reasons why general elaborative thoughts
embody a clairvoyant quality of dialogue more than any other
type of thinking. Recall that successive general elaborative
thoughts evoke excerpts which seem to move into the "face"
of awareness; they seem to be an intrinsic part of the stream of
thoughts, wherein awareness embodies their meaningful significance in a naturally flowing and direct fashion. In addition, such
excerpts are identified proactively. Proactively identified excerpts
engender both speed and a sense of knowing the unfolding,
meaning-laden nuances of thought just prior to and after them
because they are a natural, meaningfully flowing extension
between and connecting thoughts. They facilitate the forward
moving, meaningful elaboration of thinking, as opposed to their
reflective counterparts which seem to interrupt the flow.

The instant each proactively identified excerpt fully appears
to awareness, its identity is complete enough to facilitate the
thought process. Subsequently, one's entire reaction to that identified excerpt is present to awareness almost immediately, despite
the fact that the reaction has not yet been initiated. During this
instant of reflection on the proactively identified excerpt (at the
outset of the reflective conceptual portion of the thought), one
experiences a clairvoyant sense of what the thought proper will
be, just before the thought gets underway.

This clairvoyant phenomenology at the outset of reflecting

on a proactively identified excerpt occurs during every type to thinking. However, being engaged in a series of general elaborative thoughts is like being engaged in an intimate conversation with a good friend because they embody a flowing, prolonged, and deeply absorbing quality. The nature of each proactively identified excerpt contributes to this deeply absorbing quality of intimate conversation during internal dialogue because of their role in facilitating a meaningfully elaborative progression.

In sum, a series of general elaborative thoughts has a quality of intimacy, as if between two friends who are clairvoyant. This is because each predecessor thought in a series of general elaborative thoughts need not be considered by its respective subsequent thought, for awareness already knows its content as lived. Consequently, each subsequent thought takes into account its predecessor's content as a natural extension of or elaboration on it. In addition, the proactively identified excepts connecting general elaborative thoughts contribute to their flowing, absorbing quality and engender a sense of intimately knowing (being) all of the evolving meaning throughout the whole "conversation." Furthermore, the identity of and reaction to each proactively appearing excerpt is present to awareness almost immediately, creating a clairvoyant sense of what the next thought will be, even before the thought begins. Last, the nature of general elaborative thoughts is like being engaged in an intimate conversation due to their more flowing, prolonged, and absorbing nature, as compared to reflective thoughts.

In natural discourse, it's socially unacceptable to consistently depart from relevant topics, thereby taking the conversation in scattered directions. Reflective thoughts are needed to track the relevant themes in a conversation. For instance, if I'm engaged in an absorbing dialogue, I may briefly interrupt it and move into my GRO, thereby gathering a sense of the context at hand as I reflect on what I'm saying. If I'm off track, I may excerpt and acknowledge this fact to the listener and respond accordingly. In the same way, reflective thinking functions to keep me on track in relation to the direction and relevance of my own thoughts, as I dialogue with myself.

As stated above, internal dialogue often consists of general elaborative thoughts that transform the receiver of messages into a clairvoyant, superfast responder. Sometimes, however, depending on one's purpose and the content of one's thoughts, more considered reactions are necessary. A considered reaction to a predecessor thought requires reflective thinking. This is especially the case during problem-solving, for example. In my struggle to solve a problem, my most recent thought may represent a partial solution to it. Reflecting on that partial solution results in a more prolonged consideration of it, thereby facilitating a more efficient problem solving process.

### *Your Best Friend and Worst Nightmare*

Recall that a thought is an experiential duality. It is a dual entity of an identified excerpt plus a conceptual reaction to it. This single dyadic entity is experienced every time you have a thought. It manifests itself in the same basic form over and over and over no matter what the content of your thoughts. Also recall that the experience of duality occurs at the juncture where awareness stretches away from, objectifies, and initially responds to the reactively identified excerpt at hand. In addition, the phenomenology of duality or self-awareness is experienced along a continuum of increasing conscious intensity at this juncture. It's increasingly conscious across IRI, the reflective forms of RI, ERI, NCRT, and CRT/TRI. Incredibly, this experiential juncture is milliseconds long! It's extremely brief. Nevertheless, these fleeting glimpses of self-awareness, like spotting a ghost, become the entire foundation supporting your unwavering belief in and objective knowledge of being a separate self.

Imagine wishing for proof of the existence of ghosts. You're led to a door and allowed to glimpse inside. The door is closed as fast as its opened, but you're sure you saw a ghost in there. This single look will serve as experiential proof of their existence. It will become the entire foundation of your unwavering belief in ghosts. Similarly, the intermittent glimpses of self-awareness, occurring at the outset of the reflective conceptual portion of reflective thoughts, becomes an important foundation for your unwavering belief in being a separate thought-self.

Reflective thinking plays an extremely important phenomenal role during internal dialogue. At the juncture of objectifying a reactively identified excerpt of the thought-message to which you're reacting, the experience of self-awareness occurs (to varying degrees, depending on the type of reflective thinking). This belief in a separate self, supported by these intermittent and very brief experiences of self-awareness, has amazingly pervasive and significant consequences. Some of these consequences are wonderful. In fact, self-awareness itself is typically a wonderful experience; self-awareness is a thrill to itself. It embodies an *experiential* bond, creating and solidifying the relationship between two, intimate friends. Couple intermittent self-awareness with internal dialogue and it's as if you always have someone to keep you company, on whom to lean, with whom to chat and consider the meaning of life. You have a constant companion. You have a friend who can read your mind, know all of your thoughts, dreams, fears, wishes, and desires from moment to moment. She's a friend who can share all of this with you, in the most intimate, knowing fashion. She always listens and responds, untiringly engaging in an internal dialogue of give and take. She's also a working companion who studies, problem-solves, brainstorms, advises, and shares insights with you. She's capable of having the utmost compassion and concern for your plight. She can be supportive, encouraging, and loving.

In chapter 2 of *Self-Awareness: It's Nature and Development*, Thomas Natsoulas (1998) reminds us that C. S. Lewis (1967) coined the term "consciring," of sharing knowledge of something with someone. Lewis generalized this concept to reflection. He states that I can't help thinking and speaking of myself as if I'm two people, one of whom can act upon and observe the other. I can pity, hate, love, and comfort myself as if from one person to another. Lewis says that by being privy to my own acts, feelings, and thoughts, I am my own *conscius* or accomplice. And this inner accomplice has all the same properties as an external one: he is a witness against me, a potential blackmailer, or one who inflicts shame and fear.

The consequences of self-awareness and the belief in a separate self-sense can be negative as well. The internal self with whom you dialogue can be your worst nightmare. He can be critical, berating, cruel, discouraging, pessimistic, catastrophizing, hating, and shaming. He can be an endless source of suffering, wounding you at your very core day in and day out. There can be no escaping him, thereby imprisoning you in a living hell.

More typically, the consequences stemming from self-awareness and the belief in a separate self are a strange mixture of positives and negatives. At it's core, self-awareness results in a sense of specialness with the resultant sense that the self must be served. Metaphorically, the self exists in a kingdom of two. It's not only a small kingdom, it's one with two kings. A kingdom with no subjects, only rulers! In this kingdom of flesh and bones, the king (or self) must split itself in two in order to know itself. Typically, it only knows itself in its objectified form. In other words, the subjective (witnessing) form of self is usually unconscious (especially during and prior to Formal Operations). As a result, the subjective king is the servant of the objective king, not knowing that he himself is ruling from the throne (of subjective immediacy). Instead, he misconstrues the objective king as the royal one. He's convinced that the objective king exists and possesses the crown, given his fortune of occasional glimpses of him (NCRT, for example).

These glimpses of the objective king reinforce the subjective king's sense of duty and service to his counterpart. Of course, there's extra incentive to meet the objective king's needs because he construes the king as himself. Thus, in this kingdom of flesh and bone there are twin kings of a unique sort. They are twin kings in mental form. Somehow they experience themselves as one and the same person as well as two different people.

Serving the king includes meeting his desires. As ruler of a kingdom unto himself, he feels oh so important. Thus, his desires for pleasure *must* be met. Satisfaction of his pleasure reinforces his belief in his central importance in the kingdom. Pleasure is very nice and is construed as one of the perks of being king. However, the need and demand for pleasure can create problems, not the least of which is *frustration* when pleasure is expected but not forthcoming. In addition, the king is inherently fearful because *he alone* recognizes just how important he is and of all the pleasure there is to lose. His desire to maintain pleasure can turn to desperation, and his fear of losing it can be all-consuming. The more pleasure he has, the more he has to lose. Consequently, he can even be paranoid about imagined threats to his hedonistic outlets.

Along with serving and protecting the king, his image must be preserved as well. The subjective king is constantly working to maintain the positive image of his objective counterpart. This is no easy task, especially if he believes his twin brother has something to hide. And who should know his imperfections better? The subjective king is very concerned about public relations and tries to present his twin in just the right light; impression management becomes a full-time job. The king, after all, is supposed to be perfect. The royal servant has a great deal of glossing up to do because the king's perfection is difficult to maintain.

Ah, how wonderful it feels to be admired by all! But, if the king's need to seem perfect and to be admired is too great, his fears of imperfection and loss of admiration grow. In addition, if he recognizes the truth of his imperfection, he fears being exposed as an impostor, a very unpleasant reality indeed.

Death to the king is frightening as well. Lo, his kingdom is precious, and death a real threat to the awareness of his special existence. Death, of course, cannot be staved off so illusions of safety are created. The walls of his kingdom are thickened, his moat widened, and his denials of death strengthened. For instance, the kingdom of bone and flesh, extended to material worth and possessions, decreases his sense of vulnerability (Wilber, 1996b). Obtaining and retaining such possessions can become all-consuming as a result.

In a real sense, the king falls in love with his self-reflection or twin-self, and fears *losing himself to himself.* Death is the ultimate threat in this regard, and he goes to great lengths to create illusions of safety and security. Again, however, the greater his needs for safety and security, which feel very cozy, the greater his fears of losing them.

The king *sees himself* as very special. All that he thinks, believes, and speaks is taken to be special because these are embodiments of his royal essence. In turn, the king thinks he's always right and that what he says is of the utmost importance. He demands to be heard and that everyone outside the walls of his kingdom agree with him. He's easily angered if anyone should dare disagree with his infallible words of wisdom.

Like twin kings, the experiences of self-awareness created by the forms of reflective thinking, and the resultant belief in the separate self split off from experience cause us to be intensely and pervasively attached to our beliefs, opinions, and concerns, all of which take the form of thoughts. This is one of the most detrimental outcomes of self-awareness, the sense of self-importance that comes with it. As a result, we're not only prejudicial when it comes to our thoughts and opinions, regarding their so-called rightness or importance, we literally construe them as embodying who we are. Any one thought being reflected on is taken as our personal subjectivity (NCRT) or is seen as the nearest passing version thereof (CRT). Consequently, we're fiercely attached to the rightness of our thoughts.

No wonder I, as a king to myself, take the content of my thoughts so seriously; they seem to embody the very essence of who I am. My sense of self-awareness is engendered by reflecting on thought, which I take as the ultimate evidence of my unique subjectivity. To take issue with my thought-belief about such and such is to take issue with who I am, literally!

Being the champion of your beliefs and opinions leaves you feeling very strong, empowered, and in control. In addition, being self-righteous is an attitude projected about your self: "I am the self who *is* always right." Experiencing yourself as *the center* of rightness supports a sense of specialness to yourself. Yet, as with so many other consequences of self-awareness and the belief in being a separate (thinking) self, the positive ones seem inherently attached to negative ones. Intense investment in the so-called rightness and importance of all of your beliefs can create a great deal of interpersonal conflict, for example. Think of the relationships that have gone bad due to your's or another's rigid beliefs which have frequently been imposed without consideration for others involved. Think of all the people you've known who projected an attitude of arrogant self-importance and who alienated many others as a result.

Buddhist literature has been very clear about the belief that thinking is largely responsible for the experience of duality, of a separate self set apart from a so-called separate, solid, already-given reality. Buddhist teachers adhere to the belief that thinking is largely responsible for a great deal of human suffering. For example, as indicated in *Entering the Stream: An Introduction to Buddha and His Teachings*, Nyanpunika Thera (1993), a Buddhist monk and founder of the Buddhist Public Society, states:

> The world built up by the dualistic outlook that separates self and other turns out to be a shifting phantasm. Those who relate to it as solid and real are doomed to the frustration of the "First Noble Truth," the truth of suffering. (p. 83)

The British monk Bhikku Mangalo (1993) also addresses the relationship between the ego or mind and suffering:

> A chain of linked associations, hopes, fears, memo-

ries, fantasies, regrets, stream constantly through the mind, triggered off by momentary contact with the outside world through the senses. It is a blind, never-ceasing, never-satisfied search for satisfaction, bewildered, aimless, suffering. (p. 131)

The "Adept" Da Free John (1983), an important author and teacher of spiritual discipline, outlines the relationship between the ego-mind and suffering:

If "I" recoil from born experience and thus turn upon myself like Narcissus, the body-mind contracts. In that process, discomfort or dis-ease arises. The natural equanimity of the body-mind is lost in self-consciousness....In body and mind I am tempted by brief and separate illusions of what I seek, but my constant experience is deeply one of dreadful chaos, confusion, disharmony, division, fear, sorrow, anger, guilt, remorse, and torment. (p. 55)

Following the lead of Eastern spiritualists, let's outline several examples of how the self, manifesting as a thought-self, can create and engender significant unhappiness. To start, the thinking-self can turn a past event into an excerpt that can meaningfully stand for the entire occasion. This is no small feat, and carries with it incredible ramifications. For instance, as reflected in the excerpt-found reaction, a given excerpt might represent a highly pleasurable past occasion. Then I, in the form of a separating self reacting to this now identified excerpt think, "I wish it wasn't over." This thought might be a sad-laden response, given my awareness that the present moment sits in contrast to the past occasion to which I'm reacting. In other words, I'm aware that the enjoyable occasion isn't happening right now and I miss it. Thus, through this single thought process the past suddenly exists in comparative juxtaposition to the present. Furthermore, this thought-self experiences the present as unsatisfactory compared to that past occasion that no longer exists.

This comparative thought process just as easily occurs in relation to future events. A week from now I expect to have a gathering of close friends. This occasion can be represented by a single excerpt, perhaps of an image of several friends sitting in my living room. Through the excerpt-found reaction I am identifying this image as that future happy occasion. Then I, in the form of a separating self reacting to this now identified excerpt think, "I can't wait for it to happen!" This response is potentially laden with frustration given my reactive awareness that the present moment sits in contrast to the future one, which isn't yet here. Thus suddenly, the present moment takes on negatively-laden emotional qualities as well as a significance that exists only because of this comparatively based thought process.

Similarly, the present moment can be fraught with anxiety as I anticipate some personally frightening event. For instance, I could excerpt the image of an anticipated conversation when I tell my friend the truth regarding something he'll be angry about. My reaction to this identified excerpt could be laden with anxiety: "I've got to avoid him!" Through this thought process I have created fear in the present moment that would otherwise not exist.

I can also consider something negative about a past event. For example, while thinking about my school days, I experience an excerpt of making a costly mistake during a football game. The reaction to this identified excerpt embodies self-berating, depressed, and humiliated feelings: "I was such an idiot!" It's possible that I could continually revivify these feelings whenever I flash on an excerpt of that regretted experience.

In addition, I can consider the present in light of how I think it should be. Many people with anger problems become irritated when events aren't unfolding as they imagine they should or want them to. For example, I come home to discover a broken furnace and experience a flash-excerpt of having it checked three months ago. I react to that identified excerpt with the angry-laden thought, "This thing *shouldn't* be broken!"

Further reactions to the furnace scenario could occur in response to excerpts embodying the negative implications of it. For example, I might experience an excerpt of having to call the furnace company and pay an expensive bill. This, along with the excerpt of the new stereo I can no longer afford leave me with the reaction, "Nothing ever goes right for me!" To make matters worse, the thinking-self is only fleetingly conscious of the content of the excerpts to which it is reacting. As a result, it is caught up in waves of emotion with no insight about why or how this has occurred. In all of these instances, the thinking-self is immersed in the comparative thinking process between an identified excerpt and a conceptual response to it. This process colors the reality of the present in a way that need not exist. Just as clearly, a quality of emotional suffering is created that is typically unnecessary and unhelpful.

Once again, however, such thought processes, which often reflect the needs, wants, fears, and desires of the separate self, can result in positive emotions and adaptive responses. A prisoner of war in solitary confinement—utilizing the holding framework of thought—memorized the names of his fellow captives, mentally built exquisitely detailed houses from the ground up, and prayed in order to survive years of isolation. Albert Einstein invoked "thought experiments" to facilitate glorious insights about the universe that changed our lives and worldview forever. A wife and mother, grieving the death of her entire family, focuses on memories of the wonderful times they shared, creating islands of happiness in the midst of her suffering. Clearly, the power of thinking is awe-inspiring and the greatest evolutionary advancement and tool of humankind.

Thus, the realities of self-awareness, the belief of being a separate self cut off from experience, and the habit of thinking create a perpetual whirlwind existence. Our lives reflect a dizzying display of varied emotions, seemingly appearing out of nowhere, due to the ghostly vicissitudes of thought. The great insights and accomplishments of humankind are often engendered within the holding framework of thought, as are the most psychotic and hideous forms of suffering. From incessant, irrational worrying to superhuman adaptiveness and coping in the face of overwhelming odds, self-awareness and the tool of thought play a huge role.

### *Rising above Thought*

The Advaita Vedanta is one of six major orthodox schools of Indian philosophical thought that accepts the authority of the ancient scriptural Upanishadic texts, which arose between 1500 and 600 B.C.E. (Paranjpe, 1998). The Vedantic school is a systematized interpretation of these texts. The practical aspect of the Advaita Vedanta involves a procedure for the removal of erroneous concepts of self to facilitate a restoration of the self's original state. To emancipate one's self from the sufferings of a mistaken identity one should discriminate between self and non-self. The first means to self-realization, according to the Advaita Vedanta, is to launch a serious inquiry into the nature of self, taking anything impermanent as the hallmark of the not-self. Thus, the true self is that which remains unchanged. One must keep convincing oneself that the body, possessions, social roles, beliefs, name, and so on, are not-self. Any and all definitions of the self as an object are to be loosened and detached from the self-pole (the always immediate witnessing self) and moved to the object pole of the not-self.

It's common for us to identify who we are with what we believe. As reflected in the Advaita Vedanta, such beliefs are not-self and must be recognized as such (Paranjpe, 1998). In *The Ghosts of Consciousness* however, we have focused on the very act of thinking as the vehicle for our sense of self. Paranjpe's (1998) book provides an amazing overview of all that is considered not-self in Eastern and Western schools of thought as well as specifying the nature of the true self. Nevertheless, only once throughout this lengthy text does Paranjpe mention that one's sense of identity is anchored in one's *current* or just passing thoughts. He indicates, however, that believing the self to be beyond all thoughts and the current Thinker can help rid of the problematic tendencies of the ego.

Recognizing that your beliefs are not the real you, nor your name, possessions, social roles, etc., seems more obvious than the fact that your thoughts do not embody the essence of who you are. Surely your thoughts embody your true self more than anything else. This certainly appears to be the case, as reflected by the powerful phenomenology of self-awareness engendered by the various forms of reflective thinking. But by outlining the microdynamics of thoughts, their structure, types, and attendant phenomenologies, we have clearly discerned that our thoughts are not-self. Furthermore, the "passing thought" being attended to during reflective thoughts is not an actual thought. It's an excerpt or mentally fixed quasi-image and representation standing-in for the thought. The "passing thought" during NCRT is mistaken as an actual thought and as embodying one's subjectivity as a thought-self. The "passing thought" during CRT is construed as a passing version of one's subjectivity as compared to a more present, witnessing thought-self taking it as its object. This seeming splitting of experience into witnessing and observed parts, during all reflective thoughts (but especially during CRT), is actually one (elaborative) experience. Had we not specified these self-engendering reflective processes, we would lack a compelling case, and hence understanding, that objectified thoughts are not-self.

Moreover, experientially there are no objects anywhere at any time separate from any so-called self. Thus, the self is the always immediate, witnessing awareness combining with, illuminating, and illuminated by all the stimuli landing on and in it. You are the witnessing awareness embodying and creating the experience of the stars in the night sky, the grove of pine trees behind the meadow, the feeling of your lover's hand in your own, the spark of insight while solving a problem, the memories of your sixth birthday, and the separate self-sense set apart from thoughts, objects, and experiences. Yet, consistent with the insights of the Advaita Vedanta, all of these embodiments or objects of experience are not-self because they are impermanent. The witnessing awareness embodying them, however, always remains the same, and hence, *is self.*

Similarly, the theory of the microdynamics of thinking helped us realize that all thoughts and experiences are elaborative, even though an emerging reflective phenomenology overlays them. Therefore, our elaborative thoughts, as lived, are not-self. They represent one form that awareness can take, no more or less self than the flowers that illuminate and are illuminated by awareness.

Consistent with the teachings of the Advaita Vedanta, the theory of the microdynamics of thinking has helped us expose the illusory nature of the objectified thought-self, based on the structure, process, typology, and phenomenologies of thinking. The insights derived from this theory are intellectual ones, and can be invoked to challenge the phenomenologies of reflective thinking. In other words, these intellectual insights have an experiential basis and can be applied in response to the illusory phenomenologies of reflective thinking as they're noticed. At bottom, the reflective phenomenologies of a so-called separate self are not-self.

Given the sound intellectual understanding of why your thoughts are not-self, you may be motivated to initiate other practices which can facilitate a shift away from the habits of thinking, thereby promoting practical, positive outcomes in your life, while minimizing negative ones. In fact, you may be tired of being at the mercy of thinking. You may now realize that instead of using thinking as a tool, you have become the tool. Becoming thinking is like being a shell caught in an ocean wave rushing to shore: you might land in a heavenly pool of sunlit water, or be smashed to bits on the rocks.

Some people decide that, despite the utility, power, and imaginative wonder of thinking, they don't want to be at its mercy.

They become motivated to learn and practice how not to think. They can learn that their attention is habitually drawn into the act of thinking, and how not to think when they'd like a break from it. Most of us don't have the ability to realize this choice. Just try to focus on any given stimulus of your choosing without having a single thought for sixty seconds. You'll discover that it is very difficult to stop thinking for even this fleeting length of time.

Buddhists indicate that the planned and deliberate cessation of thought processes nullifies the desires and aversions that fuel self-perpetuating forms of suffering (Paranjpe, 1998). Thus, when people decide they'd like more control over when they do and don't think, Buddhists recommend that they turn to meditation as a method for learning how to do so.

Meditation is a very straightforward method of practice. In one basic meditation technique, you are asked to sit in a comfortable, upright position with your legs crossed, much like sitting around a campfire. You are then asked, often with eyes and mouth closed, to focus on the sensations of your breath at the point where air passes in and out of your nostrils. With each inhale and exhale, you silently repeat successive numbers from one to ten, or simply, "in" and "out," or other similar versions (Chah, 1993; Goenka, 1993; Rinpoche, 1993; Thera, 1993). For as long as possible, you are to fix your attention on the breath. Beginners of meditation inevitably discover that their attention has wandered into thought. Upon noticing this, they gently return their attention to their breath and begin counting each inhale and exhale anew.

During meditation, attention is withdrawn from all objects of thought, leaving the center of awareness or the witnessing-self. Once one is more firmly anchored in the witnessing mode, awareness is less habitually drawn to the array of intentional objects, the intentional stance lessens, and the subject-object distinction dominating daily experience drops away (Paranjpe, 1998). Thus, as an important goal, the meditator's experience lacks the separation between the experiencing subject, the object thought, and the construal of the object as "a tree," for example.

With meditative practice people learn to discipline their attention. They learn that awareness becomes easily consumed in thinking, and that if awareness is focused on the breath instead, thoughts do not occur as readily. They learn to be less habitually consumed in thought. They also learn that there is an observing awareness that exists outside of and other to thought. They learn to see themselves as something more than or other to thought, and as something more than thinking-selves (Chah, 1993; Goenka, 1993; Rinpoche, 1993; Thera, 1993).

Many positive outcomes can be experienced from meditative practice. For example, many practitioners discover that they are less frequently anxious, sad, depressed, frustrated, and angry because they're less at the mercy of the thought process that has these emotion-inducing tendencies. Consequently, they may be more at peace. In addition, they're often more focused and tuned into present realities rather than being in the time-machine of thought, traversing the mental creations of past and future. Furthermore, they spend less time in the imagined present regarding how it "should" be or how they would prefer it to be. They typically become less addicted to meeting their desires and avoiding their aversions. This is partly due to a lessened belief in being a king to oneself, as a separate, objectified self, and to being less vulnerable to the thought process that engenders the illusions of the separate (thought) self (Goenka, 1993; Thera, 1993).

Through meditation and other related practices, the *self-reinforcing* and addictive aspects of being a separate self begin to drop away. Our belief in being a separate (thought) self, as well as our attachment to it, begins to dissipate. We become less fearful and defensive and more open and receptive because we're not as invested in protecting that sense of self that has been so identified with its thoughts and beliefs. As a result, our relationships and communication improve through less investment in the so-called specialness and rightness of our thoughts, beliefs, and opinions. Last, our tendency to automatically and habitually grasp, desire, avoid, reject, and ignore realities that had soothed or threatened this separate self-sense will lessen.

By disidentifying with the separate thought-self or mental ego, I will be more in touch with my body as well. Becker (1973), Wilber (1996b), and the Existentialists (Bugental, 1976; Yalom, 1980), for example, believe that humans evolved to support a denial of death. As seen developmentally, a child's consciousness as a body-self (0–2 years) transitions into the mind, becoming a thought-self (2–7 years). As a result, the body has been increasingly transcended. However, instead of incorporating and embracing the realities of the body into this higher consciousness, the ego or thought-self tends to cut itself off from the body. Again, Wilber (1979) compares this to Western man's tendency to ride his body as if it were a horse, rather than being centauric: half-man, half-horse.

The egoic-mental-self is motivated to cut itself off from the body because the needs, limitations, and realities of bodily existence bring it closer to the existential givens of life. Such givens include being living creatures who eat and drink to survive, urinate and defecate, get tired and sleep, are vulnerable to pain and injury, become ill and disabled, experience lust and desire, procreate, and are aware that death is inevitable. My sense of self as a thought-self can deny or ignore all of that bodily "baggage" and the other disconcerting facts of being alive. Therein lies the motivation of the mind to dissociate itself from "its" body.

Thus, when I no longer solely identify myself with or as a thought-self because I have seen through the misleading phenomenal manifestations of thought, it will be easier to be grounded in the immediacy of the present and therefore back into my physical-bodily existence. I'm moving toward a higher state of consciousness by no longer identifying myself with the thinking-self per se, but with the always immediate, witnessing awareness. I can still be a thought-self but experience myself as other to it as well. I can now embrace my thought-self into a more overarching identity as this always immediate and boundless "field" of awareness, and embrace and include my bodily-self into this awareness as well.

The benefits of reembracing the body and its existential re-alities, according to Bugental (1976), Becker (1973), and Yalom (1980), is that one begins to live a more authentic life. Living authentically equates to feeling, thinking, and acting in accord with your most valued beliefs about yourself, others, and the re-alities of life. For example, it has been my awareness of the reality of death which has assisted my writing. If I was denying the real-ity of death by avoiding consideration of it in any way, I might be motivated to put this writing off. As a result, I would be liv-ing less authentically because I'm avoiding something extremely important to me. In fact, my death fear as reflected in my death denial could prompt me to avoid writing this book because do-ing so reminds me of death.

Most of us intuitively recognize that, in relation to really important goals, there's a finite timetable for realizing them. At-tending to our goals is often an implicit reminder of death and this can be very uncomfortable. As a result, we may avoid at-tending to our most important goals because they've often been associated with the realization that there's only a limited time for completing them.

There are innumerable ways people live inauthentically as a function of being cut off from the reality of their bodies and from the givens of being living creatures with finite lives. How many stories have you heard of people who nearly died or lost loved ones and made significant changes in the way they lead their lives thereafter? The realities of life and death aren't as eas-ily denied or avoided following such crises. Subsequently, the changes in the way they live reflect their greater awareness of the precariousness and preciousness of life.

People at all stages of development can live authentic lives. However, most of us tend not to, especially during the stages of Concrete and Formal Operations, when our mental, egoic, thought-self solidifies and dissociates from the realities of bodily existence. We live inauthentically by not attending to, and hence not being aware of physical, aspects of our experience. We also have many cognitively based strategies and beliefs to help us minimize, avoid, and deny the physical and existential realities of being living creatures who will die, because in our awareness of ourselves as thought-selves, we become overinvested and concerned about staying alive to ourselves; we want the awareness of our selves as a living presence to last forever. This is why, at the outset of the stage of Vision-Logic, when we begin to observe, understand, and discern the true nature of mind, ego, and thought, this experience of duality or self-awareness dissipates and we're less afraid of getting reacquainted with the physical, existential givens of life.

Beyond the stage of Vision-Logic, there are other stages of development that generally unfold hierarchically, if a person chooses to pursue further growth in his or her consciousness. Wilber (1995, 1996a) outlines these stages in his Full Spectrum Developmental Model of Consciousness. Optimally, each ensuing stage follows the same pattern of preserving the prior stage in its makeup while negating that stage's exclusivity by subsuming it within its more encompassing wholeness. A person progressing along this hierarchy comes to identify himself in much less narrow a fashion as he includes more and more of reality as part of his identity.

For example, through the intellectual and experiential insights gleaned from the theory of the microdynamics of thinking and self-awareness, meditation, and other related practices (Goenka, 1993), you begin to observe and understand the subjective, experiential illusions that thinking engenders, especially that of being a separate thought-self split off from experience. As a result, you may begin to identify yourself with and as the immediacy of the boundless "field" of awareness. Within this "field," when attention turns to an object, that object and awareness combine to create a single experience. This is a function of that object's physical essence, the physical stimuli in relation to it impinging on you, along with your uniqueness as a physical-mental entity, where those stimuli are trans*formed*. As a "field" of awareness, what you include as aspects of your identity widen. You no longer exclusively identify yourself to the narrower, separate thought-self. Your sense of identity can include the endless "field" of your awareness as an always immediate witness, along with all the experiential aspects and objects which occur within it. You and the panorama in front of you combine to form one experience; in every instant, the whole of your fully embodied awareness is the essence of who you are.

In sum, being a thought-based self is not the entirety of who we are. We can move beyond thought in the way we experience ourselves and the world around us, while using thought as a wonderful tool and source of self-experiencing when we so choose. To do so, however, we needed to understand the all-consuming nature of thinking in our lives and how it generated many problematic, illusory realities which are the source of a great deal of unhappiness. The theory of the microdynamics of thinking and self-awareness has facilitated this understanding of the illusory phenomenologies of thinking by outlining the structure and types of thought, their subjective manifestations, and the processes by which they're engendered. This theory may serve as the foundation for a new area of psychological study called cognitive phenomenology. Whether it does or not, the theory itself has helped us better understand and clarify the insights about thinking, self-awareness, and consciousness that Eastern religious traditions have embraced for thousands of years. Consequently, we are better acquainted with the "ghosts of consciousness" and are more appreciative of their helpful existence. We have also seen through some of their tricky illusions, and may move toward, of all things, further transcendence! As Da Free John (1983) states:

> Narcissus must go beyond the pond in the desert where he looks at his own reflection and is aware of nothing else. He must stand up from the pond and become aware of everything, high and low, to infinity. (p. 190)

# *Afterword:* The Big Prize

U NTIL THIS POINT, THE phenomena I have described were experienced firsthand. As a result, I felt confident that what I presented possessed personal accuracy and merit. It is with some trepidation then that I discuss higher states of consciousness because I am not experientially familiar with them, other than realizing fleeting tastes and glimpses; I have not engaged in the necessary practices to maintain such states. Nevertheless, it is important to touch on them because they represent the evolutionary progression in the development of the individual, once thought and its illusory manifestations have been transcended as the pervasive habit of mind (which has been the emphasis of this book).

Let's review the development of human consciousness outlined in earlier chapters, followed by a brief outline of the transpersonal stages of development which lie beyond identifying one's self as an ego or thought-based self. Remember that at each stage of development along the spectrum of consciousness, the self, taking certain experiential forms, has a specific worldview consisting of an awareness of certain objects.

According to Wilber (1995), who integrates the psychologies of world religions, sacred tranditions, and transpersonal psychology with contemporary psychological systems, from the ages of 0–1, during the Sensoriphysical stage, where the worldview is said to be Archaic, the self identifies with (takes the form of) body sensations, becoming a body-self that is increasingly aware of external objects set apart from it. Next, from the ages of 1–3 years, during the Phantasmic-emotional-sexual stage, where the worldview is Tyhonic, the self continues to be a body-self, but also identifies with developing mental images and symbols, increasingly becoming a body-mind. At first this body-mind cannot differentiate itself from the emotional body-minds' of others. The child thinks that what it feels (sees, wants, etc.) is what the world is feeling. By the end of this stage, however, the child can differentiate its self-image and feelings from its images of others and from their feelings.

From the ages of 3–7 years, during the stage of the Representational mind, where the worldview is Magical, the mind of the child consists of higher symbols and concepts representing the external world, resulting in the birth of the verbal, conceptual, narrative self; the self identifies with its thoughts, as lived. Consciousness is increasingly seated in the conceptual mind and attention is on external objects. The child's body and bodily impulses exist more separately from its thoughts/mind, and hence, exert less influence over its behavior (Wilber, 1995).

From the ages of 7–11 years, during the stage of the Rule/ Role mind, where the worldview is Mythic, consciousness is increasingly seated in the conceptual mind, but also becomes identified with particular social roles and rules. Across this stage, the child makes increasing differentiations between the roles of self versus others (Wilber, 1995).

Around the age of 11, during the stage of the Formal-Reflexive mind, where the worldview is Rational, consciousness is still very identified with and embedded in thoughts, but the child becomes increasingly capable of attending to its thoughts as objects, thereby manifesting a reflective, introspective mind. However, thoughts as objects are experienced as who the child is; instances of self are reflected in its passing thoughts. Here, the observer of thoughts is so absorbed in the thought being observed that it doesn't realize its own presence as the observer. The observer keeps losing its subjective presence in its attempts to objectify itself via observed thoughts (NCRT). Nevertheless, the child is now capable of questioning and challenging the roles and rules it once swallowed without question. Still, the separate self-sense tends to take up a single, fixed interpretation of the world. Its worldview is marked by a belief that the subjective realm is fundamentally set apart from the objective realm of nature (Wilber, 1995).

At the next stage of Vision-Logic, where the worldview is centauric, the observer of thoughts increasingly separates itself from thoughts as objects, thereby identifying itself as the witness of thoughts (CRT). In addition, its worldview expands to include multiple perspectives rather than a single, privileged one (Wilber, 1995).

Beyond these aforementioned stages of consciousness development, we move into the first of the transpersonal stages of development. At the Psychic stage, where the worldview is that of Nature Mysticism, my self-identity is further embedded in the witnessing awareness. In addition, this Witness tends to realize that all of nature arises through, in, and as this observing awareness. As a result, self-identity is expanded to include all of nature. In this first transpersonal (personal plus) stage, the locus of self-identity includes nature itself. In other words, the clouds, sun, rain, trees, and so on, are literally experienced as part of who I am. In addition, this self, existing as a witnessing awareness, recognizes that all humans possess exactly the same awareness, as that through which all gross manifestation arises. Hence, Wilber (2000) says that this psychic realm is the domain of the soul versus the personalized self of the lower stages because I recognize that the witness in me transcends the isolated person and is common to all beings. With this Oversoul or One Soul, my individual identity is negated and yet preserved in a deeper and wider ground, which includes all of nature and humanity. Wilber adds that psychic developments have one foot in the gross, ordinary realm, and one foot in the transpersonal realm. A new wordview begins to include phenomena arising in meditative states, as well.

At the Subtle stage of development, where the worldview is that of Deity Mysticism, consciousness is still identified with or as the Witness or Oversoul, but its worldview is further expanding to include phenomena beyond the gross, ordinary, waking realm (Wilber, 2000). In deep states of meditative or contemplative awareness, says Wilber, one begins to witness interior illuminations, sounds, archetypal forms and patterns, very subtle body/mind energies or currents, subtle cognitions, and expansive emotional states such as profound love and compassion. In such deep states of meditation, base patterns or forms emerge which are recognized as precursers to (the perception of) all other forms, including those in the manifest world. Experientially, it feels as if one is communing with God. It's as if God makes him/herself evident to the soul, where there is still a slight remnant of a subject-object duality (Wilber, 2000).

Next, the Causal stage of development is the realm beyond God. Its worldview is that of Formless Mysticism. Here, in deep states of meditation, the Witness settles into the Ground and Source out of which the personal God emerged in the Subtle stage of development. In other words, the Deity Mysticism of the Subtle level dissolves into the Formless Mysticism of the Causal level. The Causal level is pure awareness, consciousness as such, out of which the subtle, archetypal forms emerge. Instead of witnessing deity or archetypal forms via a slight remnant of duality at the Subtle level, those forms dissolve (do not arise) into the pure Emptiness of the Causal (Wilber, 2000).

The Causal level is the *cause* or ground of everything that emerges into awareness. When you pursue the Witness to its very source of pure Emptiness, then no objects arise in consciousness at all. This is a state of unmanifest absorption or cessation, where all objects and subjects cease to arise as experiential phenomena (Wilber, 2000).

In the Causal realm, states Wilber (2000), the Witness abides as Pure Emptiness or Pure Awareness, and this is its identity. This is a state of formless, silent awareness, and one knows this from within, as self-felt, he says. It is a state experienced as an expansive freedom, as an utter fullness, infinitely drenched in the fullness of Being. It can never be seen as an object; this pure self is Pure Emptiness.

Thus, in the Causal, the source of the Witness is realized as Pure Emptiness. As you calmly rest in the observing awareness, you will rest in a vast expanse of freedom, through which all objects come and go. You are the opening through which all manifestation arises, gross and subtle. When you rest in the pure Witness you are invisible. You are pure awareness and not anything that arises in awareness. The Witness is itself the causal unmanifest, and resting in this, all phenomena cease to arise. This is pure formless mysticism, where all objects, even God as the personal form emerging in the Subtle level, vanish into cessation. Because all objects have not yet arisen, this is a completely unmanifest state of Pure Emptiness. It is the creative Ground that finally becomes transparent to itself in beings that awaken to it (Wilber, 2000).

Beyond, above, and including the Causal and all levels below, is the Nondual. Here, the Formless Mysticism of the Causal level gives way to Nondual Mysticism as a worldview. Where the Emptiness or pure consciousness of the Causal level is a discrete state of awareness or cessation (a wooden rung of the ladder along the spectrum of consciousness), that same Emptiness (of the Nondual) is also the condition of all states and levels of consciousness; it is both the highest rung of the ladder and the wood of which the ladder is made. Therefore, the Nondual is not a separate level among other levels. It is the suchness of all levels. In other words, in the Nondual, Emptiness is recognized and experienced as the most basic reality or suchness of all states. As a result, this recognition of the Nondual is brought to all levels of the Spectrum of Consciousness, and hence, to all experience in the gross and subtle (Wilber, 2000).

Wilber (2000) says that the "experience" of this Nondual suchness is similar to the nature unity at the Psychic level, but now this unity is experienced not just with gross form "out there," but also with all the subtle forms "in here." In the Nondual, the sense of being a witness vanishes completely. You don't look at the sky because you are the sky. There is no duality, just pure seeing. Wilber says that consciousness and its display are not-two, whether the forms in consciousness are trees, thoughts, deity forms, subtle illuminations, visions, and so on.

Wilber (2000) stresses that, in the Nondual, the Pure Emptiness of the Witness turns out to be one with every Form witnessed. He says that, resting in the Witness, you realize that the sensation of the Witness and the sensation of the mountain, for example, are the same. In other words, the real world is not given to you twice, once out there and once in here. It is not severed into seer and seen. All of reality is nondual: you and the mountain are two sides of *one and the same experience*, which is the only reality in that moment. You as subject don't see the mountain as an object; you and the mountain are one in the immediacy of actual experience. Consciousness is not a separate something that has an experience of a separate something else, says Wilber. There is just One Taste in the immediateness of experience. You don't have experiences; you are experience. In here and out there are one.

I *imagine* the Nondual in terms of having no head. Pure Awareness or Consciousness is pouring out of my neck and flooding into the external surroundings. There, awareness mingles with all sensory stimuli to create my particular (human) visual experience of the display at hand, for example, as a single experience.

According to Wilber (2000), despite the Nondual nature of all experience, the dualisms of all the levels below will continue to arise and are supposed to arise; they are the very nature of lesser levels of consciousness. But with Nondual awareness, we can see through these dualisms to their Source. Nondual traditions don't try to divorce Emptiness from Form. Instead, they treasure an Emptiness that embraces all Form. The Nondual tradition is: Abide as Emptiness, embrace all Form. Emptiness is one with whatever forms arise. In the Nondual, you simply relate to all forms (in your day-to-day experience) at the lesser levels of consciousness as forms of Emptiness. You are literally one with all of them as they arise.

In sum, Wilber (2000) indicates that the cross-cultural evidence supporting an actual development or *evolution of consciousness* along a continuum from matter to mind to soul to Spirit is massive and overwhelming. He specifies that at each level of that continuum, what we consider to be our "self" changes dramatically. When consciousness is identified with the body, we experience ourselves as a body-self. When consciousness identifies with the mind, we experience ourselves as the ego, as the conceptual, thought-based, narrative sense of self. When consciousness identifies with the Subtle level, we experience ourselves as the soul, a supra-individual sense of self that begins to breathe an atmosphere beyond the gross and conventional experience of the self in the awake state. When consciousness evolves into the Causal level, it identifies with a witnessing awareness, where the last primitive remnant of the separate self exists, of a duality or tension between the Witness and everything witnessed, the tension between Emptiness and Form. This Witness is the seat of attention, the root of the separate self-sense, the subtlest duality between seer and seen. Lastly, this final duality will dissolve into the Nondual when the causal Witness itself dissolves into all forms of experience, where subject and object become One Taste, where Emptiness embraces all form, and where the Witness is everything witnessed.

A clarifying aside: In earlier chapters I stated that through the vehicle of thought and its operations (at the pretranspersonal stages of ego), you try to objectify the Witness or observer as a way to experience it. You want to see it and experience a reactive awareness to it as an object. However, I also added that the Witness can never be successfully objectified because it is needed as a subjective presence to observe any phenomenon, including a so-called instance of itself.

Remember that beyond the stage of Formal Operations, when you realize that an observed thought is never the actual observer, you begin to identify yourself as the observer or Witness of all phenomena. Perhaps without consciously acknowledging it, you are finally allowing the experience of *being* the witnessing awareness, *as lived*, to be completely satisfactory. You no longer need to objectify or see the Witness as a way to validate it.

Similarly, certain subtle realm states such as lucid dreaming—where the dreamer is both aware of himself dreaming and is aware of and can manipulate the dream—create an awareness of *being* the Witness, *as subjectively lived*. In addition, certain extra-normal experiences such as past life recall yield an awareness of *being* the witness, *as lived*, while simultaneously being aware of the visual display and passage of personal history.

Apart from experiences in the transpersonal realms and from relatively unusual experiences such as lucid dreaming and past life recall, in general, the ego or thought-based self does not have experiences in which a recognition of being the Witness as subjectively felt occur. Again, the ego uses the medium of thought and its operations to try to objectify instances of itself. It's in-love with itself and longs to admire itself in the reflective water of thought.

Now that we have outlined some basic aspects of the transpersonal stages of consciousness development, we can briefly revisit a difficult task relevant to transcending the pretranspersonal, egoic stages of development. Wilber (2000) indicates that for those of us who have evolved to the Rational level of development, identifying ourselves with the conceptual mind, "…it is only by investigating…the subtle contraction known as the separate self-sense that one's identity can expand from the mind to spirit itself." (p. 181); "…because only by bringing awareness to the mind can you begin to transcend the mind and be free of its limitations…usually through meditation and contemplation…which leads to spiritual and mystical experiences" (p. 177); "…but with radical transformation, the self itself is inquired into, looked into, grabbed by its throat and throttled to death" (p. 26). This is what *The Ghosts of Consciousness* has attempted to help you do: explore and identify the nature of thoughts, their unfolding, and interactions, which engender various phenomenologies, including that of the illusory, separate self-sense set apart from all of reality. By understanding thought and its subjective manifestations, you may be motivated to transcend the thought-based, illusory self altogether, and move into the transpersonal stages of human development, potentially realizing "The Big Prize" of Enlightenment!

Once you successfully stop experiencing yourself as a thinking-self and identify who you are with the observer or Witness of all phenomena, you move into the transpersonal stages of development. Wilber (2000) says that by engaging in practices that help you persist in relaxing in the Witness or choiceless awareness, and by watching phenomena arise without grasping, identifying with, or avoiding them, the witnessing consciousness will begin to extend from the waking state into the dream state (a Subtle realm phenomenon). In other words, you will remain conscious of dreaming throughout dreaming. Then, states Wilber, as you pass into deep, dreamless sleep you still remain conscious, but *you are aware* of nothing but vast and pure emptiness, with no content whatsoever (Causal realm). You abide in pure consciousness itself, without qualities, contents, subjects, or objects. You know that you still exist, but only as pure consciousness. Then, as you *come out of* the deep sleep state, you see the mind and the dream state arise and take form. That is, out of Causal emptiness (awareness in deep dreamless sleep) there arises the subtle mind (dreams, images, symbols, concepts, visions, forms), and you witness their emergence. The dream state continues, and then as you begin to wake up, you can see the entire gross realm arise directly out of the subtle mind. You have just taken a tour of the Great Chain of Being—from gross body to subtle mind to causal spirit. With constant consciousness or unbroken witnessing, you remain aware during all these changes of state, even into deep dreamless sleep.

As Wilber (2000) states,

> "according to the great sages there is something in
> us that is always conscious—that is literally aware at

all times and through all states. And that ever present awareness is Spirit in us. That underlying current
of constant consciousness (or Nondual awareness) is
a direct and unbroken ray of pure Spirit itself—our
pipeline straight to God."(p. 64)

Furthermore, according to Wilber,

"If we want to realize our supreme identity with
Spirit, we will have to plug ourselves into this current of constant consciousness, and follow it through
all changes of state-waking, dreaming, and sleeping-
which will (1) strip us of an exclusive identity with
any of those states (such as body, mind, ego, or soul);
and (2) allow us to recognize and identify with that
which is constant—or timeless—through all of those
states, namely, Consciousness as Such, by any other
name, timeless Spirit." (p. 65)

Appropriately, we will end this book with another quote
from Ken Wilber, the man who has introduced me and countless others to the transpersonal world of consciousness, to a new
vision of self-identity and future of unrealized potential:

Once you find your formless identity, you will take
that constant, Nondual, ever present consciousness
and reenter the lesser states and reanimate them with
radiance. You will not remain Formless and Empty.
You will Empty yourself of Emptiness: You will pour
yourself out into mind and world, and create them in
the process, and enter all of them equally...your lesser
self will become the vehicle of the Spirit that you are.
And then all things, including your own little mind
and body and feelings and thoughts, will arise in the
vast Emptiness that you are, and they will self-liber-
ate into that true nature just as they arise, precisely
because you no longer identify with any one of them,

but rather let them play, and let them arise, in the Emptiness and openness that you are." (pp. 65–66)

# Glossary

NOTE: Instead of organizing this glossary alphabetically, I have presented the concepts in a logical order regarding the unfolding components and types of thought.

EXCERPT—AN EXTREMELY FLEETING, quasi-image-like, memory association automatically triggered by internal or external stimuli, which becomes the object of a subsequent thought, or to which new excerpts or behaviors respond. It is also an object or aspect of experience that becomes briefly "fixed" and represented in awareness as a function of attention, and which becomes the object of a subsequent thought, or to which new excerpts or behaviors respond.

**Proactive Excerpt-Found Reaction**—This reaction occurs just prior to and at the outset of all thoughts and embodies the increasingly apparent identity of an evolving excerpt. The full appearance of the excerpt co-occurs with its proactively identified, implicit content, and marks the onset of all thoughts. One's phenomenal experience during a proactive excerpt-found reaction consists of moving toward an increasingly visible and identified excerpt.

**Proactively Identified Excerpt**—Marking the onset of all thoughts, this is an excerpt which awareness embodies throughout its evolution, and which is implicitly identified at the instant awareness reflects on and reacts to it via the reflective conceptual portion of an elaborative thought and via the reactive excerpt-found reaction of a reflective thought.

**Reactive Excerpt-Found Reaction**—Following the proactively identified and appearing excerpt, at the outset of *reflective thoughts,* the reactive excerpt-found reaction begins identifying the implicit content of the proactively apparent excerpt, thereby embodying an unfolding awareness of its explicit content. One's phenomenal experience consists of identify*ing* a "visible" excerpt *after* it appears to awareness, while looking at and moving away from it. This reaction then becomes the excerpted object of the reflective conceptual portion of a reflective thought.

**Reactively Identified Excerpt**—This is the second excerpt or excerpting instant which only occurs during reflective thoughts following the reactive excerpt-found reaction to the proactively identified excerpt. This reactively identified excerpt is fixed by attention and is established in its explicitly identified form at the instant awareness reflects on it at the outset of the reflective conceptual portion of a reflective thought.

**Reflective Conceptual Portion of the thought**—The initial response of awareness to the proactive or reactive excerpt-found reaction. At the outset of an *elaborative thought*, the instant of reflection on the proactive excerpt-found reaction brings it to an end, thereby establishing it as an excerpt, the content of which is now completely identified or recognized (albeit implicitly), and to which the reflective conceptual portion of thought responds. At the outset of a *reflective thought*, the instant of reflection on the reactive excerpt-found reaction brings it to an end, thereby establishing it as an excerpt, the content of which is now explicitly identified or recognized, and to which the reflective conceptual portion of the reflective thought responds. At the outset of this portion of the reflective thought, an awareness of being a separate identity in relation to the excerpted object can occur.

**Elaborative Conceptual Portion of the thought**—Following the reflective conceptual portion of the current thought, awareness is no longer attending to the identified excerpt, and disperses into and as the meaningful experiencing at hand. Awareness is in a transition period of not focusing on or reacting *to* a specific object. Phenomenally, one experiences an identity *with or as* the experiencing at hand, as opposed to experiencing a separate identity *from* some observed, objectified form of experiencing.

**Excerpt-Searching Reaction**—At the end of the elaborative conceptual portion of a thought, some meaningful nuance prompts awareness to exit the thought as a prelude to the proactive excerpt-found reaction and proactively appearing excerpt. An excerpt-searching reaction precedes the appearing excerpt prior to the outset of all the forms of "reflective identification of excerpts."

**Attentional Surfacing**—The surfacing of awareness from the elaborative conceptual portion of a thought, leading to an excerptive-clip of some meaningful aspect of that thought, which then becomes the object of a subsequent reflective thought (excluding the reflective form of RI of excerpts), or of implicit reflective identification (a type of elaborative thought).

**Excerptive Clipping**—Following attentional surfacing from an occurrent thought, this is the action of attention and awareness excerpting some meaningful aspect of that thought as it "passes," where the resulting excerptive-clip becomes the object of a subsequent reflective thought (excluding the reflective form of RI of excerpts), or of IRI.

**Excerptive-Clip**—Excerptive clips are mental "snap-shots" of internal or external stimuli. The instant awareness attentively fixates on a stimulus it becomes an excerptive-clip if a thought or action takes it as its object. Reflective thoughts (excluding the reflective form of RI of excerpts), and IRI, react to an excerptively clipped aspect of their respective predecessor-thought. Marking the outset of all the forms of "RI of excerptive clips of external objects," some object or aspect of external experience becomes fixed in awareness, thereby becoming an excerptive-clip as a function of attention to it.

**Excerptive Reminder**—An excerpt prompted by an aspect of one's present experiencing related to one's personal sphere, but which is not autobiographical. For example, seeing the long grass near the porch prompted an excerpt of the lawnmower in the garage.

**Excerptive Memory**—An autobiographical excerpt prompted by an aspect of one's present experiencing. For example, hearing friends talk about biking trips prompted excerpts of one's own biking excursions.

**Excerptive Solution**—An excerpt or memory association which is not explicitly personal or autobiographical in nature and has little to do with information from one's personal sphere. It typically represents factual information in the form of memory associations or answers to academic questions or about new events. It represents what one knows about things outside of one's personal circumstances.

**Excerptive Decision**—An excerpt prompted by an aspect of one's present experiencing which embodies a reminder of a prior decision or which has decision-influencing potential. It is followed by the reflective conceptual portion of the thought, consisting of the decision proper, as a direct response to the excerpt.

**Reflective Thinking**—The act of attending to, excerptively clipping, and explicitly representing a "passing thought's" meaningful content. It can also include an explicit awareness of the thought as a presence per se.

**General Elaborative Thinking**—The outset of the current thought attends and implicitly reacts to an excerpt *prompted* by the predecessor-thought, and not to some meaningful aspect, identity, or "presence" of the "passing thought." During general elaborative thoughts, one's phenomenology takes the form of the reaction which awareness presently embodies; there is no experience of duality. A general elaborative thought is preceded by an excerpt-searching reaction, and is initiated by a proactive excerpt-found reaction and any one of a variety of proactively identified excerpts, excluding excerptive-clips.

**Implicit Reflective Identification**—A type of elaborative thinking, at the outset of which, some aspect (a fleeting image) of the just prior thought is attended to and excerptively clipped. Having taken into account some meaning embodied in the prior thought is subjectively implied in the present thought's reaction to the excerptive-clip. In other words, the reaction is a response to the excerptive-clip rather than about it. Implicit reflective·

identification takes into account some meaning in its predecessor-thought more directly than does a general elaborative thought. Implicit reflective identification reacts to an excerpted aspect *of* the predecessor-thought, whereas the predecessor-thought *prompts* an excerpt to which a general elaborative thought reacts. Implicit reflective identification is preceded by attentional surfacing and is initiated by a proactively identified excerptive clip.

**Explicit Reflective Identification**—A type of reflective thinking, at the outset of which, the explicit identity and/or presence of the predecessor-thought is attended to and excerptively clipped. Having taken into account that thought's identity and/or presence is explicitly embodied in the excerptive-clip and in the current thought's reaction to that clip. Explicit reflective identification is preceded by attentional surfacing, is initiated by a proactively identified excerptive-clip, and a reactive excerpt-found reaction.

**Reflective Identification of Excerpts (elaborative form)**—A type of elaborative thinking preceded by a predecessor-thought (usually a question) which prompts awareness to actively seek one or more excerpts in response to that thought. The excerpt seems to come out of the periphery of awareness, as if outside the stream of thought itself. It entails an elaborative phenomenology wherein the content of a proactively identified and appearing excerpt is implicitly reacted to in the form of a thought. It is preceded by an excerpt-searching reaction marking the end of the predecessor-thought, and is initiated by one of a variety of proactively identified, appearing excerpts (excluding excerptive-clips).

**Reflective Identification of Excerpts (reflective form)**—A type of reflective thinking preceded by a predecessor-thought (usually a question) which prompts awareness to actively seek and expectantly wait for one or more excerpts in response to that thought. The excerpts seem to come out of the periphery of awareness, as if outside the stream of thought itself. Reflective identification of excerpts entails a reflective phenomenology wherein a proactively identified and appearing excerpt is explicitly identified by a reactive excerpt-found reaction. Unlike ERI, which reacts to content *inherent to* the "passing thought," "RI of excerpts" reacts to the excerpt *prompted by* the "passing thought." Reflective identification of excerpts is preceded by an excerpt-searching reaction marking the end of the predecessor-thought, and is initiated by one of a variety of proactively identified, appearing excerpts (excluding excerptive-clips), a reactive excerpt-found reaction, with its unfolding, explicit representation of the excerpt's identity.

**Reflective Identification of Excerptive-Clips of External Objects (elaborative form)**—A type of elaborative thinking which takes excerptive-clips of external stimuli as objects. The reaction to the excerptive-clip embodies an elaborative phenomenology and implicit identification of the stimulus represented by the excerptive-clip. It is preceded by attentional surfacing from a prior thought or action, is initiated by a proactively identified excerptive-clip of an external object, and subsequent implicit identification of the excerpt's content during the reflective conceptual portion of the thought at hand.

**Reflective Identification of Excerptive-Clips of External Objects (reflective form)**—A type of reflective thinking which takes excerptive-clips of external stimuli as objects. The reaction to the excerptive-clip embodies a reflective phenomenology and explicit identification of the stimulus represented by the excerptive-clip. It is preceded by attentional surfacing from a prior thought or action, is initiated by a proactively identified excerptive-clip of an external object, and a reactive excerpt-found reaction, with its unfolding explicit representation of the clip's content.

**Noncomparative Reflective Thinking**—A type of reflective thinking engendering a sense of self-awareness, at the outset of which a "passing thought" is excerptively clipped and mistakenly construed as one's immediate subjectivity in the form of an objectified thought-self. It is preceded by attentional surfacing from the predecessor-thought, a proactively identified excerptive-clip, and a reactive excerpt-found reaction.

**Comparative Reflective Thinking**—A type of reflective thinking engendering a sense of self-awareness, at the outset of which a "passing thought" is excerptively clipped and construed as a just prior thought-self or version of subjectivity, unfolding in relation to a present thought-self or more immediate form of subjectivity witnessing that thought-object. It is preceded by attentional surfacing from the predecessor-thought, and is initiated by a proactively identified excerptive-clip, and a reactive excerpt-found reaction.

**Transparent Reflective Identification**—A type of reflective thinking engendering a sense of self-awareness, at the outset of which a "passing reflective thought" is excerptively clipped, with a subsequent explicit awareness of the content and phenomenology of that "passing reflective thought," and co-occurring awareness of experiencing another reflective act in the present. It is preceded by attentional surfacing from its predecessor-thought, and is initiated by a proactively identified excerptive-clip, and a reactive excerpt-found reaction.

**Something More**—A form of self-awareness occurring at the outset of reflective thoughts, during which the present thought-self recognizes and knows everything the observed thought-self knew, plus something more; it now knows that thought-self as a whole, from a stand point seemingly outside of and subsuming it. Its phenomenology is that of feeling more important, more knowing, and superior to the thought-object being observed.

**The True Me**—A form of self-awareness occurring at the outset of reflective thoughts, when, in the act of correcting, falsifying, or validating the "passing thought," the present thought-self grasps its predecessor's meaningful vantage point, along with its own, which is a meaningful elaboration on it. This creates a sense of self-awareness, as if one's *true self* is being manifested: "This is what I truly am and stand for, not that."

**The Intending Self**—A form of self-awareness occurring at the outset of reflective thoughts, during which one feels like a controlling, directing, decision-maker in the form of a reactive decision to a recognized excerpt which embodies either a reminder of a prior decision or a piece of meaning-laden ground of decision-influencing potential.

**Having Thoughts**—A form of self-awareness occurring at the outset of reflective thoughts, when, following the act of excerptively clipping a "passing thought," one construes it as a whole and completely identified thought-object, resulting in experiencing oneself as a thinker who "has" separate, already-given thoughts as objects.

**Elaborative Experiencing**—The act of being so absorbed in the experiencing of the moment that one is not attending to, and hence, not aware of oneself in context. Its phenomenology is a singular experiencing in the form of a reaction to and as the object of attention at hand; one does not experience a separate identity in relation to the object of attention.

**Reflective Experiencing**—The act of attending to aspects of one's present experiencing, with an awareness of *being* a separate identity or observer in relation to the objectified experience being observed.

**General Reality Orientation**—Typically considered as one's ordinary state of waking, conscious experience, consisting of intermittent attention to and awareness of self in relation to surrounding concrete realities. It is synonymous with reflective experiencing.

**Externally-Based General Reality Orientation**—Attending to oneself as a physical-behavioral presence in relation to one's surroundings in this time and place, resulting in the experience of self-awareness. It is synonymous with reflective experiencing.

**Partially-Based Internal General Reality Orientation**—Excerptively clipping and conceptually reacting to one's thoughts as explicit objects of attention, resulting in the experience of self-awareness as a thinking-self in relation to externally-based aspects of time and place. It is synonymous with noncomparative reflective thinking.

**Internally-Based General Reality Orientation**—Excerptively clipping and conceptually reacting to one's thoughts as explicit objects of attention, resulting in the experience of self-awareness in the form of a witnessing self in relation to a "passing" or less immediate thought-object. This results in the experience of self-awareness in relation to mental time and space. It is synonymous with comparative reflective thinking.

# Bibliography

Bandler, R., and Grinder, J. (1979). *Frogs into Princes.* Real People Press.

Bateson, G. (1972). *Steps to an Ecology of Mind.* New York: Ballantine.

Bateson, G. (1979). *Mind and Nature: A Necessary Unit.* New York: Dutton.

Bears, B. (1988). *A Cognitive Theory of Consciousness.* Cambridge, England: Cambridge University Press.

Becker, E. (1973). *The Denial of Death.* New York: Free Press.

Berne, E. (1972). *What Do You Say after You Say Hello?* New York: Free Press.

Brandt, A. (1980). "Self-confrontations." *Psychology Today*, Oct.

Brentano, F. (1973). *Psychology from an Empirical Standpoint* (O. Kraus, ed.; A. C. Rancurello, D. Terrell, & L. L. McAlister, trans.). New York: Humanities Press.

Broughton, J. (1975). The Development of Natural Epistemology in Adolescence and Early Adulthood. Doctoral dissertation. Harvard.

Bugental, J. F. T. (1976). *The search for authenticity: An Existential-Analytic Approach to Psychotherapy.* (enlarged edition). New York: Irvington.

Carrington, P. (1977). *Freedom in Meditation.* New York: Anchor Press.

Chah, A. (1993). "Our real home." In S. Bercholz & S. C. Kohn (eds.), *Entering the Stream: An Introduction to Buddha and His Teachings* (86–95).

Chalmers, D. J. (1996). *The Conscious Mind: In Search of a Fundamental Theory.* Oxford & New York: Oxford University Press.

Crick, F. H. C. (1994). *The Astonishing Hypothesis: The Scientific Search for the Soul.* London: Simon & Schuster.

Da Free John. (1983). *Easy Death.* USA: Dawn Horse Press.

Dasgutpa, S. N. (1975). *A History of Indian Philosophy* (Indian ed. Vols. 1–5). Delhi, India: Motila Banarsidass (original work published 1922).

D'Aulaire, E. P. and D'Aulaire, I. (1982). *D'Aulaires' Book of Greek Myths.* New York: Dell Publishing Group.

Dewey, J. (1925). *Experience and Nature.* (La Salle, IL: Open Court Publishing (299).

Eccles, J. C. (1989). *Evolution of the Brain: Creation of the Self.* London: Routledge.

Ecker, B., and Hulley, L. (1996). *Depth Oriented Brief Therapy.* San Francisco: Jossey-Bass.

Erickson, M., Rossi, E., and Rossi, S. (1976). *Hypnotic Realities.* New York: Irvington.

Erickson, M. H., Rossi, E. L., and Ryan, M. O. (1985). *Life Reframing in Hypnosis.* New York: Irvington.

Farah, M. J. (1984). "The Neurological Basis of Mental Imagery: A Componentical Analysis." *Cognition,* 18: 243–61.

Fromm, E. (1941). *Escape from Freedom.* New York: Farrar, Straus & Giroux.

Gardner, H. (1983). *Frames of Mind.* New York: Basic Books.

Gardner, H. (1985). *The Mind's New Science: A History of the Cognitive Revolution.* New York: Basic Books.

Gazzaniga, M. (1985). *The Social Brain.* New York: Basic Books.

Gendlin, E. T. (1962). *Experiencing and the Creation of Meaning: A Philosophical and Psychological Approach to the Subjective.* USA: Free Press of Glencoe.

Gennaro, R. J. (1996). *Consciousness and Self-Consciousness: A Defense of the Higher-Order Thought Theory of Consciousness.* Amsterdam/Philadelphia: John Benjamins Publishing Group.

Goenka, S. N. (1993). "Moral Conduct, Concentration, and Wisdom." In S. Bercholz & S. C. Kohn (eds.), *Entering the Stream: An Introduction to Buddha and His Teachings* (96–121).

Goldstein, J. and Kornfield, J. (1987). *Seeking the Heart of Wisdom: The Path of Insight Meditation.* Boston & London: Shambhala.

Harvey, O. J., Hunt, D. E., and Schroder, H. M. (1961). *Conceptual Systems and Personality Organization.* New York: Wiley.

Hughes, C. L. and Flowers, V. S. (1978). *Value Systems Analysis: Theory and Management Application.* Dallas: Author.

Hughes, C. L. and Flowers, V. S. (1982). *Value Systems Analysis: An Introduction.* Dallas: Author.

Jackendoff, R. (1987). *Consciousness and the Computational Mind.* Cambridge, England: Cambridge University Press.

James, W. 1950 (1890). *Principles of Psychology.* 2 vols. New York: Dover.

Jaynes, J. (1976). *The Origins of Consciousness in the Breakdown of the Bicameral Mind.* Boston: Haughton Mifflin Company.

Johnson-Laird, P. N. (1983). *Mental Models.* Cambridge, MA: Harvard University Press.

Johnson-Laird, P. N. (1988). *The Computer and the Mind: An Introduction to Cognitive Science.* Cambridge, MA: Harvard University Press.

Kihlstrom, J. F. (1987). "The Cognitive Unconscious." *Science.* 237: 1445–52.

Koestler, A. (1976). *The Ghost in the Machine.* New York: Random House.

Kohut, H. (1977). *The Restoration of the Self.* New York: IUP.

Kosslyn, S. M. (1978). "Imagery and Internal Representation." In E. Rosch and B. B. Lloyd, eds., *Cognition and Categorization.* Hillsdale, N.J.: Lawrence Erlbaum.

Kosslyn, S. M. (1980). *Image and Mind.* Cambridge, MA: Harvard University Press.

Kosslyn, S. M. (1983). *Ghosts in the Mind's Machine: Creating and Using Images in the Brain.* New York: W. W. Norton.

Levy-Bruhl, L. (1985) (1910). *How Natives Think.* (L.A. Clare, trans.). Princeton: Princeton University Press.

Lewis, C. S. (1967). *Studies in Words.* (2d ed.) Cambridge, England: Cambridge University Press.

Loevinger, J. (1976). *Ego Development.* San Francisco: Jossey-Bass.

Lunberg, M. J. (1974). *The Incomplete Adult: Social Class Constraints on Personal Development.* Westport, CT: Greenwood.

Luria, A. R. (1976). *Cognitive Development: Its Cultural and Social Foundations* (M. Cole, ed., & trans.; M. Lopez-Morillas, L. Solotaroff, trans.). Cambridge, MA: Harvard University Press.

MacLean, P. D. (1973). *A Triune Concept of Brain and Behavior.* Toronto: University of Toronto Press.

MacLean, P. D. (1990). *The Triune Brain in Evolution: Role in Paleocerebral Functions.* New York: Plenum.

Mahler, M., Pine, F., and Bergman, A. (1975). *The Psychological Birth of the Infant.* New York: Basic Books.

Mangalo, B. (1993). "The Practice of Recollection." In S. Bercholz & S. C. Kohn (eds.), *Entering the Stream: An Introduction to Buddha and His Teachings* (130–40). Boston: Shambhala.

Maslow, A. (1968). *Towards a Psychology of Being.* New York: Van Nostrand Reinhold.

Maturana, H. R. and Varela, F. J. (1980). *Autopoiesis and Cognition: The Realization of Living.* Boston: D. Reidel.

Merleau-Ponty. (1945). *Phenomenologie de la perception.* Paris: Callimard.

Natsoulas, T. (1998). "Consciousness and Self-Awareness." In M. Ferrari & R. J. Sternberg (eds.), *Self-Awareness: Its Nature and Development* (12–33).

Neisser, U. (1976). *Cognition and Reality.* San Francisco: W. H. Freeman.

Newcott, W. R. "The Hubble Telescope." *National Geographic* 191(4) (1997): 2–17.

Ornstein, R. E. (1986). *Multimind.* Boston: Houghton Mifflin.

Ornstein, R. E. (1991). *The Evolution of Consciousness: Of Darwin, Freud, and Cranial Fire—The Origins of the Way We Think.* New York: Prentice Hall.

Paranjpe, A. C. (1998). *Self Identity in Modern Psychology and Indian Thought.* New York: Plenum Press.

Piaget, J. (1977). *The Essential Piaget.* H. Gruber & J. Voneche (eds.). New York: Basic Books.

Pylyshyn, Z. W. (1979). "Imagery Theory: Not Mysterious—Just Wrong." *The Behavioral and Brain Sciences* 2: 561–62.

Pylyshyn, Z. W. (1981). "The Imagery Debate: Analogue Media versus Tacit Knowledge." *Psychological Review,* 88: 16–45.

Pylyshyn, Z. W. (1984). *Computation and Cognition: Toward a Foundation for Cognitive Science.* Cambridge, MA: MIT Press.

Restak, R. M. (1979). *The Brain: The Last Frontier.* Garden City, NY: Doubleday.

Rinpoche, S. (1993). *The Tibetan Book of Living and Dying.* San Francisco: HarperCollins.

Robins, R. W., Gosling, S. D., and Craik, K. H. (1999). "Empirical Analysis of Trends in Psychology." *American Psychologist,* 54, 117–28.

Saussure, F. (1966) (1915). *Course in General Linguistics.* New York: McGraw-Hill.

Searle, J. R. (1998). "Consciousness and Self-Awareness." In M. Ferrari & R. J. Sternberg (eds.), *Self-Awareness: Its Nature and Development* (12–33).

Shebar, W. (1979). "Mental Imagery: A Critique of Cognitive Psychology." Paper submitted for A. B. with honors in philosophy, Harvard University,

Cambridge, MA.

Shepard, R. N., and Metzler, J. (1971). "Mental Rotation of Three-Dimensional Objects." *Science*, 171: 701–3.

Shor, R. (1959). "Hypnosis and the Concept of the Generalized Reality Orientation." *American Journal of Psychotherapy*, 13: 582–602.

Suzuki, S. (1970). *Zen Mind, Beginner's Mind.* New York: Weatherhill.

Thera, N. (1993). "Seeing Things as They Are." In S. Bercholz & S. C. Kohn (eds.), *Entering the Stream: An Introduction to Buddha and His Teachings* (83–5).

Tulving, E. (1983). *Elements of Episodic Memory.* Oxford: Clarendon.

Wade, J. (1996). *Changes of Mind.* New York: SUNY Press.

Watt, H. J. (1905). "Experimentelle beitrage zur einer theorie des denkens." *Archiv fur Geschite der Psychologie* 4: 289–436.

Werner, H. (1980) (1940). *Comparative Psychology of Mental Development.* New York: International University Press.

Wilber, K. (1979). *No Boundary.* Boston: Shambhala.

Wilber, K., Engler, J., and Brown, D. (1986). *Transformations of Consciousness: Conventional and Contemplative Perspectives on Development.* Boston: Shambhala.

Wilber, K. (1995). *Sex, Ecology, Spirituality: The Spirit of Evolution.* Boston: Shambhala.

Wilber, K. (1996a) (1980). *The Atman Project: A Transpersonal View of Human Development.* Wheaton, IL: Quest.

Wilber, K. (1996b) (1981). *Up from Eden.* 2d ed. Wheaton, IL: Quest.

Wilber, K. (1996c) (1983). *Eye To Eye: The Quest for the New Paradigm.* 3d ed. Boston: Shambhala.

Wilber, K. (1997). *The Eye of Spirit: An Integral Vision for a World Gone Slightly Mad.* Boston & London: Shambhala.

Wilber, K. (2000). *One Taste: Daily Reflections on Integral Spirituality.* Boston and London: Shambhala.

William, W. R. (1993). "Lightning: Nature's High-Voltage Spectacle." *National Geographic* 184(1): 83–103.

Yalom, I. D. (1980). *Existential Psychotherapy.* New York: Basic Books.

Zimbardo, P. G. (1980). *Essentials of Psychology and Life.* 10th ed. USA: Scott, Foresman and Company.

# Index